Reading Dewey

Donette Considine

EDITED BY LARRY A. HICKMAN

Reading Dewey

Interpretations for a Postmodern Generation

INDIANA UNIVERSITY PRESS
Bloomington and Indianapolis

The paper used in this publication meets the minimum requirements of
American National Standard for Information Sciences—Permanence of
Paper for Printed Library Materials, ANSI Z39.48-1984.

Manufactured in the United States of America

Library of Congress Cataloging-in-Publication Data

Reading Dewey : interpretations for a postmodern generation / edited
  by Larry A. Hickman.
      p.   cm.
   Includes bibliographical references and index.
   ISBN 0-253-33384-9 (hardcover : alk. paper). — ISBN 0-253-21179-4
(pbk. : alk. paper)
   1. Dewey, John, 1859–1952. I. Hickman, Larry.
B945.D44R43 1998
191—dc21   97-40911

 1 2 3 4 5   03 02 01 00 99 98

Contents

Acknowledgments

This volume was prepared at the Center for Dewey Studies during 1996. Its timely completion is due in large measure to the efforts of three members of the Center's staff. Diane Meierkort and Barbara Levine exhibited the diligence with respect to matters of style and proofreading that has characterized their work during more than twenty years at the Center. And Karen O'Brien spent many hours at her computer attending to the details of references and endnotes.

The poem by William Carlos Williams quoted in the essay by Thomas M. Alexander is from: William Carlos Williams, *The Collected Poems of William Carlos Williams, 1909–1939*, vol. 1. Copyright 1938 by New Directions Publishing Corporation. It is reprinted by permission of New Directions.

Standard references to John Dewey's work are to the critical edition, *The Collected Works of John Dewey, 1882–1953*, edited by Jo Ann Boydston (Carbondale: Southern Illinois University Press, 1969–1991), and published as *The Early Works: 1882–1898* (EW), *The Middle Works: 1899–1924* (MW), and *The Later Works: 1925–1953* (LW). These designations are followed by volume and page number. For example, page 101 of volume 12 of the *Later Works* would be cited as "LW12:101." An electronic edition, based on the critical edition, is now available as *The Collected Works of John Dewey, 1882–1953: The Electronic Edition*, edited by Larry A. Hickman (Charlottesville, Va.: InteLex Corporation, 1996).

Introduction

Larry A. Hickman

John Dewey (1859–1952), hailed during his lifetime as "America's Philosopher," is now generally recognized as one of the seminal thinkers of the twentieth century. His critical work ranged more broadly than that of either of his great contemporaries, Martin Heidegger and Ludwig Wittgenstein, and he anticipated by several decades some of their most trenchant insights. Dewey's groundbreaking contributions to philosophy, psychology, and educational theory continue to animate research on the cutting edges of those fields.

The twelve original interpretive essays in this volume locate Dewey's major works within their historical context and present a timely reevaluation of each of the major areas of his broad philosophical reach. They explore his contributions to logic, ethics, social and political philosophy, the philosophy of religion, the philosophy of art, metaphysics, and the philosophy of the human sciences. They also locate Dewey's work as it relates to the dominant strands of modern philosophy, as it participates in the major debates of continental philosophy from phenomenology to poststructuralism, and as an early contribution to feminist thought.

This collection is thus designed to introduce Dewey's basic insights and to provide a context for understanding the current revival of interest in his thought. The last previous comprehensive collection of original essays to do this was *Guide to the Works of John Dewey*, edited by Jo Ann Boydston and published in 1970. Although her collection still serves as a benchmark for Dewey studies, developments during the quarter-century since its publication have demonstrated the need for a reinterpretation of Dewey's basic insights by, and for, a new generation.

The Breadth of Dewey's Philosophical Reach

Dewey disliked the idea of "systematic" philosophy and said so early in his career. Nevertheless, no major philosopher during his time or since has exhibited a broader philosophical reach. When he accepted a faculty position at the University of Chicago in 1894, it was as head of a department that included philosophy, psychology, and pedagogy. He was to make major contributions in each of these fields.

His contributions to psychology include the seminal 1896 essay "The Reflex Arc Concept in Psychology," which served both as a fatal blow to introspectionism and a manifesto of the new functionalism. In 1942 a panel of seventy of America's prominent psychologists voted it the most influential essay published by the *Psychological Review* during the journal's fifty-year history.

In that essay Dewey criticized the concept of the reflex arc on the grounds that it had failed to take into account the situatedness of the organism. He argued for the then novel thesis that the interests and habits of the organism, its active situations, influence how its stimuli are chosen.

Dewey's research in psychology profoundly influenced his work in logic. Skillfully avoiding the pitfalls of psychologism, he nevertheless argued that inquiry is a form of behavior, and that an account of its genesis and development as habit-formation must be a part of its theoretical dimension. In his view, logical forms accrue to subject matter in inquiry; they are not given prior to inquiry.

In the field of pedagogy, or the philosophy of education, Dewey established a laboratory school where he and his colleagues could apply their innovations in psychology and philosophy to the education of young children. He published groundbreaking works on the developmental stages of learning, on techniques by which the native talents and interests of children can inform and be informed by the curriculum, and on the complex interactions between classroom education and the institutions of the wider society.

Dewey's philosophical work was both rich and varied. During his decade at the University of Chicago (1894–1904), he founded and led a school of instrumental pragmatism that made major contributions to ethics, logic, and social psychology.

Following his move to Columbia University in 1905, Dewey increasingly turned his attention to the construction of a "philosophy of culture." In *How We Think* (1910) and *Democracy and Education* (1916), he sought to develop a theory of deliberation as it operates in the best examples of day-to-day learning and decision making. In *Experience and Nature* (1925), he developed a version of evolutionary naturalism that continues to provide insights into current environmental and technological problems. It is a matter of continuing significance that Dewey's *Experience and Nature* announced and examined the consequences of the end of western metaphysics-as-usual well in advance of Heidegger's 1927 *Sein und Zeit,* and that it anticipated by some two decades both Wittgenstein's rejection of private language arguments and his instrumental view of language.

In *Individualism Old and New* (1930) and *Liberalism and Social Action* (1935), Dewey addressed the problems associated with changing notions of individualism and liberalism within technological cultures. In *Art as Experience* (1934), he argued that aesthetic experience has both cognitive and non-cognitive dimensions, and that the value of a work of art lies in its instrumentality for the enlargement, consolidation, and consummation of the meanings of human experience. In *Logic: The Theory of Inquiry* (1938), he worked against the grain of the increasingly formal logic of that time in an attempt to demonstrate how inquiry is always situated, always in a context, and consequently always much richer than the practitioners of formal logic had imagined. *The Knowing and the Known* (1949), written in collaboration with Arthur F. Bentley, represents Dewey's attempt to move beyond the models of "self-action" utilized in classical philosophy and the "interactional" models of modern mechanistic physics in order to develop a "transactional" way of thinking that honors the dynamic features of human behavior.

In these and other major works, Dewey developed rich accounts of the relations between the scientific method and the methods of democracy, the transactional relationships between knowing subjects and the objects of their knowledge, and the role of philosophical inquiry in the reconstruction of technological culture.

Sources and Legacy: Dewey's Place in American Thought

Dewey assessed what he took to be his relation to fellow pragmatists C. S. Peirce and William James in his 1925 essay "The Development of American Pragmatism." Peirce's pragmatic maxim provided him with the insight that the meaning of an idea lies in its conceivable consequences. For Peirce, as for Dewey, action is far from being the end of deliberation; it is instead a phase within the formation of a new general habit of action that is applicable across a wide range of situations. Dewey was also influenced by Peirce's complex theory of categories. Throughout his published work, but especially after 1925, Dewey utilized and developed what Peirce had termed "firstness" (presence or quality), "secondness" (force or fact), and "thirdness" (habit or law).

Dewey also owed a debt to the work of William James. James's 1890 *Principles of Psychology* provided him with a rich sense of the edges and fringes that lie just beyond the focal points of our experience. James's radical empiricism furnished Dewey with the idea that relations, too, and not just what analysis later reveals as their relata, are objects of experience. James's insight that there are cognitive dimensions of belief, his incipient instrumentalism, and his notion that evolution is not yet finished—each of these themes was taken up and developed in Dewey's mature work.

Even before his death in 1952, Dewey's version of pragmatism began to be eclipsed by new philosophical movements. Captivated by the attempts of the positivists of the Vienna Circle and their allies to purge philosophy of all that they regarded as unscientific, by the ideal language philosophy of Wittgenstein's *Tractatus* period and the ordinary language philosophy of his *Investigations* period, and by a growing preoccupation with German and French phenomenology and existentialism, American philosophers began to regard Dewey's work as old-fashioned and of little relevance.

But by the end of the 1960s this situation began to change. Dewey's published work, much of it scattered and out of print within just a few years after his death, began to be reissued in a critical edition of thirty-seven volumes, edited by Jo Ann Boydston. His insights began to receive renewed attention by social and political philosophers and philosophers of education. Major interpretative studies of Dewey's philosophy of culture, his philosophy of art, his metaphysics, his ethics, his logic, his philosophy of religion, and his theories of radical democracy began to appear. Today, Dewey's work is once again in the forefront of American philosophy. Its contributions to environmental studies, feminist studies, multicultural studies, and even cognitive science are the subject of ongoing investigation by a new generation of philosophers.

Dewey's Basic Ideas in their Historical Context

Dewey's Aesthetics and Philosophy of Art

For Dewey, the aesthetic is one of the basic moments of human experience, and the making of art is one of the most basic ways in which the meanings of human life are enriched. It was on these grounds that he argued that the traditional distinction between the fine and the instrumental arts signals a failure of integration of ends and means, and an impoverishment of experience.

In "The Art of Life: Dewey's Aesthetics," Thomas M. Alexander begins with a brief presentation of the historical context of Dewey's *Art as Experience*. He then discusses its relationship to *Experience and Nature*, which Dewey had published nine years earlier, and its reception by Dewey's colleagues and critics.

Even though Dewey had written little about art *as such* prior to 1925, when he was already in his sixty-sixth year, it is clear from his remarks in these two volumes that he regarded art as a pivotal aspect of human experience.

When Dewey writes about art, he is writing about the means of overcoming debilitating dualisms—the splits within experience that tend to make it either chaotic, on the one side, or rigid and repetitious, on the other. And just as refined works of art grow organically out of those that are cruder and less developed, our experience of the fine arts comes alive only as it is grounded in concrete, lived experience. Nor must art be unfailingly happy or comforting in order to be "good" art. In a well-chosen series of examples, Alexander demonstrates how the arts have embraced, clarified, and enriched experiences that would otherwise have been enervating or destructive.

Alexander's essay emphasizes Dewey's understanding of perception as more aesthetic than epistemic, as more participatory than passive, and as capable of opening humans outward to the full range of possibilities afforded by their environing conditions. It also illuminates the ways in which Dewey thought that aesthetic experience implicates enriched notions of democracy, communication, education, and religious experience.

Dewey's Idea of Communication and Community

Rooted in the ideals of the Progressive Era of American history and the typically American faith in the ability of communication to achieve consensus, Dewey's vision of community is one in which misunderstanding and even initial intransigence is overcome as parties to conflict come together to recast and reconfigure common problems in ways that lead to novel solutions. "Of all affairs," writes Dewey in *Experience and Nature*, "communication is the most wonderful. . . . Where communication exists, things in acquiring meaning, thereby acquire representatives, surrogates, signs and implicates."

In his essay "Dewey's Conception of Community," James Campbell explores Dewey's understanding of the ways in which groups are formed and how they function, how they develop and maintain their values, and how they grow, or deteriorate, as they respond, or fail to respond, to opportunities for their reconstruction.

Campbell reminds us that the social pragmatism developed by Dewey and his colleagues George Herbert Mead and James Hayden Tufts drew on notions of community that had been central to the American experience since the earliest days of European colonization. Internally, communities must exhibit shared interests. Externally, they must interact freely with other modes of association. The work of community building is never easy; it demands a strong commitment to mutual respect and the pooling of experiences.

Dewey and the Human Sciences

Dewey's contribution to the human sciences, particularly social psychology, was deeply influenced by his commitment to evolutionary naturalism. In collaboration with George Herbert Mead, Dewey developed first a functionalist, then a social behaviorist view of the human sciences that substituted "interests" for "desires" and placed heavy emphasis on the role of social and cultural institutions as platforms for continuing adjustive activity. In his mature work, the problems of psychology were absorbed into his accounts of inquiry within the many areas of human endeavor such as art, politics, and law. He argued that psychological phenomena, far from being the sources of social phenomena, were more often their consequences.

In "Dewey and American Social Science," Peter T. Manicas develops what he terms Dewey's "scattered views" on the social sciences. Although they are still largely misunderstood and for the most part unappropriated, he suggests, they nevertheless hold considerable promise as tools for reconstituting those disciplines.

Especially in his 1938 *Logic: The Theory of Inquiry,* Dewey roundly rejected positivism and attempted to establish an instrumentalism that would increase our understanding of the continuities within actual social relations. One consequence of this view is that science and commonsense inquiries are, and must be understood as, continuous. Another is that if social scientists are to facilitate the growth of a Great Community, then they will have to get beyond the fragmentations and abstractions that are current features of their disciplines.

Dewey's Philosophy of Education

The clearest statement of Dewey's philosophy of education is found in his 1897 essay, "My Pedagogic Creed." In that essay he argued that education involves the development of the learner's capacities and interests in ways that empower her or him to assume the role of constructive participant in the life of the wider society. Nevertheless, in Dewey's view schools *are* communities and not simply sites of preparation for community life. Constructive educational practice begins with "the primitive unconscious unity of social life" from which it then differentiates the various academic disciplines. Schools are the foremost agents of social progress, and it is the moral duty of a society to provide educators with the tools necessary for this task.

In "Dewey's Philosophy as Education," James W. Garrison invites us to consider the ramifications of Dewey's famous remark that "if we are willing to conceive education as the process of forming fundamental dispositions, intellectual and emotional, toward nature and fellow-men, philosophy may even be defined as the general theory of education."

As a part of his extended discussion of Dewey's treatment of dispositions, habits, emotion, and character, Garrison argues that philosophy *is* education because one of its aims is to develop a holistic vision of human growth. If life is to be meaningful, and if human beings are to increase the store of its meanings, then philosophy as education must foster transactions between organism and environment with a view to establishing continuities.

Garrison argues that the flowering and fruit of philosophy as education is a kind of moral poetics, in which lifelong learning converts what would otherwise be disconnected and discordant into experience that is refined and harmonious.

Dewey's Social and Political Philosophy

Dewey's extensive writings on social and political issues present his attempts to rethink and recast traditional notions of individual and society, public and private, liberalism and conservatism, and above all, democracy. Democracy is, in his view, not so much a form of government as it is a process—a body of tools and methods for undertaking the ongoing reconstruction of social life. "Democracy," he wrote in 1939, "is belief in the ability of human experience to generate the aims and methods by which further experience will grow in ordered richness."

In "Dewey's Social and Political Philosophy," John J. Stuhr reminds us of Dewey's observation that there are no global social or political theories that are adequate for all times and places. If we are to avoid the academic sin of "chewing a historic cud long since reduced to woody fibre," then we must work in the *practical* arena to bring about positive change. Such efforts must remain cognizant of actual cultural forces and changes, and they must be prepared to persist over the long haul. Faith in democracy is radical, since it works toward ends that have never yet been realized in any nation or society.

Do Dewey's recommendations in the areas of social and political philosophy have a future? Stuhr admits that he does not know. The answer, he suggests, depends on the extent to which we decide to work together to establish and realize common goals, to cast aside old ways of thinking and imagine new alternatives, and to face the future with fresh energy.

Dewey's Ethics

Dewey's work in ethics is the flower of both his aesthetic theory and his theory of inquiry. In its aesthetic dimension, ethics grows out of the affective moments of human life. Feeling, and feeling *with,* are the sources of both the felt pleasures of harmonious living and the disruptions and displacements that occasion inquiry. For its part, inquiry in ethics involves the evaluation and resolution of the conflicting claims of experienced values. Dewey rejected traditional notions of fixed duties and rights, and he thought that the moral atomism of some of his predecessors had led to disastrous social practice.

In "Dewey's Ethics: Morality as Experience," Gregory F. Pappas presents Dewey's attempt to carve out a middle position between what he regarded as two equally extreme views of ethics. At one extreme there are those who regard morality as the application of eternal verities. According to this "rulebook" view, advocated by deontologists and some "virtue" ethicists, ethical norms exist prior to experience and are imposed upon it. At the other extreme are the extreme relativists and subjectivists who think that ethical norms are more or less arbitrary. Rejecting both views, Pappas reminds us, Dewey called for an ethics that placed the center of moral gravity within the concrete processes of living, rather than within an ivory tower.

Dewey's Philosophy of Religion

Early in his career, Dewey withdrew from participation in organized religion. Nevertheless, his work retains a deep sense of the importance of ideals within human life and of the energies and enthusiasms that men and women marshal in order to realize their profoundest commitments. During the years surrounding the publication of *A Common Faith* in 1934, Dewey joined in extensive discussions with theologians and philosophers of religion regarding the extent to which a religious humanism was possible.

In "Dewey's Philosophy of Religious Experience," Steven C. Rockefeller draws our attention to the tortuous path taken by the evolution of Dewey's own religious experience. His childhood, influenced by his mother's sharp sense of sin and alienation, had left the adolescent Dewey with what he would later call an "inner laceration." But his undergraduate study of science and philosophy convinced Dewey that the ruptures between soul and body, and especially between religion and science, could be healed. During his twenties and thirties Dewey turned to the palliatives offered by neo-Hegelian idealism. But finally, in the years that followed his move to Chicago in 1894, he began to develop his own naturalistic understanding of religious experience.

Rockefeller reminds us that Dewey was attacked by religionists of the right for his alleged atheism and relativism, and of the left for his alleged failure to take evil seriously. But in the end, he suggests, the type of faith that Dewey recommended may turn out to offer precisely the resources that will be required if human life on earth is to have a future.

Dewey's Metaphysics

In 1925 Dewey described metaphysics as a "statement of the generic traits manifested by existences of all kinds without regard to their differentiation into physical and mental." To this he added that "Any theory that detects and defines these traits is therefore but a ground-map of the province of criticism, establishing base lines to be employed in more intricate triangulations." There has been considerable debate regarding whether

Dewey intended his own ground-map to be a metaphysics of existence, which would have been yet another contribution to the ontological metaphysics of the western tradition, or a metaphysics of experience, which would have effected a radical departure from the tradition.

In "Dewey's Metaphysics: Ground-Map of the Prototypically Real," Raymond D. Boisvert draws extensively on this fecund metaphor of metaphysics as "ground-map of the province of criticism." He argues that this conceptual link between maps and metaphysics has a threefold pertinence: first, both types of description are constructed; second, neither rests on any ultimate foundation; and third, both are open to revision.

In this matter, as elsewhere, Dewey attempted to chart a course between extremes. He rejected the claims of those such as Descartes and Kant who had accepted metaphysics as the study of "supersensible reality." But he was also critical of the claims of positivists such as A. J. Ayer that metaphysics is "impossible" or "meaningless."

In a further development of Dewey's leading metaphor, Boisvert suggests that Dewey's metaphysics should be thought of not as *one* map, but as *many*—as a kind of atlas which gains plausibility as it becomes thicker.

Dewey's Theory of Inquiry

Dewey defined inquiry as "the controlled or directed transformation of an indeterminate situation into one that is so determinate in its constituent distinctions and relations as to convert the elements of the original situation into a unified whole." He thought this idea of sufficient importance that he advanced it on several different levels. In his presentations to teachers, he laid out a five-stage process of deliberation that moves from the vague awareness that something is unsettled to the consummatory moment in which a warranted conclusion is reached. His logics of 1903, 1916, and 1938 represent a fuller and more technical treatment of these matters. In his *Logic: The Theory of Inquiry* (1938), for example, Dewey turned several elements of traditional logic on their head, arguing for example that logical forms accrue to subject matter in inquiry and are not imposed upon it. In the face of the formal logics of his time and ours, Dewey's contention is that inquiry is always situated and contextual, and that it is undertaken in response to actual perceived problems.

In "Dewey's Theory of Inquiry," Larry A. Hickman presents Dewey's logic in terms of some of its central, and most controversial, features. Unlike much of contemporary epistemology, for example, Dewey argued that judgments cannot be separated from the contexts in which actual inquiry takes place. He also identified inquiry as a form of organic behavior and argued that it is instrumental to what he called "warranted assertibility," which was his reconstruction of the much used (and abused) term "truth."

One of Dewey's most controversial claims was that forms accrue to subject matter in inquiry and are not imposed on it from without. In holding this position he broke with over two thousand years of tradition. Dewey's treatment of judgments and propositions also breaks new ground. He denied, for example, that propositions have truth values. He preferred instead to characterize them as valid or invalid, which was his way of assessing whether they are effective, strong, and relevant with respect to the advancement of inquiry. Finally, coming full circle, Dewey argued that inquiry is essentially social. It promotes cooperation among reflective organisms because it allows them to rehearse actions before making irretrievable commitments.

Dewey's Feminism

Dewey was an early feminist who supported university co-education for women, the dissemination of information about methods of birth control, and women's suffrage at a time when those issues were still the source of considerable strife. Dewey's views were no doubt informed by his wife, Alice Chipman Dewey, and by Jane Addams, with whom he had a close personal and professional relationship. Dewey thought that gender issues were central to enhanced understanding of self and society. His feminism is thus a part of his wider commitment to the enlargement of human community by means of the development of shared meanings and the undertaking of joint social action. For Dewey, the work of social reconstruction requires that every member of society, male and female alike, should experience the liberation of her or his capacities for enhanced appreciation and growth.

In her essay "John Dewey's Pragmatist Feminism," Charlene Haddock Seigfried argues that pragmatist theory itself provides strong resources for feminist thinking since it is committed to pluralism and perspectivism, it understands experience as dynamic, and it rejects representational realism. As a result of its deployment of these resources, pragmatism has been able simply to ignore some of the issues that have preoccupied academics and to turn its attention instead to the problems of those, such as women and people of color, who bear the brunt of adverse social and economic conditions.

Seigfried thinks that pragmatism's claim that theory must be intimately related to experience and its insistence that inquiry have a central place within experience were particularly attractive to the first generations of feminists since of all its many features these are the ones that tend most to undermine established power relations. In all this Seigfried demonstrates the relevance of Dewey's thought for some of the most persistent conflicts of our time.

Dewey's Response to Modern Philosophy

Dewey's response to the theories of knowledge advanced during the modern period of philosophy, from Descartes to Nietzsche, was to undercut their assumptions and to propose radical alternatives to their stated projects. As a part of his assault on the modernist "quest for certainty," Dewey criticized attempts to provide a firm foundation for knowledge based on the priority of the thinking self (Descartes), directly experienced impressions (the Empiricists), and the individual transcendental ego (Kant). In Dewey's view, experience does not constitute an epistemological problem to be explained from an external standpoint. Dewey also criticized the Romantic reaction to Enlightenment rationality that was mounted by Hegel and his followers. He contended that its lack of concreteness had vitiated its underlying project. The weakness of both movements, he argued, was their failure to recognize that human experience is the situated awareness within which feeling occurs and within which problems are felt, articulated, and resolved. Characteristically, however, Dewey took up and advanced what he regarded as the best and most enduring elements of both Enlightenment and Romantic thinkers.

The final pair of essays in this volume locate Dewey with respect to the modernist tradition, which began with Newton and Locke, and the "Continental" tradition, which owes much of its authority to the work of Husserl and Heidegger.

In her essay "The Contemporary Significance of the American Philosophic Tradition: Lockean and Redemptive," Thelma Z. Lavine locates Dewey squarely at the intersection of two competing philosophical frameworks, each of which sought to dominate the course of modernity. What she terms "Enlightenment Modernity" was preoccupied with eternal truths discoverable by reason and universally applicable. "Romantic Modernity," on the other hand, countered the claims of universal reason with its own claims on behalf of particularity and creativity.

Lavine argues that it was Dewey, uniquely among American philosophers, who understood the competing claims of these movements, and who attempted to take into account what was best in each.

Dewey in Dialogue with Continental Philosophy

Dewey's rejection of many of the central assumptions and aims of modern philosophy places him in dialogue with Continental philosophers from Husserl and Heidegger to Derrida. Like Heidegger, he thought that experience is always situated and inevitably caught up within the presuppositions of a particular life-world. But Dewey could accept neither Heidegger's privileging of poetry over the other forms of *technē*, his deep pessimism regarding technology, nor his now famous flight, evident in his later work, into the mysteries of "Being."

In his imaginative essay "Dewey in Dialogue with Continental Philosophy," Joseph Margolis sheds a great deal of light on these complex issues. He does this first by drawing our attention to Richard Rorty's seminal 1974 essay "Overcoming the Tradition: Heidegger and Dewey," which he thinks fails to capture the essential differences between Dewey and Heidegger.

Margolis thinks that the path to understanding the most trenchant differences between Dewey and Heidegger leads through an appreciation of the work of Merleau-Ponty. This is to say that Dewey asserts a continuity between the natural and the phenomenological in a way that Heidegger never did, but which was an essential part of Merleau-Ponty's effort to come to terms with Husserl.

In the long run, Margolis submits, the most promising prospects for dealing with big problems of philosophy will come from the convergence of pragmatic and phenomenological approaches since they undercut skepticism, reject all forms of cognitive privilege, and freely admit the historical context of inquiry.

Reading Dewey

1   The Art of Life: Dewey's Aesthetics

Thomas M. Alexander

The Place of Aesthetics in Dewey's Philosophy

Experience and Nature appeared in 1925 and was immediately recognized as the most synoptic, systematic statement of Dewey's philosophy. Yet it contained several surprises, not least of which was an important chapter discussing the nature of art and aesthetic experience. Aside from a few comments, the subject of art as such had not occupied Dewey after 1903 in the writings which had made him the preeminent spokesperson for the new generation of pragmatists and naturalists. Dewey had been identified as a philosophical psychologist, an educational theorist, a naturalist in the debates with the idealists, an instrumentalist in the debates with the realists, an advocate for progressive, social democracy, and, perhaps above all, an advocate who urged that empirical, scientific methodology be used to illumine and guide all modes of life. But in *Experience and Nature,* just before the closing chapter on the ideal of wisdom, instead of extolling the scientific method, Dewey spoke on "Experience, Nature, and Art."

The reaction by the critics was confused and diverse. C. J. Ducasse, for example, stated that "Professor Dewey's conception of the nature of art is in harmony with his well-known instrumentalism," but he went on to say that this merely shows "what a strange picture of life such an instrumentalist must paint," a life consumed with making tools for making tools, endlessly fatiguing and drained of joy.[1] Such confused responses became more pronounced nine years later in 1934 when *Art as Experience* appeared. For example, Stephen Pepper, an admirer of Dewey, had already been working on a pragmatist (or "contextualist") aesthetics and was surprised to see that he and Dewey diverged on several key issues. His rather uncharitable conclusion was that Dewey had dredged up some old Hegelian notions on art from his early idealist days "contrary to the spirit of pragmatism" in order to round out his otherwise naturalistic system. This view would be repeated a few years later by Benedetto Croce, an Italian Hegelian and no lover of pragmatism or naturalism. Croce insinuated that Dewey had actually "borrowed" ideas from Croce's famous *Aesthetic* (1902, trans. 1909) without acknowledging the source and thus had been forced, in spite of himself, to acknowledge the truth of idealism. A bitter exchange between Dewey and Croce ensued that continued sporadically until 1952, the year both of them died.[2]

It would have been better if readers had focused upon the careful structure of *Experience and Nature* itself and listened to Dewey's language, as powerful and delicate as the branching roots of a great tree grappling with the earth. Let us look at the organization of the chapters. Dewey opened the book with a discussion of his methodology, his "naturalistic humanism," describing what today we might call the "ecological" context of human-experiencing-within-nature. He moved on in chapter 2 to point out the fundamental interplay of order and disorder, stability and precariousness, that affects all living beings. Chapter 3 dealt with immediate, qualitative experience, sudden joys and losses, which in their vividly given but transitory impact, make us learn to pursue them as ends. Chapter 4 showed how, in order to reexperience those qualities, we frame projects and recognize means, and thereby subsequently expand our understanding of the interrelationships of the world. This transforms elements in our situation into being known rather than merely "had." These chapters laid the basis for the subsequent discussion of the rise and flowering of intelligence in conduct.

The next four chapters (5–8) dealt, respectively, with: the rise of symbolic behavior or communication (the social basis of meaning or "mind"), the nature of subjectivity as a creative response to situations (the "reconstructive" moment in the process of action), the emergence of our embodied mentality from organic existence, and finally a discussion of consciousness itself, ranging from the penumbral horizon of subconsciousness and dim feeling to the intensive focus of ideational thinking as well as the perception and enjoyment of meanings. These neglected chapters present Dewey's longest, sustained argument against dualism and his alternative emergentistic view of mind and body, consciousness and matter, self and world.[3]

It was then, in chapter 9, that Dewey chose to introduce his discussion of art. To overcome the separation of theory and practice, inherited from the Greeks, Dewey states, we must accept a remarkable conclusion:

But if modern tendencies are justified in putting art and creation first, then the implications of this position should be avowed and carried through. It would then be seen that science is an art, that art is practice, and that the only distinction worth drawing is not between practice and theory, but between those modes of practice that are not intelligent, not inherently and immediately enjoyable, and those which are full of enjoyed meanings. When this perception dawns, it will be a commonplace that art—the mode of activity that is charged with meanings capable of immediately enjoyed possession—is the complete culmination of nature, and that "science" is properly a handmaiden that conducts natural events to this happy issue. Thus would disappear the separations that trouble present thinking: division of everything into nature *and* experience, of experience into practice *and* theory, art *and* science, of art into useful *and* fine, menial *and* free. [LW1:268–69]

The idea of experience as art, Dewey continues, "sums up in itself all the issues which have been previously considered," that is to say, the whole exposition of *Experience and Nature* up to that point.

Dewey's discussion of art also anticipates the tenth and final chapter of the book insofar as it is concerned with the application of criticism and philosophy toward the end of making life intelligent, of guiding action by ideals that illumine ends that intrinsically fulfill us. "The characteristic human need," Dewey claims, "is for possession and appreciation of the meaning of things, and this need is ignored and unsatisfied in the traditional notion of the useful" [LW1:272].[4] Our utilitarian outlook has made us concentrate on activities whose ends do not serve the ultimate enhancement of the human encounter with meaning and value, and so "we optimistically call them 'useful' and let it go at that," Dewey wryly notes. "If we were to ask useful for what? we should be obliged to examine their actual consequences," which, for Dewey would involve seeing what they lead to in terms of "narrowed, embittered, and crippled life, of congested, hurried, confused and extravagant life" [EN, 362; LW1:272]. Aesthetic experience and intelligence exemplified in art are necessary conditions to achieving wisdom, the shared life of intelligent conduct.

In other words, Dewey is making three pivotal comments. First, he holds that human life is guided by a desire to experience the world in such a way that the sense of meaning and value is immediately enjoyed. This is the "human eros," in my terms, the desire that lies behind the various motivations and aims of life. Second, our utilitarian obsession with means apart from ends makes us ignore the widespread poverty and emptiness of human experience, what Marx calls "alienation." Utilitarian reasoning (or a "means first," linear type of pragmatism, one which uncritically takes ends as arbitrarily given and forever immune to any critical evaluation) is the opposite of instrumentalist intelligence.[5] Third, Dewey claims that in the idea of art we find the moment in which human alienation is overcome and the need for the experience of meaning and value is satisfied. Through art, in the aesthetic experience, the rift in the world that frustrates our primordial desire for encountering a sense of meaning and value is healed. Art and the aesthetic experience thus move to the forefront in importance: it is there that we possess a paradigm of experience which all other aspects of Dewey's philosophy in some way point to and presuppose. The trick will be not to read "art" and "aesthetic experience" in such a way that reduces Dewey's philosophy to an effete, purist "aestheticism" of the Pre-Raphaelite or Bloomsbury variety.[6]

That Dewey was explicitly aware of the radical import of this conclusion is evident from the discussion in *Art as Experience* called "The Challenge to Philosophy." Not just aesthetic experience is imaginative, he says, but "all *conscious* experience has of necessity some degree of imaginative quality"; indeed, given that imagination is the temporal transformation of experience in which novelty and continuity fuse and meanings are experienced, "Imagination is the only gateway through which these meanings can find their way into a present interaction" [LW10:276]. Through imagination, experience becomes expressive. In art, unlike mechanical production, ends and means are thoroughly integrated; through this experience, the self grows.

> This fact constitutes the uniqueness of esthetic experience, and this uniqueness is in turn a challenge to thought. It is particularly a challenge to that systematic thought called philosophy. For esthetic experience is experience in its integrity. Had not the term "pure" been so often abused in philosophic literature, had it not been so often employed to suggest that there is something alloyed, impure, in the very nature of experience and to denote something beyond experience, we might say that esthetic experience is pure experience. For it is experience freed from the forces that impede and confuse its development as experience; freed, that is, from factors that subordinate an experience as it is directly had

to something beyond itself. To esthetic experience, then, the philosopher must go to understand what experience is. [LW10:278][7]

Dewey immediately adds that the aesthetic theory of a philosopher "is a test of the capacity of the system he puts forth to grasp the nature of experience itself. There is no test that so surely reveals the one-sidedness of a philosophy as its treatment of art and esthetic experience" [LW10:278]. Given that Dewey's own philosophy is one prolonged effort "to grasp the nature of experience itself," such a remark cannot be easily dismissed.

It should be sufficiently clear by now that whatever Dewey's critics may have held, Dewey himself had come to formulate in his concept of art and the aesthetic a central, ultimate response to the issues that motivated his philosophy as such. In art, properly understood, one finds the overcoming of dualisms which Dewey had struggled against from the start. Beyond that, in art and the aesthetic one finds "the culminating event of nature as well as the climax of experience" [EN, xvi; LW1:8]. Whether this shift in Dewey's philosophy reflects a deep reorientation, like Heidegger's "turn" or *Kehre*, or a natural development, a blossoming, of Dewey's earlier thought, cannot be addressed here.[8] In my view, Dewey's thinking about art crystallized major themes that characterize his philosophy as it took shape in the late 1890s and certainly by the early 1900s.[9] The articulation of these themes allowed Dewey to develop his original interpretation of art later on. But in trying to deal directly with the issue of art and the aesthetic, Dewey often integrated and clarified these themes far more successfully than elsewhere. And so, I maintain, Dewey's discussion of "art as experience" is essential to understanding his mature philosophy as well as the import of much of his earlier thought.

The Roots of Aesthetic Experience

Dewey begins *Art as Experience,* oddly enough, by warning us against museums. It is not so much that Dewey hated museums (in fact he worked for one at the Barnes Foundation) as that he worries about beginning our *reflection* upon the nature of aesthetic experience and art by thinking of our experiences of fine art. First we are tempted to isolate our museum experiences from other experiences in life at large. Thus, we fail to see how the works we encounter in museums (or their equivalents for other artforms, such as concert halls or classrooms) have actually grown from those common conditions in life which we share with the artists who made those works. Having done this, we may make a second mistake. In believing that aesthetic experience belongs to a segregated realm, we will fail to see how the artists' success in making expressively meaningful, intrinsically fulfilling objects from the raw material of life can be applied across the whole spectrum of human existence. The great moral to be learned from the arts for Dewey is that *when ideals cease to be confined to a realm separated from our daily, practical experience, they can become powerful forces in teaching us to make the materials of our lives filled with meaning.*

Many interpreters of Dewey's philosophy of art, like Ducasse, have missed this point, arguing that Dewey wished to forget the fine arts entirely or devalue them as "upper class" arts in contrast to popular "democratic" arts. Others have tried to take Dewey as meaning that all popular arts or folk crafts are on a par with the fine arts. On this view, the moral pointed out above would be rendered invisible: why should one try to develop something which, in its crude form, is judged to be adequate? What Dewey deplores is that the *continuity* between popular arts and fine arts is covered up so that, instead of a *process* of growth we set up a dysfunctional dichotomy. Thus, museums are fine and good, as long as we are aware of *how* art arises from daily life, functions in contexts, and is rooted in the vital dimensions of a culture. There is an aesthetic and artistic aspect of our ordinary experience which can be developed to a high degree, and the fine arts are living proof of that, provided they are not set off on Mount Olympus, operating as a mere refuge from the failure of the rest of our experience to be deeply meaningful. The purpose of aesthetics is "to restore continuity between the refined and intensified forms of experience that are works of art and the everyday events, doings, and sufferings that are universally recognized to constitute experience" [LW10:9]. This is the task of *Art as Experience.*

Thus, Dewey proposes that we begin with "raw" aesthetic experience. He means here those experiences that suddenly call forth attention and compel us, making experience "come alive," as it were. Dewey cites such dramatic events as a fire engine going by, our interest in large construction machines, the drama of steel workers catching hot bolts on the high beams, or the "tense grace of the ball-player" [LW10:11]. But he also includes more sedate activities: a woman tending houseplants or working in the garden, people watching the shifting flames and crumbling embers of an evening fire, a skillful mechanic lovingly at work, a parent mindfully caring for a child [see LW10:268]. These are moments in which we indeed *live;* the otherwise dim or submerged potentiality of experience to be deeply meaningful and expressive is consciously realized.

These incidents are not merely "vivid" or "tranquil" islands in the vast monotony of ordinary experience. They are revelatory. Our ordinary consciousness may not see just how revelatory they are, but the artist and the aesthetic philosopher can discern their power. Take Dewey's example of the fire engine. On his way to visit the studio of his friend Marsden Hartley, the poet William Carlos Williams experienced a fire engine rushing by in a torrent of color and sound. Standing in a doorway, he wrote out a poem, "The Great Figure," which he showed to Hartley and another painter, Charles Demuth:

> Among the rain
> and lights
> I saw the figure 5
> in gold
> on a red
> firetruck
> moving
> tense
> unheeded
> to gong clangs
> siren howls
> and wheels rumbling
> through the dark city.

Demuth himself was so struck by this clear-sighted depiction of a moment of excitement in which the bigness, the redness, the clanging of the bell, and the scream of the siren were fused together and rushing past with immanent dangerous speed, that he decided to turn it into a painting, *I Saw the Figure 5 in Gold.*[10]

Monet's serene paintings of water lilies and gardens evoke a spreading sense of tranquility where light and water seem to converge in a fragile moment of pure life itself. Or think of Edward Hopper's painting *Early Sunday Morning:* the deep sense of eerie quiet, desolation where there normally is life and activity, reveals in the clear, slanting light an unsuspected order and rhythm of form which otherwise would be concealed by the restless weekday crowds.

The artist does not have to focus on experiences that are exciting or peaceful, but may instead work with elements drawn from fear, alienation, or terror. Kafka has us engage a world where the nightmare simply does not allow us to awake. The work of painter James Ensor explores a world where every face is denuded of its bland bourgeois mask to expose true characters of imbecility, greed, hatred, and death. Edward Munch's painting *The Scream* evokes the soundless terrifying isolation of insanity. Novelist Eli Weisel gives us a concentrated look at Hitler's final solution with relentless lucidity and poetic exactness.

This is an important point since Dewey's so-called "optimism" often leads readers to doubt that his aesthetic theory embraces such negative or disturbing aspects of the human condition. It is true that Dewey does not dwell on such items, though he does mention violent illness, storms, a near-death experience and the shattering of friendship.[11] It is not that such experiences are "fulfilling" in the sense of making us feel better about ourselves and the world. Such shallow existence is not the self-realization Dewey sees as desirable or fundamental. A life of superficial self-satisfaction is not growth. But such experiences do reveal the expressive power of experience that is due to the fact that in order to grow we must "undergo," that is, suffer. Life has depth because we can sense its precariousness. The power of art comes from the power of life itself to be expressive. This does not mean that all that life has to say is comforting. To hold, as Dewey does, that all experience involves some degree of "undergoing" or "suffering" and to emphasize, as he does, that the precarious aspect of existence is pervasive so that even armed with keen intelligence and the best intentions in the world we may yet work toward our own disaster, bespeaks neither an "optimistic" view of life nor a "pessimistic" one, but one in which the tragic and the comic are basic existential features of the human condition. Art has the ability to bring these deep meanings before us in fused experiences that give us some understanding of life.

The Ecological Dynamics of Aesthetic Experience

Experience is basic for Dewey, and he gives one of his best accounts of this central term in the first three chapters of *Art as Experience*. "The first great consideration is that life goes on in an environment; not merely *in* it but because of it, through interaction with it" [LW10:19]. We are engaged in a rhythmic dance with our environment; "undergoing" means to be open, to be vulnerable, to have outwardly directed needs. Lungs do not merely "intend" the air, they suck it in as gasp when they cannot get it.

"Doing" is more than acting or reacting; it is responding, organizing our energies *toward* the world in a coordinated, discriminating way. When undergoing and doing are integrated, there is intelligence, there is art. As Maurice Merleau-Ponty once said, walking is more than a series of arrested falls. But that is how it begins. Gradually we are able to move and respond in an upright way that is flowing and continuous. Our walking may even develop artistically and take on deep aesthetic meaning, as in Buddhist "walking meditation."

Our rhythmic movement with the world also means that at times we fall out of step and then recover. But, as Dewey observes, "the recovery is never mere return to a prior state, for it is enriched by the state of disparity and resistance through which it has successfully passed" [LW10:19]. In short, we grow, we learn. Dewey then adds a crucial comment: "These biological commonplaces are something more than that; they reach to the roots of the esthetic in experience" [LW10:20]. The vital harmony that our body itself establishes with the world is tensive through and through. This is the organic root of the very idea of "form" itself. Rather than a static, intellectual structure or drop of frozen Being, form is due to the temporal recovery of action through engagement with the precarious power of the environment. Form is that "reconstruction" arising from doing and undergoing that involves growth and the establishment of continuity. In Dewey's terse phrase, "order itself develops" [LW10:20].

Carried out at the level of art, form is the capacity for a work of art to renew itself and grow in human experience. [See LW10:14 f.] What distinguishes functionally well-designed utilitarian objects from objects that have aesthetic form is that the latter *also* serve the larger end of enlivening perception. "Objects of industrial arts have form—that adapted to their special uses," says Dewey. "When this form is liberated from limitation to a specialized end and serves also the purposes of an immediate and vital experience, the form is esthetic and not merely useful" [LW10:121]. Thus *"Form may then be defined as the operation of forces that carry the experience of an event, object, scene, and situation to its own integral fulfillment"* [LW10:142].

The dynamically ordered relationships we achieve with the world also have emotional depth. Emotion for Dewey is as functionally and environmentally understood as bound up with form. Emotion is "the conscious sign of a break, actual or impending" with the continuity of action; it arouses attention to focus upon aspects of the world. All action begins with the "blind surge" of what Dewey calls "impulsion," the "hunger and demand" of the organism in its entirety for "complete experience" [LW10:64]. As movement becomes specifically directed and establishes definite coordinated relationships with the world, blind surge becomes purposeful and meaningful [LW10:65].

> Impulsion from need starts an experience that does not know where it is going; resistance and check bring about the conversion of direct forward action into reflection; what is turned back upon is the relation of hindering conditions to what the self possesses as working capital in virtue of prior experiences. As the energies thus involved reenforce the original impulsion, this operates more circumspectly with insight into end and method. Such is the outline of every experience that is clothed with meaning. [LW10:66]

Meaningless organic energy is transformed into meaningful, conscious experience. In this process both self and world become imbued with felt, emotionalized, or expressive significance. There is no expression without this coordination; mere "discharge" of feeling with articulation is not expression for Dewey. Thus he says, "Expression is the clarification of turbid emotion" [LW10:83]. Art is a cultivated development of the natural capacity for objects in experience to acquire expressive, emotional meaning.

This is why, Dewey speculates, artists tend to cultivate "moments of resistance and tension" for their own sake, thereby "bringing to living consciousness an experience that is unified and total" [LW10:21]. Recall the French poet Rimbaud's experiments with the "disordering of all the senses." [12] Out of these experiments he produced such works as the *Illuminations* which present an utterly strange world apprehended in pure moments of total self-composed lucidity. [13] Dewey would understand. There is no natural dualism between reason and the emotions. We come to distinguish "reason" from "emotion" insofar as they reflect different phases in dealing with a tensive situation: we have an emotional reaction, then we think what to do. But as action integrates conduct once again, the two flow and work together. The resulting order is both intelligent and emotionally expressive. "The difference between the esthetic and the intellectual is thus one of the place where the emphasis falls in the constant rhythm that marks the interaction of the live creature with his surroundings" [LW10:21]. This is the reason, too, why we do not need to speak of emotions being "projected" into surroundings: from an ecological point of view the *world* is expressive and emotionally colored from the start. Art cultivates this potentiality.

These issues lead Dewey to a profound and far-reaching conclusion. The rhythmic flow of life is the basis for our experience of meaning and value in the world.

> There are two sorts of possible worlds in which esthetic experience would not occur. In a world of mere flux, change would not be cumulative; it would not move toward a close. Stability and rest would have no being. Equally is it true, however, that a world that is finished, ended, would have no traits of suspense and crisis, and would offer no opportunity for resolution. Where everything is already complete, there is no fulfillment. . . . Because the actual world, that in which we live, is a combination of movement and culmination, of breaks and re-unions, the experience of the live creature is capable of esthetic quality. [LW10:22]

This passage can be read as a gloss on the history of metaphysics, at least in the west, which has tried to identify Being and meaning with the "God's eye view" that sees everything essentially from an atemporal, timeless, changeless vantage. Whereas the medievals reserved such a view for God, the moderns, beginning with Galileo and Descartes, have tried to describe nature and the elements of the human mind from just such an ideal so that we easily speak of "states of affairs" or "brain states," as if the world were really composed of completely fixed, discrete atoms, physical, mental, logical or otherwise. In such a world the aesthetic is altogether absent or, where present and acknowledged, meaningless. It is no accident that as G. E. Moore was expounding his beliefs that there were ultimate moral qualities and Russell was working on his logical atomism, Clive Bell argued that aesthetics was only concerned with pure, fixed, "aesthetic" emotions, entirely unrelated to anything in the object.[14]

Dewey, by contrast, is deeply aware of how temporality infuses all experience. In the midst of turmoil and conflict, there is the mute memory of equilibrium and harmony, "the sense of which haunts life like the sense of being founded on a rock" [LW10:23]. For some, caught in the failure of the present, "the past hangs upon them as a burden," filling our lived sense of the present with awareness of missed opportunity, regret; we live carrying a weight. But for what Dewey calls "the live creature," the one existing in the aesthetic flow of experience, the past is adopted, making friends even with its stupidities, as Dewey says, so that "living experience owes its richness to what Santayana well calls 'hushed reverberations' " [LW10:23]. The future fills the present with a "halo" and its possibilities are imminently felt in the here and now. Dewey concludes, "Art celebrates with peculiar intensity the moments in which the past reenforces the present and in which the future is a quickening of what now is" [LW10:24].

The Alienation of the Senses

The very resistance to integrate art with life betrayed to Dewey a pervasive feature of modern life. Our dualistic habits not only affected our theoretical discussions and isolated intellectual from existential issues: they affected the very way we felt and lived in the world. In a similar way Marx spoke of the alienation of the senses.[15] Dewey puts it blandly, "The institutional life of mankind is marked by disorganization" [LW10:26]. By "disorganization" Dewey means "static division into classes," the evaluation of classes as "high" (or good) and "low" (or base),[16] compartmentalization of life, the separation of spirituality from daily experience, a mechanistic market-driven system of desire and productivity, and, ultimately, because of the compartmentalization of all spiritual and intellectual disciplines, the existence of systematic or collective stupidity throughout the social order.

The tragedy is that by nature human beings crave experience that is felt to be meaningful and value rich, as noted above. "Only occasionally in the lives of many are the senses fraught with the sentiment that comes from deep realization of intrinsic meanings." More poignantly: "We see without feeling; we hear, but only a second-hand report. . . . We touch, but the contact remains tangential because it does not fuse with qualities of senses that go below the surface" [LW10:27; see 34 f.]. The fundamental problem for Dewey is not to account for the *presence* of aesthetic experience, but to account for its *absence*. The tragedy of the human condition is that we have accepted a maimed version of experience as "normal" and so have had to explain genuine experience as "abnormal," "transcendent," or "pure."

"Sense" is a rich term for Dewey, ranging from the use of the senses, to sensitivity, to the felt immediacy of meaning, of what "makes sense." This range bespeaks no vagueness or ambiguity, but the incarnation of spirit in the flesh, the blossoming of the body into a lived meaning. Space and time are not conceptual abstractions or formal intuitions: they are the dramatic ranges of possible action, the anticipations of events performed and experienced. The act of recognition is no bare identification, but the sudden crystallization of experience suffused with memory. Perception itself is essentially an aesthetic rather than an epistemological category.

To see, to perceive, is more than to recognize. It does not identify something present in terms of a past disconnected from it. The past is carried into the present so as to expand and deepen the content of the latter. There is illustrated the translation of bare continuity of external time into the vital order and organization of experience. Identification nods and passes on. . . . The extent to which the process of living in any day or hour is reduced to labeling situations . . . marks the cessation of a life that is a conscious experience. Continuities realized in an individual, discrete, form are the essence of the latter. [LW10:30]

Perception has been poorly conceived in epistemology as an inward flow of "ideas" or "sense data" which are then recognized and catalogued by a dispassionate observing intellect or "mind." For Dewey, however, perception involves an "opening outward" of the body to the world, an exploratory and intensely receptive activity—and this means a capacity to suffer, a vulnerability. To be able to experience the world we must be willing to be wounded by it. Dewey notes that without the element of "undergoing, of suffering in its large sense" there "would be no taking in of what preceded." For "taking in" is no mere addition to what has gone before: "It involves reconstruction which may be painful. . . . there are few intense esthetic experiences that are wholly gleeful" [LW10:47–48].

The moral that Dewey draws from this is momentous. Not only is "Art . . . thus prefigured in the very processes of living," but "The existence of art is the concrete proof . . . that man uses the materials and energies of nature with intent to expand his own life. . . . Art is the living and concrete proof that man is capable of restoring consciously, and thus on the plane of meaning, the union of sense, need, impulse, and action characteristic of the live creature" [LW10:30–31]. Art, when placed in its natural, ecological context, points the way for the liberation of the sensuous human body from its institutionalized alienation. Perhaps this is why Dewey describes the *idea* of art as "the greatest intellectual achievement in the history of humanity" [LW10:31].

The Consummatory Experience

What, then, is the nature of experience when it is most fully realized *as* experience? It should be evident now that Dewey's description of aesthetically consummated experience is central to his philosophy as a whole and not merely to his aesthetic theory. Dewey addresses this topic most directly in the chapter "Having an Experience." The emphasis here is on the indefinite article *an* which denotes the pervasive continuity and intense, qualitative integration of the experience as a whole that marks it off from ordinary experience which is filled with "distraction and dispersion." "In contrast with such experience," says Dewey, "we have *an* experience when the material experienced runs its course to fulfillment.... Such an experience is a whole and carries with it its own individualizing quality and self-sufficiency. It is *an* experience" [LW10:42]. Such experiences have a beginning and an end. The beginning is initiated by a tensive excitement that compels us to focus on the unfolding experience. Dewey calls this "seizure" or "impulsion."[17] The field of experience is rendered focused and kept within limits by what Dewey terms "closure" or "fusion," which also brings about the sense of drawing the experience to an end.[18] While such phases can be predominantly marked out as "beginning" and "ending" the experience, it must be emphasized that they coexist and mutually determine each other throughout the experience of the artwork, there is "opening" and "closing" going on all the time in the encounter.[19] As we listen to a piece of music, there is a felt "tendency toward integration and converging" going on at the same time as a "felt tendency toward novel development and expansion"; as we look at a painting, our eyes are kept within the limits of the work by the frame and the inner organization while we visually explore the different regions within the painting itself. In this way emotion and thought are both alive and united through their perceived and felt interrelationship.

Thus, every experience which is *an* experience is a consummation, a bringing-to-completion, in which the world opens itself to us and reveals a felt or sensed meaning and embodied value (in a nonverbal way). No matter how brief, it is marked by the correlative temporal dynamics of seizure-closure. An analysis of even such minimalist artforms as haiku manifests such an event structure. A haiku depicts a momentary crystallization of a situation that is inherently transitory and that evokes a sense of a seasonal world and an individual's sudden, poignant mood. It must be stressed yet again that by "consummation" or "completion" Dewey does not mean that works of art cannot deal with themes that involve "alienation" or "fragmentation." A bad work of art, whatever its theme, fails to integrate its materials so that they are expressive and realize a felt meaning to the work. Our interest is not provoked and our senses are not brought into a fresh synthesis. On the other hand, a good work of art, like Picasso's *Guernica* which deals with the destruction of civilization, achieves its power through the focal, integrated intensity of its composition. An experience of seeing *Hamlet* well performed does not leave us with a sense that there is either a triumph of order in the universe or that everything works out for the best. But it does achieve "consummation" and "completion" because of its integrity and depth as a work of art. This completion is the realization of dynamic continuity:

> In such experiences, every successive part flows freely, without seam and without unfilled blanks, into what ensues. At the same time there is no sacrifice of the self-identity of the parts. . . . In an experience, flow is from something to something. As one part leads into another and as one part carries on what went before, each gains distinctness in itself. The enduring whole is diversified by successive phases that are emphases of its varied colors. [LW10:45]

One of the major points that Dewey makes regarding consummatory experience is that the pervasive qualitative "feel" of the situation is consciously manifest throughout the course of the experience. "An experience has a unity that gives it its name, *that* meal, that storm, that rupture of friendship. The existence of this unity is constituted by a single *quality* that pervades the entire experience in spite of . . . its constituent parts" [LW10:44]. There is a bounding horizon which constitutes the "sense of the context" within which all our conscious awareness of meaning, aesthetic or not, occurs. But most of the time this is not in our conscious awareness. When we are engaged in sheerly routine work or in "problem solving" in its most limited, utilitarian sense, we are not explicitly aware of the "feel" of the experience as such. We are "getting work done" or "fixing the sink."

As experience becomes aesthetic, whatever we happen to be doing, this pervasive quality that marks it out as whole, continuous, and meaningful is vividly present. Thus, the "quality" of the experience is not some specific *part* of the experience that remains *in spite of* the diversity. The experience may go through complete transformation (and usually does in aesthetic experience). *King Lear* begins with a sense of the complacency and shallow authority of tradition; by the end of the play nothing of this is left. We have traveled through a harrowing reduction of human nature to its most contemptible and noblest elements. Yet all parts of the play are felt as *belonging* to the play; they are *about* it. Nor is the pervasive quality easily identifiable, repeatable, or nameable. It is what marks off "*an* experience" as a whole, as *that* experience and no other. It is this elusive but meaningful dimension of the aesthetic that artists point to when they refuse to put the "meaning" of their art into words or, in the case of verbal arts, into different words: The work is about *that!* they will say.

The final point to note about consummatory experience is that it involves a *perceived* relationship between the phases of experience which are had or undergone and those which are done. "An experience has pattern and structure, because it is not just doing and undergoing in alternation, but consists of them in relationship" [LW10:50–51]. Dewey's common term for this is "intelligence."[20] What makes ordinary experience fail to be consummatory is just the failure to integrate these two. As doing is ignored we verge toward passive, bland neutrality or else, in the name of experience, indulge in chaotic, meaningless intensity. Rimbaud's experiments in the "disorganization of the senses" eventually went to the extreme of nearly driving him insane and in the end made him abandon poetry for running guns to Ethiopia. As we come to emphasize doing for the sake of doing, we head toward the rat-race vision of life of which Ducasse spoke. Thus, for those who would make the aesthetic dimension of experience passive and merely intuitional, Dewey would urge the instrumental nature of all meaningful experience; for those who would make the instrumental a means-first or a means-without-ends activity, Dewey would have us look at the intelligence in the aesthetic. By carefully reflecting on experience in its wholeness, the consummatory experience, Dewey points to what the rest of his philosophy is about.

Conclusion: A Philosophy of Democratic Civilization

Art as Experience proceeds to offer an in-depth analysis of the cardinal issues of aesthetics: expression, form, the relation of subject matter to the work of art itself, the relationships of the arts to each other, and so on. Given the way Dewey has integrated aesthetics into the heart of his vision of experience, these issues have implications for his philosophy as a whole, for his theory of communication in particular as well as for his critique of anti-aesthetic or "aestheticicist" philosophies of experience. But the larger implications of his work are more far reaching. "Aesthetics" has usually been equated with a "philosophy of fine art," and so has been completely unrelated to ethics or political philosophy. Likewise "ethics" has been narrowly conceived as limited to matters of moral conduct and rules of moral judgment, and "political theory" has focused on constitutional mechanics, the origins of legitimacy, and the problem of "rights."

Dewey achieved his most radical insight, in my view, in driving the implications of his aesthetic theory toward a broad vision of the aims of the democratic life, toward a philosophy of civilization. Democratic society seeks the liberation of experience, Dewey believed. But liberation does not come by merely removing barriers. The powers of human beings to engage the world so that it funds their lives with a vibrant sense of meaning and value must be nurtured. Thus, ethics and the philosophy of education naturally become part of the political for Dewey.

But democracy is not primarily a political theory in Dewey's way of speaking. It is the culture of a whole society in which experience is engaged in its power of fulfillment of life through cooperation and communication. The basis of democracy is the community, a localized place where human life is nurtured, where a willingness and power to listen precede any given speaking.[21] Above all, a community is a source of ideals. Without a sense of what human fulfillment can be, we cannot give any intelligent direction to our practices. To be sure, these ideals must be submitted to experimental implementation and critical reevaluation. Competing ideals must be entertained as intelligence warrants. But if democracy is to have a future, it must embrace an understanding of the deepest needs of human beings and the means of fulfilling them. Dewey has argued that our deepest need, the "human eros" as I have termed it, is for the experience of meaning and value in our lives. In art, we have a concrete instance that this is possible. What if the lesson taught there could be applied across the board? The aesthetic could become a possibility of human experience at large.

Obviously, Dewey did not think that any and all types of experiences could or should be made "aesthetic." Drudgery and boredom, disease and death cannot be eliminated, and our abilities to adapt or respond may be limited (though the great religions, most of which are constituted by what Dewey calls "arts of acceptance" indicate how far an aesthetics of mortality and fatality can be developed).[22] Dewey cannot deny that the skills of a torturer or executioner are not arts, for experts can be clearly recognized there. Whether they belong as ideals for a *democratic* society, however, is another matter. James Joyce recalled his experience of being punished by a school master who excelled in the art of fear, but not at all in the art of education, which, of course, was the ultimate purpose of the school.[23]

At the beginning of *Democracy and Education*, Dewey notes that we have education because culture *must* be passed on. Each one of us is fated to die, but because of the act of communication, shared, cumulative experience can pass along and with it the possibility of a deeper, wiser, more intelligent, and more humane response to the enduring problems of the human condition. From the inevitability of death and the demands of the human eros to experience the world with meaning and value, civilization is born. "Instruction in the arts of life," says Dewey, "is something other than conveying information about them. It is a matter of communication and participation in values of life by means of the imagination, and works of art are the most intimate and energetic means of aiding individuals to share in the arts of living" [LW10:339]. Dewey sardonically adds, "Civilization is uncivil because human beings are divided into non-communicating sects, races, nations, classes, and cliques."

How can we generate mutual understanding across such barriers? Before there can be effective political debate, perhaps there must be a capacity to hear each other's stories, experience the world from the other's body, be at least momentarily held by their visions of paradise. We may not be Buddhists or Christians or Moslems, but we may be suddenly stunned by the beauty of a Gandharan statue of the Buddha, a stained glass window in a great cathedral, or the shining glazed tiles of the mosques of Isfahan. Through their images of beauty we may be able briefly to enter the aesthetics of other cultures' worlds. We may become open at least to the *possibility* of their experience, of their way of meaning. As we develop an "epistemology of the ear" we may be able to hear the voices of other cultures, of marginalized people in our own culture, of women everywhere. As we learn to listen, so may others. When there is mutual listening, perhaps we may at last speak. Listening does not mean passive acceptance. It means receptivity combined with imagination. This is the condition of criticism and change. In that process, where a community gradually emerges through the mutual imagination of the participants, the aesthetic possibility of experience effects a transformation, "the light that never was on sea or land," to which Dewey gave the name of "the religious."[24]

Notes

1. C. J. Ducasse, *The Philosophy of Art* (New York: Dial Press, 1929), p. 86. The passage deserves to be read in full since it illustrates the typical misreading of pragmatism that Dewey's critics perpetuated over the years:

The life of man, or rather of intelligent man, that is to say man as he supposedly ought to be, is in effect depicted by it as a life of toolmaking, all the tools made (whether physical or psychological) being themselves essentially tools for toolmaking. In a life of that sort there is no such thing as tool-using except for the making of other tools; and the only satisfactions acknowledged are those arising from the process of toolmaking itself, or from the perception of the utility of some tool for toolmaking. Immediate satisfactions are paradoxically said to be "their own excuses for being just because they are charged with an office" [LW1:274].

Such a life would avoid the "dust and ashes of boredom" to which Professor Dewey says that a consummatory object which is not also instrumental also turns in time; but it would bring to replace it a characteristic evil of its own,—the fatigue and weariness which no less surely result in time from the ever renewed stimulation of the ever instrumental; and the ingrained restlessness and incapacity for contemplation,—all too widespread today,—which insistence on somehow turning everything into means, produces.

2. See Stephen Pepper, "Some Questions on Dewey's Esthetics" in *The Philosophy of John Dewey,* 3d edition, ed. Paul A. Schilpp and Lewis Hahn (La Salle, Ill.: Open Court, 1971), p. 371, and Benedetto Croce, "On the Aesthetics of Dewey," *The Journal of Aesthetics and Art Criticism* 6 (1948), pp. 203–207. An extended discussion of this problem can be found in my *John Dewey's Theory of Art, Experience, and Nature: The Horizons of Feeling* (Albany: State University of New York Press, 1987), ch. 1. This work will hereafter be cited as *The Horizons of Feeling.*

3. Emergentism argues that nature is capable of generating or evolving new modes of order and creating new features which are irreducible to the conditions which produced them. Thus, matter is necessary for life, but life cannot be reduced to physics; life is necessary for consciousness, but consciousness cannot be reduced to neurophysics. It is important to emphasize, for Dewey's Emergentism at least, that (1) the emergent traits are not "supervenient properties" but creative transformations or reconstructions of nature, (2) nature cannot be identified with the object of physics, as in materialistic naturalisms but is the creative environment within which events of all kinds occur, and (3) novelty, individuality, and relation are pervasive features of nature. It is thus a serious mistake to read Dewey as belonging to the mechanistic, reductionist naturalistic tradition of Democritus, Hobbes, Spencer, or Dennett. Nor is he an epiphenomenalist regarding consciousness as an impotent byproduct like Santayana or Paul Churchland.

4. This passage occurs only a few pages from the phrase quoted by Ducasse cited above; had Ducasse made a careful study of Dewey's own text, instead of projecting upon it a perfect inversion of Dewey's meaning, his criticisms could not have been raised. Again, I point to this because such a misreading of Dewey is endemic in the literature about him.

5. For a discussion contrasting linear or "straight-line" means-ends thinking, often confused with Deweyan instrumentalism, see Larry Hickman's discus-

sion in *John Dewey's Pragmatic Technology* (Bloomington: Indiana University Press, 1990), ch. 1.

6. See Oscar Wilde's essay "The Critic as Artist" for an example of the former and Clive Bell's essay "Art" as an example of the latter.

7. Compare: "Experience in the degree in which it *is* experience is heightened vitality" [LW10:25].

8. The influence of the industrialist–millionaire–art collector Albert Barnes upon Dewey from 1917 on cannot be discounted. Barnes, otherwise a pugnacious and autocratic man, became a devoted friend of Dewey and took Dewey with him on his artistic jaunts to Europe. Dewey eventually became associated with Barnes's institute and museum. Dewey dedicated *Art as Experience* to Barnes, just as Barnes had dedicated his *Art in Painting* to Dewey.

9. Some of the themes I have in mind are: (1) Dewey's attention to the "fringe" or "horizon" of experience as an integral part of the meaning of the focal, intentional object of conscious thought and as a structuring matrix for it, (2) the pervasive qualitative nature of "sense" as what is sensed as well as what makes sense, (3) the themes of situation, reconstruction, and evaluation, and (4) his view of nature as emergent and creative.

    Usually the problem of Dewey's "turn" is placed on his shift away from idealism toward pragmatism in the 1890s. But critics of his mature philosophy, like Pepper and Croce as well as, more recently, Richard Bernstein and Richard Rorty, see Dewey's position as deeply contradictory, pulled one way by metaphysical idealism and the other by empiricism and naturalism. Thus, one could say that unless a case is successfully made for *Experience and Nature* and *Art as Experience,* the two works where critics find these "opposing strains" most in evidence, the real "turn" in Dewey's thought is *away* from the "naturalism" of 1903 to 1925 toward an idealistic philosophy that underlies most of his "great" works from *Experience and Nature* on. Such an approach does not seem at all necessary to me. The consequence, however, of rejecting this alternative is to undertake a serious and prolonged investigation of just these two works. I have attempted this in *The Horizons of Feeling.*

10. William Carlos Williams recalls the initial experience in his autobiography: "Once on a hot July day coming back exhausted from the Post Graduate Clinic, I dropped in as I sometimes did at Marsden's studio on Fifteenth Street for a talk, a little drink maybe and to see what he was doing. As I approached his number I heard a great clatter of bells and the roar of a fire engine passing the end of the street down Ninth Avenue. I turned just in time to see a golden figure 5 on a red background flash by. The impression was so sudden and forceful that I took a piece of paper out of my pocket and wrote a short poem about it." *The Autobiography of William Carlos Williams* (New York: New Directions, 1967), p. 172. Demuth's painting is also a testimony to his friendship with the poet. See Dickran Tashjian, *William Carlos Williams*

and the American Scene (Berkeley: University of California Press in association with the Whitney Museum of American Art, 1978), p. 71.

11. The examples come from Dewey's attempts to describe the "pervasive quality" of "an experience." See Later Works 10, p. 43, and the Introduction to Essays in Experimental Logic [MW10:322].

12. See Rimbaud's A Season in Hell, "Delerium": "I invented the color of vowels!—A black, E white, I red, O blue, U green.—I regulated the form and the movement of every consonant, and with instinctive rhythms I prided myself on inventing a poetic language accessible one day to all the senses. I reserved all rights of translation. At first it was an experiment. I wrote silences, I wrote the night. I recorded the inexpressible. I fixed frenzies in their flight" (trans. Louise Varèse). See also his poem "Voyelles" ("Vowels").

13. Dewey makes an important observation here that artists, like scientists, engage in experimental thinking (just as we saw above, Dewey thinks that scientists engage in artistic thought): "The odd notion that an artist does not think and that a scientific inquirer does nothing else is the result of converting the tempo and emphasis into a difference in kind. The thinker has his esthetic moment when his ideas cease to be mere ideas and become the corporate meanings of objects. The artist has his problems and thinks as he works" [LW10:21].

14. See Clive Bell, Art (1913; New York: G. P. Putnam's Sons, 1958).

15. See Karl Marx, Economic and Philosophical Manuscripts of 1844, trans. Martin Milligan (Buffalo, N.Y.: Prometheus Press, 1988), esp. "Estranged Labor," pp. 74–80, and "Private Property and Communism. Various Stages of Development of Communist Views. Crude, Equalitarian Communism and Communism as Humanism Coinciding with Humanness," pp. 103–107.

16. Compare here Nietzsche on the creation of values and social dominance in The Genealogy of Morals.

17. See Later Works 10, pp. 64 and 150, and my discussion in The Horizons of Feeling, p. 140 f. and p. 243 f., where I analyze this as "the dawning sense of the promise of meaning."

18. See Later Works 10, pp. 47 and 196, and my discussion in The Horizons of Feeling, p. 204 f. and p. 251 f.

19. This aspect of aesthetic experience occurs in Heidegger's own analysis in "The Origin of the Work of Art." It was also a major theme in Chinese aesthetics, which referred to it as "k'ai ho" or "open-closure." See George Rowley, The Principles of Chinese Painting, 2d ed. (Princeton, N.J.: Princeton University Press, 1959), p. 48 f.

20. See the especially important essay "Qualitative Thought" [LW5:243 ff.].

21. See the very last paragraph of The Public and Its Problems [LW2:371–72].

22. See The Quest for Certainty [LW4], ch. 4.

23. The incident is described in *The Portrait of the Artist as a Young Man.*

24. See Dewey's *A Common Faith* [LW11]. The phrase "the light that never was on sea or land" comes from Wordsworth's "Elegiac Stanzas Suggested by a Picture of Peele Castle in a Storm." Dewey uses the phrase in *Reconstruction in Philosophy* [MW12:201 and LW10:279].

2 Dewey's Conception of Community

James Campbell

This chapter explores aspects of Dewey's conception of community. It begins with a discussion of his understanding of the nature of society, emphasizing the relationship between groups and their values, and the role of the social critic. Then it explores aspects of Dewey's analysis of the qualities and marks of community, focusing upon his understanding of community as a moral place. Finally, it briefly considers the reasons Dewey offers for emphasizing one's place in the community and some of the problems that are inherent in a focus upon the common good.

I

Community has long been an important topic in American thought. The question of who we are, and why, could never have been far from the surface of discussion in a society that saw itself engaged in an ongoing process of self-creation. Whatever their model of human perfection, Americans have stressed that the community provides the emotional and moral place where individuals can approximate it. Our current uneasiness about the direction of American society—an uneasiness full of assumptions that we have fallen from some true path and worries about where we are leading our children—has had many precursors, going back to our earliest discussions as a country.

The topic of community has been one of the central themes of American philosophy as well; and it holds a special place in the work of John Dewey and his Social Pragmatist colleagues, George Herbert Mead and James Hayden Tufts. Tufts writes, for example, of the importance of constructing and reconstructing social institutions so that the community can carry forward its gains and avoid remaking prior mistakes: "the individual's span is at best short. His working years are soon counted. He can accomplish little alone. But man has learned to build institutions."[1] Mead's many discussions of community include consideration of the essential moral role of the social critic, who "appeals, so to speak, from a narrow and restricted community to a larger one."[2] Discussions of the role of communal institutions in human fulfillment and of the nature of social criticism play a major role in Dewey's thought as well.

In any consideration of the nature and role of community in human life it is necessary to consider the individuals, the selves that create and sustain and benefit from the community. The Social Pragmatists discuss the origin of the self as something not present at the birth of the individual but emerging, developing in the course of living communally with other individuals. In their view, individuals grow to a sense of self-consciousness *through* the communities in which they live, not simply *in* them. Thus, rather than seeing selves in terms of either separateness from others or faithfulness to some pre-set trajectory, the Social Pragmatist analysis emphasizes the emergence of the self within the social context. Emergent selves are social through and through, growing within and because of their communal life, developing in a situation of shared living.

For Dewey, human individuals are inherently social, creatures for whom community is natural. For Dewey, moreover, communities are essential: we need groups to *become* human. We develop our humanity, our individuality, in the midst of community living. "To learn to be human," he writes, "is to develop through the give-and-take of communication an effective sense of being an individually distinctive member of a community; one who understands and appreciates its beliefs, desires and methods, and who contributes to a further conversion of organic powers into human resources and values." This process is one that, as he continues, "is never finished" [LW2:332]. Participation in a community is essential to a fulfilled human existence because such participation makes possible a more diversified and enriching experience for all members.

Another fundamental aspect of human individuals to which Dewey and the other Social Pragmatists point is the role of habit in our lives. Habits give continuity and stability to our activities; they enable us to act, free from the need to think through and plan our actions at every particular step. Habits, moreover, are remarkably persistent. "No matter how accidental and irrational the circumstances of its origin, no matter how different the conditions which now exist to those under which the habit was formed," Dewey writes, it persists "until the environment obstinately rejects it." He continues: "Habits once formed perpetuate themselves, by acting unremittingly upon the native stock of activities. They stimulate, inhibit, intensify, weaken, select, concentrate and organize the latter into their own likeness. They create out of the formless void of impulses a world made in their own image" [MW14:88]. Because of the centrality and importance of habits, we cannot hope to gain some sort of liberation from them. We need, on the contrary, a recognition of their general importance to life and of the specific impact of particular habits. Habits "of whose import we are quite unaware," Dewey writes, "possess us, rather than we them. They move us; they control us." And they will continue to do so until such time as "we become aware of what they accomplish, and pass judgment upon the worth of the result" [MW9:34–35].

Of particular importance to the present topic of community are those social habits that we call customs. Of them Dewey writes: "Most of the important habits of the individual are dependent for their origin and growth upon prior customs in society." Included among these habits is "a large part of the content of morality" [MW6:413]. These social customs or traditions are set ways of organizing conduct, ways with which we are in general comfortable and which we are for the most part willing to defend and carry forward. These institutions are able to order our shared lives in large part because of the importance of institutions to the successful life of the community. Given the virtually infinite number of possible ways for ordering the necessary ongoing activities of our group—activities like reproduction and the raising of children, the allocation of work and disposing of the economic output of the group, the management of our place in nature through health care and agriculture and religion, and so on—the institutional system employed must be, and must be felt to be, both proper and powerful.

While individuals more open to the rich variety of other possible approaches may view the procedures of their societies as largely arbitrary, more typically members of groups see these procedures as natural and proper, and superior to the procedures in effect elsewhere. Dewey writes that, because of social embellishments, these customs are integrally ours: "If social customs are more than uniform external modes of action, it is because they are saturated with story and transmitted meaning" [LW10:329]. So essential and fundamental is the role of custom to the self that we seldom notice how powerfully it shapes our actions. Dewey continues that: "our tendency to ignore the influence of tradition as a controlling factor is itself very largely due to the fact that when we begin to reflect, to invent, and to project new methods and aims, tradition has already done its work so completely that we take it for granted without thinking about it, so that we deliberate and project within limits set by custom" [MW6:414]. Again here, as with individual habits, our goal is not liberation from custom but recognition of its powerful role. As Dewey puts it: "the choice is not between a moral authority outside custom and one within it. It is between adopting more or less intelligent and significant customs" [MW14:58; cf. LW1:23].

These considerations lead us to a further Deweyan point that people all "require moral sanctions in their conduct: the consent of their kind" [MW4:49]. Most frequently this sanctioning comes indirectly, through these very social customs. The traditional way of doing things—what we like to call "our" way—carries with it a special moral status that enables it to bypass many uncomfortable justificatory questions. Dewey writes that "[i]n customary society, it does not occur to anyone that there is a difference between what he ought to do, i.e., the moral, and what those about him customarily do, i.e., the social." In other words, he continues: "The socially established *is* the moral" [MW5:387]. Even in societies like our own, which we take to be more informed and reflective, people often "take their social relations for granted; they are what they are and, in being that, are what they *should* be" [LW7:314]. He continues that we find "multitudes of men and women who take their aims from what they observe to be going on around them. They accept the aims provided by religious teachers, by political authorities, by persons in the community who have prestige. Failure to adopt such a course would seem to many persons to be a kind of moral rebellion or anarchy" [LW7:184; cf. MW9:21].[3] Dewey's reminder of the intimate relationship between the familiar and the proper rings true, especially with regard to our contemporary near-equation of what is traditional and what is valuable. His point moreover is particularly useful to us because his use of *customary* is not related primarily to some presumed historical or anthropological setting but rather to the nature of the moral justification that is being offered. The sense of *customary* that he has in mind refers to "the centre of gravity in morality," and its opponent is not *modern* but *reflective*. His intention is to bring about a shifting in this center of gravity, from justification through conformity with "ancestral habit" to "conscience, reason, or to some principle which includes thought" [LW7:162].

We normally adopt the values of our groups—of our sex and class, of our religion and family—and we evaluate ourselves, at least initially, as measuring up to or not measuring up to these groups' general ideal of a good person. Dewey presents this internalization as follows: "An assembly is formed within our breast which discusses and appraises proposed and performed acts. The community without becomes a forum and tribunal within" [MW14:216]. As growing and developing selves, we receive our enemies and our friends, our goals and our taboos, from our groups. Because the way our groups do things becomes the proper way, we all too often find our moral and political and aesthetic values as easily—and with as little serious thinking—as we find our idioms of speech and familiar telephone numbers. In other words, our socially derived values just seem obvious; and they seem obvious because they are not the external restraints upon us that the familiar individualistic analysis suggests they are. Rather, these values are reinforcing elements within our selves. These socially derived values are, for good or ill, parts of us; they are habitual elements of our beings that are not easily changed.

When we consider the related question of challenging and perhaps reconstructing our customary values, traditions, and institutions to adapt them to changes in the contemporary world, one particular difficulty is prominent. Many of our customs—especially those that are felt to be closest to our social core, like sexual values and religious and political symbols—are not the sorts of topics about which we are likely to think critically. We have felt the need, on the contrary, to sacralize them, perhaps to make them better tools in shaping our children's behavior, perhaps to increase their power as a justification for punishing those among us who fail to conform, perhaps simply to help us quiet any lingering doubts we might have about their validity. Whatever the reason(s), the sacralization of our customs short-circuits potential evaluation. As a result, we often find ourselves unable to change our customs without abandoning what we see as part of ourselves. To the extent that our traditions make us what we are, to change them would make us something else. So we live in conflict, unable to adapt. For example, we are a people who, oblivious to contemporary realities, champion heterosexual monogamy as the proper form of coupling. We are a people who long so strongly for a bygone era of public civility that we forget that this civility masked grievous inequalities. We are a people who find it necessary to defend the literal interpretation of religious texts and the idolization of political objects, even though both are more properly seen as symbolic. We hold on to sacralized elements of our past because to reject them is to reject ourselves.

Even when we can minimize this sacralization, we recognize the difficulties that we will encounter when we attempt to challenge the familiar. Dewey writes that customs persist primarily "because individuals form their personal habits under conditions set by prior customs." As a consequence, he continues, a person "usually acquires the morality as he inherits the speech of his social group." And, just as "[t]here is no miracle in the fact that if a child learns any language he learns the language that those about him speak and teach," we should find it in no way surprising that individuals also adopt customs other than the linguistic. The persistence of custom can thus be attributed to the normal process of developing a habituated self by individuals whose "imagination is thereby limited," and change will be difficult [MW14:43]. "Ways of belief, of expectation, of judgment and attendant emotional dispositions of like and dislike," he writes, "are not easily modified after they have once taken shape" [MW14:77].

This discussion of Dewey's understanding of the role of society and custom in the shaping of the self is not yet completed. Human individuals are not just members of groups. Just as important to our lives is our ability to transcend these groups. In addition to the conventional and habitual aspect of the self, there is also a reactive or responsive aspect. Each of us develops, at the time when she or he becomes a self with a conscious recognition of what it is to be a good person according to any group's ideal, the ability to step outside of this ideal. We recognize, of course, that this ability to separate ourselves from the collective flow of the group grows slowly, by means of the gradual realization of the degree to which our actions are ordered for us by society's customs. We recognize as well that this realization takes place largely through encounters with other actual modes of living. We also recognize the difficulty that individuals have trying to balance this knowledge of other modes of living off against our own frequent sacralizations without succumbing to some form of crippling relativism. The young have an especially difficult time keeping alive the pursuit of the morally justifiable as they become increasingly cognizant of our frequent equations of the traditional with the right. It is the job of an educational system to help prepare these future adults to use customs without being overcome by them; but our schools and other educational institutions are acutely sensitive to the pressures to sacralize.

Effective social critics, as Dewey recognized, are individuals firmly rooted in the life of their community who see there problems and possibilities of resolution and who try to bring this perspective before the public. In doing so, the critic does not simply attack his or her society. Rather, as we saw with Mead above, individuals appeal "from a narrow and restricted community to a larger one." As Mead formulates this point elsewhere, individuals attempt to uncover "the principles" that have been overwhelmed by "the prejudices of the community."[4] Our group has by accident or choice adopted customary ways of acting that overlook important values, usually values that it itself upholds in some weakened or distorted form; and the individuals who have cultivated a sense of the larger community can recognize and point this out. If successful, social critics make the community a richer place by causing it to confront and overcome the contradictions between its values and its current practices. A central point in this community building is the process of discussion that makes social growth happen. The effective social critic thus attempts to justify proffered social proposals through interaction with others, and through this process of cooperative inquiry we discover together values upon which we can build.

This role of social critic is played by all of us at one time or another, because we are all able to step back and evaluate our communal situation. We are all members of more than one group and are familiar with many more; and, just as even young children can criticize the decisions of their own parents in the light of what they consider to be the more enlightened policies operating in other families, we can by comparison suggest alternate ends and means for our community. The complex self that should be cultivated in anyone who lives in our multicultural world is a storehouse of historical and contemporary facts and relationships of importance to social evaluation. In his own life and work, Dewey attempted to play this role of rooted social critic, advocating the advancement of the common good and the growth of individuals. Central to his work was the belief that we could build communities that would be both enduring and supportive of individuals, that we could foster individual lives that would be both rooted and growing. For the social self, this growth means not disengagement but greater involvement, not independence but responsibility. The ideal is to develop as a contributor to the efforts of the community to address the problems of social life.

II

If we move from this broadly social and moral standpoint to a more narrow consideration of aspects of community itself—especially of ideas on how to understand and advance community—we reach the philosophical core of Dewey's work on community. Underlying this work is the belief that social reconstruction is a complex process. It is a process that depends in part upon the careful analysis of our intellectual materials—our ideas and concepts—and in part upon the forging and enactment of fundamental institutional changes. On the one hand, we need to think more clearly about what our inherited notion of community means, and how it might be improved; on the other, we need to work to develop better communities. In this essay, the former aspect will predominate.

Throughout his career, Dewey concerned himself with the reconstruction of the full range of political concepts. In each case, he was interested in uncovering how the terms had been used and were being used in his day; but in no case did he suggest that we remain trapped within their habitual senses. Underlying his work on conceptual reconstruction are three separable claims, each of which is fundamentally pragmatic in nature. The first was that conceptions of political terms are tools to be used in our attempts to settle our social problems, and that they thus have no *absolute* or *final* meanings. So, for example, while it is necessary to be guided by the meanings contained in the admittedly incoherent set of traditions and documents that we have inherited, the requirements of an adequate sense of community cannot simply be uncovered in this way. Neither can we hope to create on our own some final sense of the term to be enforced in the future. Rather, the functional adequacy of conceptions must be evaluated in the context of their particular situations. His second claim was that the various historically bound conceptions of political terms that we have inherited did once make reasonable contemporary sense, the fact to which they owe their survival. The third claim that Dewey was making was that by his day many of these inherited conceptions no longer worked to advance the common good. These conceptions had become, in other words, merely habitual, and they continued to function largely by default. Some conceptions were necessary for ordering discourse and they, as the traditional ones, benefitted from the advantage of being familiar and in place.

To begin our consideration of community, we remember that for Dewey human individuals are inherently social—creatures for whom association, community, is essential. Communities or "publics" (to use Walter Lippmann's less contested term)[5] are natural; we need groups to *become* human. We develop our humanity, our individuality, in the midst of community living. The efforts of the members of the community benefit each other as they all attempt, through cooperative inquiry, to address their common ills. Dewey's claims about the important contribution of communal living to individual fulfillment should not suggest, however, a belief on his part that all groupings are necessarily beneficial.

In fact, Dewey uses the term *community* alternatively both in descriptive and in eulogistic senses. He writes sometimes of all kinds of "societies, associations, [and] groups" [LW2:278], "scattered communities" [LW2:306], "the business community" [LW2:354], "street gangs" and "trade unions" [MW12:194], and "criminal bands" [LW2:278]. At other times, Dewey focuses on what we might call "good" communities: democratic or moral community [cf. LW2:328–32]. Besides groups that we think anyone would be proud to be part of, like the community of scholars or "the republic of letters" [MW9:25], Dewey writes that we must also include within the scope of the term individuals "banded together in a criminal conspiracy, business aggregations that prey upon the public while serving it, political machines held together by the interest of plunder" [MW9:88]. He does not believe that this dual usage betrays any ambiguity on his part. Rather, he believes that he is pointing to the ambiguity of the terms themselves. Terms such as *community*, he writes, "have both a eulogistic or normative sense, and a descriptive sense; a meaning *de jure* and a meaning *de facto*" [MW9:88]. While there are these two meanings, and while it is thus possible to say without confusion that a gangster "is as highly 'social' in one connection as he is anti-social in other connections" [LW15:221], Dewey's central interest is upon how we *should* understand the term, upon the moral sense of *community*.

This intention to focus upon these moral aspects brings Dewey immediately to the question of how to evaluate communities. Any attempt to develop criteria, he writes, must be rooted in the societies with which we are familiar: "We cannot set up, out of our heads, something we regard as an ideal society. We must base our conception upon societies which actually exist, in order to have any assurance that our ideal is a practicable one. But . . . the ideal cannot simply repeat the traits which are actually found. The problem is to extract the desirable traits of forms of community life which actually exist, and employ them to criticize undesirable features and suggest improvement" [MW9:88–89]. Operating within these restraints, Dewey offers two distinct criteria, both of which are drawn from his analysis of growth. The first criterion is an *internal* one: "How numerous and varied are the interests which are consciously shared?" The second criterion is *external:* "How full and free is the interplay with other forms of association?" [MW9:89; cf. 105]. So, for example, in the case of a gangster mob, whatever quality the association might possess under the former criterion would be overridden, Dewey maintains, by its inadequacy under the latter. "The robber band cannot interact flexibly with other groups; it can act only through isolating itself" [LW2:328]. Consequently, we recognize that vibrant community results from individuals' efforts to develop both internal and external relations, places within our various groups and places for our groups within the larger life of the society. These various places are mutually contributory: "fullness of integrated personality is therefore possible of achievement, since the pulls and responses of different groups reenforce one another and their values accord" [LW2:328]. Individuals in such communities recognize their multiple locations and the resultant balanced sense of self-identity precludes individual absorption into any one group.[6]

In addition to his position that we would be mistaken to consider all human groupings as full examples of community, Dewey points to two other misunderstandings often found in our inherited notions. The first is the equation of community with the institution of the state or the government. Dewey is careful to indicate that he intends a distinction between community and its external forms. As he writes at one point, "I mean by 'state' the organization of the resources of community life through governmental machinery of legislation and administration" [MW2:81]. Further, the state is properly subordinated to the community. Dewey writes that there are social "agencies that lie deeper than the political" and that "the real needs of the American people must be met by means more fundamental than our traditional political institutions put at our disposal," namely the voluntary agencies of a vital and concerned community [LW3:135]. "We are held together by non-political bonds," he continues, "and the political forms are stretched and legal institutions patched in an *ad hoc* and improvised manner to do the work they have to do" [LW2:306]. He notes further that it is by means of these "social forces" that changes in "our inherited political machinery" will be made [LW3:135; cf. LW5:193].

A second possible misunderstanding that Dewey rejects is the belief that a community has to display the homogenized and monochromatic sameness with which some of its critics identify it. He recognizes that no community can be a community without some high degree of sharing. However, this communality should also imply a richness or complexity of possible perspectives that can be entered into, not the simplicity of identity. The advancement of community does not require, Dewey believes, "a sacrifice of individuality; it would be a poor kind of society whose members were personally undeveloped" [LW7:345].[7] In particular, Dewey emphasizes the value of the diversity brought to this country through the various streams of immigration, and the continued loss that results from our ongoing failure to appreciate what this multiplicity of cultures could mean. He writes, for example, that "one cannot contemplate in imagination that every people in the world should talk Volapük or Esperanto, that the same thoughts should be cultivated, the same beliefs, the same historical traditions, and the same ideals and aspirations for the future. Variety *is* the spice of life, and the richness and the attractiveness of social institutions depend upon cultural diversity among separate units. In so far as people are all alike, there is no give and take among them. And it is better to give and take" [MW10:288]. In the context of a living American community, "unity cannot be a homogeneous thing." Our efforts should focus rather on creating a unity "by drawing out and composing into a harmonious whole the best, the most characteristic which each contributing race and people has to offer" [MW10:204].

In Dewey's attempts to develop a conception of community adequate for our current situation, he offers three marks of increasing richness. The first of these is simple *association* or *interaction*. Of course, this first mark functions more as a reminder of Dewey's overall conception of natural existence: "Everything that exists in as far as it is known and knowable is in interaction with other things" [LW1:138]. This level of interactive association is just a precondition for community. As he writes, "no amount of aggregated collective action of itself constitutes a community" [LW2:330]. Moreover, it is this level of association that in the modern world increases the need for a full community, for shared activity and common values. Secondly, then, for interaction to result in community, it must become *shared action*. Dewey's model here is broad. For him, such shared activity is similar to "taking part in a game, in conversation, in a drama, in family life" [LW7:345]. There must be cooperation on the part of individuals for addressing the common ills of their common lives and for achieving the common goals which are fashioned. "Wherever there is conjoint activity whose consequences are appreciated as good by all singular persons who take part in it," Dewey writes, "and where the realization of the good is such as to effect an energetic desire and effort to sustain it in being just because it is a good shared by all, there is in so far a community" [LW2:328].

This shared activity makes possible the emergence of *shared values* and thus gives rise to the possibility of a fuller community. Thirdly, then, Dewey tells us that people live in a community in virtue of the "aims, beliefs, aspirations, knowledge . . . which they have in common; and communication is the way in which they come to possess things in common" [MW9:7; cf. LW13:176]. He continues that "[t]o have the same ideas about things which others have, to be like-minded with them, . . . to attach the same meanings to things and to acts which others attach" [MW9:35] is to live in community with them. For individuals who live in this way, he writes, " 'we' is as inevitable as 'I' " [LW2:330]; but, before there can be such a "we," such a community, "there must be values prized in common" [LW13:71], values that have arisen in shared activity. "A society that is largely held together by the aim of many individuals to get on as individuals is not really held together at all," Dewey writes [LW9:179]. There must thus be a central core of common felt values that operate as significant values for the community. In a vibrant community, Dewey concludes, each individual "feels its success as his success, its failure as his failure" [MW9:18].

III

From Dewey's suggestion that individuals should feel the success of the community to be their own success, I derive the two main themes of this final section: an examination of his reasons for seeing ourselves as members of communities and a consideration of his call for focusing our efforts upon the common good. After discussing these two themes, the chapter will close with a brief exploration of Dewey's thoughts on how we might advance toward such community.

As to the initial question of whether we ought to understand ourselves as social beings and emphasize community, we can begin with Dewey's central claim: "Shared experience is the greatest of human goods" [LW1:157]. To formulate a direct response to this point, as a critic might, would be to suggest that we should not advocate Dewey's social sense of human fulfillment, nor should we increase our efforts to advance community. Rather, what we should advocate is a largely individual sense of fulfillment to be advanced through increasing personal freedom and expanding private goods, and to operate within the more narrowly circumscribed realm of family and close friends. Shared experience, in other words, is simply not the greatest of human goods.

While I do not believe that choosing between these two options is a purely emotive matter, it is not clear how to respond here. How would we attempt to convince individualists of the correctness of Dewey's social analysis of human nature and human fulfillment, or how would they attempt to convince us of theirs? Such ideals can be *presented*, of course. They can be *defended* as well; but they cannot, in any real sense, be *proven*. Facts about human nature certainly play a role in choosing ideals; but the answers to questions like what are the facts and what role do they play in a value discussion like this one are unclear. Even if we assume that Dewey is correct, by what method can we hope to convince others that they will improve their level of fulfillment by adopting the ideal of human community?

One possibility is a sort of *prudential* argument that is found running through Social Pragmatist thinking. The essence of this position is that the successful life of a democratic community requires of the citizens a level of commitment to the common welfare that precludes the kind of privatism that the individualistic perspective advocates. While Dewey is in agreement on this point, he also seems strongly drawn by the possibility of an *ethical* argument for adopting a social stance based in obligations of justice. According to this egalitarian approach, we have all received unearned benefits from the prior efforts of the human community and this debt must somehow be repaid. "The things in civilization we most prize are not of ourselves," Dewey writes, but exist, on the contrary, "by grace of the doings and sufferings of the continuous human community in which we are a link." The just response in our situation is some attempt at repaying this social debt through efforts to benefit those who are following us. Dewey formulates this at the conclusion of *A Common Faith* as follows: "Ours is the responsibility of conserving, transmitting, rectifying and expanding the heritage of values we have received that those who come after us may receive it more solid and secure, more widely accessible and more generously shared than we have received it" [LW9:57–58; cf. MW14:19]. Dewey thus defends his call for adopting the communal ideal—that human fulfillment is greatest for those who play a cooperative role in the ongoing life of the community—by means of the moral claim that we have a duty to expand the range of shared experience. Individuals supportive of another ideal, one downplaying this social understanding of human fulfillment, are not likely to be converted by such a defense. Dewey's ethical argument, designed to call out greater efforts in those who accept the communal ideal, cannot prove to those who do not that they should accept it. Current political trends suggest that they are not convinced by the prudential argument either.

The second theme which I wish to consider here is that of the complexity of the common good, a theme that stands behind all that has been considered so far. It is clear that throughout the work of all the Social Pragmatists for advancing collective well-being runs the assumption that our society can legitimately be spoken of in collective terms, like "the people" or "the common good." We find Dewey, for example, writing that our attempts to address social conflicts are attempts to discover "some more comprehensive point of view from which the divergencies may be brought together" [MW9:336]. Without the existence of such a common good, the adoption of the social focus that he is advocating would be self-destructive, since attempts to advance this phantom good would disproportionately favor those individuals and groups who were successful in presenting their particular interests as representing the common good.

The complexity of the issue of a general welfare is brought out in the reminder of C. Wright Mills, that *we* is "the most tricky word in the vocabulary of politics." He emphasized that, when we are focusing on the collective well-being of the community, we are especially vulnerable to sliding over important distinctions and failing to recognize potential conflicts. "What is a 'problem' to one 'group' is not at all problematic to another," Mills continues, "it may well be a satisfactory 'solution.' "[8] To recognize the complexity of this issue is not necessary to admit its insolubility; it is to remind ourselves that it is necessary for all who focus upon community to emphasize as well fostering a critical distance from it. As we have seen, the Social Pragmatists foster such distance through an emphasis upon our memberships in multiple groups.

However complex it is, our sense of the common good usually seems to be negative in content. From the point of view of the *common*, we tend to think of the common good as a situation in which sectional and private and special interests do not play a disproportionate role in our decision making. From the point of view of the *good*, we tend to think of it as a situation in which specific, easily recognizable social problems—epidemic disease, environmental pollution, overpopulation, continued poverty among the employed, and so on—have been minimized or eliminated. Dewey's explanation of the negative nature of our normal sense of the common good connects it with group problems and with the origin of communities. He writes that "human acts have consequences upon others," and it is the recognition of these consequences that leads "to sub-sequent effort to control action so as to secure some consequences and avoid others" [LW2:243]. We determine the ones that we wish to secure and avoid by comparing our situations with more ideal possibilities.

It is this recognition of, and attempts to deal with, the "[i]ndirect, ex-tensive, enduring and serious consequences of conjoint and interactive be-havior" that call into existence a public with "a common interest in con-trolling these consequences" [LW2:314]. A public is thus "all those who are affected by the indirect consequences of transactions" to such an extent that they realize the existence of the problem and determine it "necessary to have those consequences systematically cared for" [LW2:245–46]. The development of a self-conscious public is vital to the potential problem-solving activities of the society.

While we recognize how necessary such a public is, we also recognize that there are severe limitations on developing a public adequately self-conscious to the task of sifting through and evaluating the available infor-mation. Some of these limitations have been considered above in the dis-cussion of custom. Dewey maintains in addition that "the machine age in developing the Great Society has invaded and partially disintegrated the small communities of former times without generating a Great Commu-nity" [LW2:314]; and, in the decades since he wrote, this process has con-tinued unabated. Part of the problem here is admittedly the complexity of the issues that we face; but another part of the problem is that the profes-sionalization of intellectual expertise that we have developed to respond to these issues has itself increased fragmentation by removing the discus-sion of social problems from the realm of public discourse. Dewey contin-ues that as a result of society's lack of intellectual understanding of our social problems "many consequences are felt rather than perceived; they are suffered, but they cannot be said to be known, for they are not, by those who experience them, referred to their origins." Without an adequate pub-lic to help us, individuals cannot understand the meaning of the constant stream of events and its attendant information. We can neither compre-hend the importance of the facts we uncover nor place the consequences of our actions in understandable future orders. A public that is as yet "in-choate" will be able to organize, Dewey writes, "only when indirect conse-quences are perceived, and when it is possible to project agencies which order their occurrence" [LW2:317; cf. MW8:443].

It is in the analysis of information and the selection among policy op-tions that publics—or, to revert to the more familiar term, communities—

must play a central role. The fact that these are plurals, multiple groups, is important to emphasize here as well, because we are all members of numerous overlapping and telescoping groups. In discussion and interaction, in carrying on the shared activities and developing the shared values that comprise each group's sense of the common good, and in coordinating these various senses of the common good, communities focus the activities of individuals upon common problems. This perception of problems and projection of responses involves moving from events to meanings. "Events cannot be passed from one to another," Dewey writes, "but meanings may be shared by means of signs." When our wants and impulses are associated with common meanings they are "transformed into desires and purposes, which, since they implicate a common or mutually understood meaning, present new ties, converting a conjoint activity into a community of interest and endeavor." A community, he continues, thus "presents an order of energies transmuted into one of meanings which are appreciated and mutually referred by each to every other on the part of those engaged in combined action" [LW2:331]. In such an intellectualized community life, marked by the interchange of meanings, the narrowed sense of the common good against which Mills warns us would seem unlikely.

When community grows in this way, we can advance the conversion of mere interaction into shared activity and common values, what Dewey refers to as "transforming physical interdependence into moral—into human—interdependence" [LW13:180]. In line with his social focus he continues, "the greatest experiment of humanity" is that of "living together in ways in which the life of each of us is at once profitable in the deepest sense of the word, profitable to himself and helpful in the building up of the individuality of others" [LW13:303; cf. MW10:233]. This experiment can be enhanced by the recognition that the well-being of each individual is bound up with the well-being of others within the community and throughout the world, and by the recognition that cooperative effort is needed to address our common ills. This recognition of common interests can also lead to the improvement of our communities through a development of "the interests which are consciously shared" and a furtherance of "the interplay with other forms of association" [MW9:89]. The more that we can live this way, emphasizing our place within the fulfilling community and focusing upon the common good, developing community through cooperative efforts, the more that we can develop a mood of social hope.

This enhanced level of "local communal life" [LW2:370] will be approached, for Dewey and the other Social Pragmatists, through improvements in the medium of education. Education in this sense is far more than what we traditionally understand as schooling. It is the lifelong process of bringing all that we have gained in past experience to bear on the present and the future. These improvements can be considered under the two themes that we have just been examining: education must help to make future thinking more social, and it must help to direct future thinking toward uncovering and solving common problems.

Beginning with the former, we can consider one task of education in community building as that of helping individuals learn to live more cooperatively, to appreciate their role in the social process, to work together to accomplish tasks that cannot be accomplished individually. "Education should create," Dewey writes, "an interest in all persons in furthering the general good, so that they will find their own happiness realized in what they can do to improve the conditions of others" [LW7:243]. This need for "the definite substitution of a social purpose . . . for the traditional individualistic aim" [LW9:180] is especially important as we attempt to fill out the broader possibilities that our contemporary situation has given us.

At times, cautioned by Mills, we may be tempted to draw back from placing this social lever in the hands of educational administrators, civic and religious leaders, and political figures—all of whom have in the past misused "we," especially in ways that undervalued individuality. Dewey, of course, emphasizes the importance of fostering individuality, both to the life of the individuals and to the success of the society; and, even in his call for "saturating [students] with the spirit of service" [MW1:20], we find no compromise with the need to develop individuality. On the contrary, for Dewey, "the unsolved problem of democracy is the construction of an education which will develop that kind of individuality which is intelligently alive to the common life and sensitively loyal to its common maintenance" [MW11:57]. His hope is to increase individuality by preparing the young to become "good citizens, in the broadest sense," citizens who are capable of "recognizing the ties that bind them to all the other members of the community, recognizing the responsibility they have to contribute to the upbuilding of the life of the community" [MW15:158]. Also, although Dewey calls for the development of "public-mindedness, a sense of public service and responsibility" [MW10:183], this public-mindedness is in no way to be a simple-minded trumpeting of the status quo. Education must help us all become more critical: better able to recognize values and more conscious of the nature of possibilities of social progress. In this way, students and adults would grow in the "ability to judge men and measures wisely and to take a determining part in making as well as obeying laws" [MW9:127].

This emphasis upon criticism leads us directly to the second task of education in community building: making it a better means for uncovering and advancing the common good. While our goal is to help students become more critical citizens, better at dealing with problems in the new and difficult situations of our contemporary world, we cannot hope to achieve this goal by means of a narrow problem-solving approach. We must direct education toward the development of "sound and whole human beings" [LW13:336]. As Dewey writes, the ultimate goal of education is to produce adults capable of sound judgments, people who are able "to pass judgments *pertinently* and *discriminatingly*" on the problems of human living [LW8:211]. This focus of education on judgment rather than simply on the accumulation of knowledge is part of his emphasis on wisdom. Wisdom, he writes, is "a moral term": "By wisdom we mean not systematic and proved knowledge of fact and truth, but a conviction about moral values, a sense for the better kind of life to be led" [MW 11:44]. And, because of our need for ongoing evaluation and criticism, he emphasizes the need to foster ongoing inquiry: "The most important attitude that can be formed is that of desire to go on learning" [LW13:29]. In this way the young will be able to make more sense of their experience at present and make a more orderly entry into their role as contributors to the lives of their various groups in the future.

It has surely become clear by this point how important Dewey's conception of community is to the rest of his thought, and how closely it is connected to his understanding of democracy as a kind of cooperative experiment. The values of democratic community—"mutual respect, mutual toleration, give and take, the pooling of experiences" [LW13:303]—pervade all aspects of his thought. As with the other Social Pragmatists, for Dewey the success of the community depends upon cooperative efforts to seek the common good in a democratic way. We may be drawn together to solve our problems, but it is the togetherness, not the solution, that is the primary result. In our attempts to build and further democratic community, the process of developing shared activity and values held in common is what matters. We need to foster, he maintains, the kind of long-term focus that sees beyond particular issues to the cultivation of dialogue and long-term cooperation. We should continue to trust in community life in spite of occasional and even severe setbacks because democracy is "a moral ideal." Democracy is, Dewey continues, "the faith that the process of experience is more important than any special result attained" [LW14:228–29]. And this faith in democratic process, this belief that shared living is itself the goal of human life is the core of Dewey's conception of community.[9]

Notes

1. James Hayden Tufts, *Selected Writings of James Hayden Tufts*, ed. James Campbell (Carbondale: Southern Illinois University Press, 1992), 344.

2. George Herbert Mead, *Mind, Self, and Society from the Standpoint of a Social Behaviorist*, ed. Charles W. Morris (Chicago: University of Chicago Press, 1934), 199; cf. 389.

3. Cf. Mead: "As a rule we assume that this general voice of the community is identical with the larger community of the past and the future; we assume that an organized custom represents what we call morality" (*Mind, Self, and Society*, 168).

4. Mead, *Mind, Self, and Society*, 217.

5. See Lippmann's two volumes: *Public Opinion* (New York: Harcourt, Brace, 1922) and *The Phantom Public* (New York: Harcourt, Brace, 1925). See also: MW13: 337–44 and LW2:213–20, 308, 334.

6. A related theme that deserves to be mentioned here is what Dewey calls "a mystical sense of fusion" [LW13:89], the almost complete rejection of the external criterion that can occur in societies especially in times of social crisis. I have discussed this theme of social fusion in two related essays: "George Herbert Mead on Social Fusion and the Social Critic," in *Frontiers in American Philosophy*, ed. Robert W. Burch and Herman J. Saatkamp, Jr. (College Station: Texas A&M University Press, 1992), 1:243–52, and "Community without Fusion: Dewey, Mead, Tufts," in *Pragmatism: From Progressivism to Postmodernism*, ed. Robert Hollinger and David Depew (Westport, Conn.: Praeger, 1995), 56–71.

7. Cf. Mead: "the attainment of that functional differentiation and social participation in the full degree is a sort of ideal which lies before the human community. The present stage of it is presented in the ideal of democracy" (*Mind, Self, and Society*, 326).

8. Mills, *The Marxists* (New York: Dell, 1962), 19; idem, *Sociology and Pragmatism* (New York: Oxford University Press, 1966), 412.

9.   I have developed the themes discussed in this essay further in "Buchler's
      Conception of Community," in *Nature's Perspective: Prospects for Ordinal
      Metaphysics*, ed. Armen Marsoobian, Kathleen Wallace, and Robert S. Cor-
      rington (Albany: State University of New York Press, 1991), 326–32, and in
      Understanding John Dewey: Nature and Cooperative Intelligence (LaSalle, Ill.:
      Open Court, 1995).

3 John Dewey and
American Social Science
Peter T. Manicas

It has not been an easy matter to judge John Dewey's relation to the social sciences in America. Most writers have held that his influence was significant. Some of these think that this influence was a good one; others are critical, since for them it contributed to what is seen to be a technocratic version of social science.[1] It is easy to infer what seems to have propelled this view: Pragmatism was an important and culturally influential philosophical movement in the United States; Dewey was at Michigan and then at Chicago (with G. H. Mead) at what was the crucial period in the genesis of the social sciences in America; Dewey was distinctly interested in promoting a view that incorporated science and the scientific frame of mind; hence, Dewey's pragmatism must have left its mark on American social science. Those who find that this influence was salutary also believe, I think, that on the whole academic social science provides us with much needed knowledge.[2]

Although the premises are all true, the argument doesn't work—mainly because the key ideas are mostly either mushy or ideological (or both?). To see this, one must be clear not only about Dewey's version of pragmatism, still very much contested, but about the character of social science in America. This last requires some concrete history governed by a philosophically sophisticated understanding of science and its possible goals. For me, what may be termed "mainstream" social science is generally a disaster for substantially the reasons pointed to by Dewey's erstwhile colleague, Thorstein Veblen. Veblen insisted that social science had as its task, "inquiry into the nature and causes, the working and the outcome, of [the] institutional apparatus." Such inquiry need bear "no colour of iconoclasm," since even if it did not, its outcome "will disturb the habitual convictions and preconceptions upon which they rest." Instead, "usages and conventions that have by habit become embedded in the received scheme of use and wont, and so have been found to be good and right" are given scientific legitimation. The result is "a 'science' of complaisant interpretations, apologies, and projected remedies."[3] Veblen's objection, like mine and Dewey's, is not that social scientists were reformers but rather that they were not good scientists.

As regards Dewey, we are just now, I think, beginning to get clearer about his instrumentalism, despite the ill-conceived effort to appropriate it for postmodernist purposes, and even if the two most recent full-length accounts, one by a historian, the other by a political theorist, say precious little of any use about how it bears on Dewey's conception of science, including social science.[4] In this essay, accordingly, I want to develop Dewey's scattered views on social science, both as he came to understand what they had become, and what they might be. Much of what he did say gave ample room for both misunderstanding and misappropriation.[5] Still, there remains in Dewey's philosophy some untapped resources for reconstituting social science.

The Origins of Social Science in America

It is of considerable importance to notice that the modern disciplines of the social sciences are an American invention, that European universities had nothing like what we now take for granted as social science. Indeed, some of the disciplines were not part of European higher education until after World War II when, as with so much else, Americanization became the order of the day.[6]

America provided the nearly perfect conditions for the modern idea of the social sciences.[7] There was, first of all, "the social problem" produced during the Gilded Age by rapid industrialization, urbanization, and massive immigration. Second, America had a "weak state" in the sense that it lacked both significant state bureaucracies and a strong central government. This promoted responses from "civil society," but especially from the private colleges and universities. Third, lacking a feudal past, America was "bourgeois" from its beginnings. As Bledsoe put it, "Americans lacked tradition as a source of authority, but they did not lack 'science.'" Before Johns Hopkins became a university in 1876, there were no universities in America—the educational upshot of the absence of a feudal past. Educational entrepreneurs could convince the John D. Rockefellers, Carnegies, and Mellons that science was just what was needed and that it could be produced with good effect in the new institutions. Finally, as science had itself been industrialized, a group of European philosopher/physicists had articulated a thoroughly positivist understanding of the successful sciences, from the practically irrelevant idea of "science" as *theoria*, to a *practically* relevant productive and predictive *instrument* whose ultimate vindication was its capacity to generate technologies "for the relief of man's estate."[8]

Indeed, for the men [*sic*] in "the institutions of higher learning," the problem was not class war, but ignorance. Social problems surely were no less subject to "scientific" solutions than other problems. Moreover, since for them there was nothing fundamentally wrong with America's basic institutions, these problems could be dealt with as technical questions in a piecemeal, ameliorative fashion. But if social scientists were to be *professional* with legitimate claims to authority and autonomy, they must mark out their scientific territories, clear away all that was nonscientific, and establish their own system of credentialling. What this meant was clear enough. It meant establishing distinct disciplines exactly in the terms in which they believed any true science must be constituted. The outcome, settled between the wars, was the disciplines of the social sciences as we know them today. This was, then, the context in which Dewey reflected. Where, we may ask, did he fit in?

Dewey and the Origins of Academic Social Science

Dewey said little about the social sciences and although one finds throughout the corpus references to science, one finds too little in the way of a systematic account of science. Most of the terms descriptive of science and in general use were—and are—vague and uncritically employed: for example, *cause, law, theory, explanation,* and *experimental method.* Dewey, like most writers today, could take these terms for granted even if, as I would insist, one can get contradictory conceptions of science from different analyses of them. This unclarity should not surprise us. What we now think of as an important subdiscipline of philosophy, philosophy of science, emerged only in the 1950s and it was only in the 1970s that there was a genuine competitor to the positivist interpretation of science.

Logic: The Theory of Inquiry, published in 1938, is surely the main exception to the overall absence of texts on Dewey's theory of science. What is there is very important, but there are many important questions that Dewey did not address and, typically, he does not make much effort to place his work in the context of other writers on science, such as Vienna positivism, for example. When the *Logic* was published, as Ralph Sleeper has argued, it was both ignored and misunderstood, so thoroughgoing were entrenched assumptions about logic and science. Moreover, by this time, systematic misunderstanding of Dewey was also well entrenched.[9] Accordingly, it was not then and is not now a genuine competitor for the received view.

At bottom is an ill-developed conception of science that is distinctly Deweyan. In the positivist, technocratic conception, the aim of science is prediction and control. To achieve this one needs only confirmed regularities, laws, or law-like statements. In this view, since they can be no part of science, ends are given or assumed and the only question is means. Since it is not within the realm of social science to decide on goals, the social scientist (qua social scientist) is "neutral" regarding who his or her work serves.

For Dewey, none of the foregoing was true, but for reasons noted, it is not an easy matter to get a firm grip on Dewey's alternative view. There is a sense in which it is utterly unique, the consequence of his radical position in epistemology. His "instrumentalism" involves a rejection of the "epistemological problem" and thus of the fact/value dichotomy. It offered a unique conception of "control" and a confusing conception of the character of theory and of the goals of science. I will try to keep my account focused, as much as possible, on what Dewey had to say about social science.

Dewey's Rejection of the Epistemological Problem

I noted that Dewey's theory of science presupposed a radical rejection of "the epistemological problem." Failure to see this has misled many otherwise astute commentators. Dorothy Ross, for example, singles out Dewey's lecture, "The Significance of the Problem of Knowledge" (1897) as a critical intervention on the side of the technocrats. But this is far from being the case. Its thrust is against traditional foundationist epistemology: rationalist, sensationalist, and Kantian. Dewey writes that: "knowledge can define the percept and elaborate the concept, but their union can be found only in action. The experimental method of modern science, its erection into the ultimate mode of verification, is simply this fact obtaining recognition" [EW5:21]. Contrary to the epistemologists, there is no *problem* of knowledge *in general:* philosophy is "not an original fountainhead of truth." And this means that for answers to questions about how knowledge is possible we need to look to psychology and social ethics— "including in the latter term all the related concrete social sciences, so far as they may give guidance to conduct" [EW5:22]. Dewey's project was to naturalize epistemology *and* moral theory.[10] "Psychology is naught but the account of the way in which conscious life is . . . progressively maintained and reorganized. Psychology is the attempt to state in detail the machinery of the individual considered as the instrument and organ through which social action operates" [EW5:23]. Similarly,

> The sociologist, like the psychologist, often presents himself as a camp follower of genuine science and philosophy, picking up scraps here and there and piecing them together in somewhat aimless fashion. . . . But social ethics represents the attempt to translate philosophy from a general and therefore abstract method into a working and specific method; it is the change from inquiring into the nature of value in general to an inquiry of the *particular* values which ought to be realized in the life of everyone, and of the conditions which shall render possible this realization. [EW5:23]

This is a stunning research program for social science, stunningly ignored. We need to be clear about this. Dewey believed, rightly, that human sciences could help us to understand ourselves: how we think and inquire and why, when thinking and inquiry are successful, they are successful. They would then give us insight into our genuine interests and purposes and their relations, and most obviously, they would give us an understanding of the obstacles in present arrangements that keep us from realizing our genuine interests and purposes. The human sciences would be emancipating in exactly the sense that they would clear away misconceptions about ourselves and our arrangements and empower us to reconstruct the social world more in accordance with our wants and aims.

Central to this project was the rejection of the bifurcation of fact and value, a further consequence of the mistaken assumptions that had generated "the epistemological problem." In his *Logic*, Dewey argued that "most current social inquiry" was marked by "the separation of theory and practice" [LW12:487]. It is sound principle, Dewey says, that one should avoid making social judgements "on the ground of moral preconceptions, conceptions of what is right and wrong, vicious and virtuous" [LW12:489]. But this is mistakenly converted to the principle that one should make no evaluations about ends. These are, accordingly, precluded from inquiry. But "only recognition in both theory and practice that ends to be attained (ends-in-view) are of the nature of hypotheses and that hypotheses have to be formed and tested in strict correlativity with existential conditions as means, can alter current habits of dealing with social issues" [LW12:490–91].

If one wants a ready current example, consider poverty. What, indeed, are the possible ends-in-view of current policy and what, accordingly, are the existential conditions that are demanded for their satisfaction? It is easy to deal here with high abstractions, "getting people off welfare," "getting people to work," "ensuring that people can acquire skills and knowledge which will make them employable," and to leave up in the air, unexamined, the requisite "existential conditions." Although I cannot prove this here, I would insist that the modern social sciences must take large measure of responsibility for the shallowness of the usual understanding of problems like poverty and crime.[11]

Moreover, it is easy to assume that "the problems which exist are already definite in their main features," and if so, then inquiry could be aimed at finding the best methods of solution. The result is that "methods for resolving problematic situations are proposed without any clear conception of the material in which projects and plans are to be applied and to take effect," with often a worsening of the situation which generated the inquiry [LW12:487]. The analogy between current modes of inquiry in social science and prescientific medicine was apt. As Dewey noted elsewhere, such practice was a combination of empiricism and quackery. Without analysis, symptoms were responded to in terms of handed down remedies. Of course, these sometimes worked. But as regards medicine at least, "it is now recognized that choice of remedial measures looking to restoration of health is haphazard until the conditions which constitute the trouble or disease have been determined as completely and accurately as possible" [LW12:488].

The poverty example again illustrates this. It is held that people are not working and that present arrangements make them welfare-dependent. The solution is obvious: eliminate welfare. But it does not take much to see that the conditions which constitute the trouble begin with the absence of jobs that would pay enough to take a family out of poverty and that one would need here to be clear about a host of other attending steps and conditions to make this possible.

The self-imposed constraints of "allegedly scientific social inquiry" also explain the positivist penchant for "fact-gathering." Dewey had attacked this idea in his 1931 essay, "Social Science and Social Control." Dewey offered that "the existing limitations of 'social science' [Dewey's quotation marks] are due mainly to unreasoning devotion to physical science as a model, and to a misconception of physical science at that" [LW6:64]. In the *Logic*, Dewey held that methods adopted "in the professed name of social science" are merely the form of genuine science since they fail "to observe the logical conditions which in physical science give the techniques of observing and measuring their standing and force" [LW12:492]. There are many places where Dewey assessed current social science as deficient. Moreover, it is surprising that the foregoing explanation of the deficiency is overlooked by Ross and other writers who accuse Dewey of contributing to "scientism." In this essay (as in the *Logic*), Dewey held " . . . [T]he facts of social 'fact finding' remain a miscellaneous pile of meaningless items." "Since their connections with human wants and their effect on human values are neglected, there is nothing which binds them together into an intelligible whole" [LW6:65].

Dewey was surely aware that his colleagues, among them Merriam at Chicago and Ogburn at Columbia, had by then established "fact-gathering" as *the* goal of social science.[12] This was, of course, a main target of Robert Lynd's *Knowledge for What?* (1939), a book which was both very Deweyan and very much out of the mainstream. Indeed, in a related section of the *Logic*, Dewey developed an argument that C. W. Mills picked up in his 1959 *Sociological Imagination*. Dewey saw two one-sided distortions. The "positivist" school (his term) single-mindedly directs itself as "fact-finding"—what Mills had called "abstracted empiricism." But the opposing tendency "places its entire emphasis on conceptions" [LW12:497]—what Mills called "Grand Theory." "Facts are subsumed directly under 'principles,' the latter being regarded as fixed norms that decide the legitimacy or illegitimacy of existing phenomena and that prescribe the ends towards which endeavor should be directed" [LW12:497].

There is another issue, part of his more general instrumentalist theory of inquiry that needs to be introduced if we are to have any hope of grasping Dewey's thoughts on science.

Instrumentalism and Science

Dewey's commitments to scientific method, his persistent attacks on inquiry detached from human concerns, and his extensive use of technological metaphors have caused enormous confusion, almost certainly because as Dewey himself saw, modern science had not been the salvific force that it was once hoped to be.[13]

Surely the most far-reaching attempt to illuminate Dewey's philosophy in terms of "technology" is Larry Hickman's *John Dewey's Pragmatic Technology*.[14] It may be that Hickman goes too far in asserting that "late in his life, technology became a synonym for the very method of inquiry,"[15] but Hickman wisely glosses Dewey's "instrumentalism" by arguing that "Dewey goes beyond theory and beyond praxis to production: his concern is with the making and testing of new entities including extra-organic tools as well as goals and ideals."[16] "Science" in this sense is a more refined and developed form of all inquiry.

Thus, in the *Logic*, Dewey insists that "there is still no sharp dividing line between common sense and science." "Gradually and by processes that are more or less tortuous and originally unplanned, definite technical processes and instrumentalities [were] formed and transmitted" [LW12:77]. It was just these that allowed for "control." "Control"—as Hickman says, a synonym for knowledge—does not refer to the subordination or domination of something. Rather, as Dewey makes clear enough, "control" refers to our capacity to apply intelligence successfully: to produce, adapt, adjust, accommodate, achieve, institute, identify, order, discriminate, and to "resolve" problems in many other sorts of ways. "Control" has been achieved when the problem which generated inquiry has been resolved.

It is in this sense, also, that "practical" must be understood. These "technical processes and instrumentalities" then become "a background of materials and operations . . . we term science" [LW12:77]. And, indeed, "genuine scientific knowledge revived when inquiry adopted as part of its own procedure and for its own purpose the previously disregarded instrumentalities and procedures of productive workers. This adoption is the radical characteristic of the experimental method of science" [LW12:99].[17] But this does entail a collapse of science into technology in the sense that all inquiry has some immediate practical aim and surely not in the sense that we can and should seek to dominate nature. All knowing is technological in the sense that if the problematic situation is to be brought under "control," language, mathematics, and/or artifacts of various kinds are required. But the difference between science and common sense is exactly that while commonsense inquiry "occurs for the sake of settlement of some issue of use and enjoyment," scientific inquiry occurs "for its own sake" [LW12:66–67].

Dewey's position here is almost always overlooked. Dewey did not reject the (Greek) idea that inquiry could be aimed solely at understanding. He rejected the bifurcation of theory and practice, the idea that one could understand *anything* without "tools" and without "experimental operations, involving definite techniques" [LW12:151, 420, 455]. Of course, it would be hard to deny that understanding may well promote the development of technologies—a key feature of late-nineteenth-century industrialized science. This leaves open the question of whether this was, as Dewey would sometimes at least seem to suggest, the ultimate justification of science.[18]

I want to say more about "experimental operations," but we need here to notice that the continuity between science and common sense creates a very special burden for social science. Cultural conditions impact all inquiry—a critical point for a sociology of science—but because "the physical" is "relatively independent of social issues," "the influence of cultural conditions" is "indirect." For example, "it is not possible . . . to separate nineteenth century devotion to exclusively mechanical conceptions from the needs of industry of that period." In social science, by contrast, "prejudices of race, nationality, class and sect play such an important role that their influence is seen by any observer of the field" [LW12:482]. It is, however, more than annoying to notice that Dewey did not, as far as I can tell, say much about how such prejudices were influencing the social sciences.

Scientific Laws and Causality

Critical to any understanding of science is the conception of law and causality. We can turn here to chapter 22 of the *Logic*. Dewey begins by rejecting the most characteristic, even defining features of empiricist philosophy of science: that "scientific laws are formulations of uniform and unconditional sequences of events," and that causality must be defined in terms of such sequences [LW12:437]. Of all the doctrines that currently inform mainstream social science, these are surely the most pernicious. Once accepted, we are committed to an event ontology and a regularity determinist view of the universe. Whenever this, then that. It is then also easy to assume a covering law model of explanation, and thus to hold also that prediction and explanation are symmetrical. One final consequence is the inability to conceptualize agency: the fact that persons make things happen. But as Dewey rightly sees, "there are no such things as uniform sequences of *events*" [LW12:445].

It is important to see that these doctrines are empiricist in that they disallow reference to unwitnessable "powers" inherent in "the things themselves." In my view, there is no necessity that this move be "occult" or unscientific. If I am right, the successful sciences make such appeals all the time.[19] Moreover, such moves are quite consistent with his idea that commonsense inquiry is continuous with advanced science. Dewey gives some examples: "A good rain will cause the seeds that have been planted to grow." The expectations are "explained" by the unscientific person by attributing a power to rain. The empiricist disallows this, but content with an effort to establish the validity of the expectations, he does not seek to understand the "power." Dewey sees, rightly, that "from the standpoint of scientific inquiry, these expectations are but material of *problems*," but he seems to miss the main point [LW12:446]. For him, the scientific problem is to try to give a more refined regularity and to fill in ever-larger numbers of "variables."[20] But this succumbs to the regularity determinist conception. The scientific problem is not, as positivists would have it, to make better predictions. The scientific problem is to identify what it is about the nature of water and seeds such that a good rain will (ceteris paribus) cause the seeds to grow.

Indeed, in *Experience and Nature*, he seemed to hold to such a view, best termed "realist." He there argued that "atoms and molecules show a selective bias in their indifferences, affinities and repulsions . . . to other events" [LW1:162]. These "selective biases," he says, define their "essence," a term Dewey used without prejudicing his fully processual view of the universe. But since in a realist view, the "things" of the universe are always related to other "things," outcomes are never guaranteed. Thus, "iron as such exhibits characteristics of bias or selective reactions," but "iron as a genuine constituent of an *organized* body acts so as to tend to maintain the type of activity of the organism to which it belongs" [LW1:195]. In a living organism, it functions not to produce iron oxide—as it would in a hinge—but to contribute to metabolism.

In *Quest for Certainty*, he argued against empiricist ontology, both of the naive realist sort characteristic of Greek science and of modern sensationalist versions. The experimental method, he writes, "*substitutes data for objects*" [LW4:79; emphasis in text]. "By data is signified subject-matter for *further* interpretation; something to be thought about. . . . Hot and cold, wet and dry, light and heavy, instead of being self-evident matters with which to explain phenomena, were things to be investigated; they were 'effects,' not causal principles" [LW4:80]. Hot, for example, is surely an effect of what is a most complicated "causal nexus," a nexus that includes not only the properties of bodies, but organisms that experience.

Nevertheless, Dewey's view needs to be distinguished from a scientific realism which holds that "things" have "causal powers." For Dewey, causality is a logical category, not an ontological one. This seems very Kantian. We cannot know "things in themselves" but we can offer "generalizations" that abstract from the existential milieu. The empiricist makes the error of supposing that the abstracted logical characters—which are related necessarily—are the existential relations of events. It is, he says, a "confusion of operational means of procedure with the existential result of their application" [LW12:444]. For Dewey, the empiricist rightly ruled out "occult" qualities, but then offered "a hybrid notion which took from common sense the idea of succession and from science the idea of invariability of conjunction" [LW12:445]. But "the contents which are *invariably* related in a law are not events, and . . . their relation is not one of sequence" [LW12:446]. As a rejection of regularity determinism, this seems right. And while I do not think that Dewey's positive account of causality is satisfactory, his rejection of regularity determinism was all that is needed to distinguish his views from the prevailing positivisms in social science. This is often missed.

Ross holds that Dewey's "Psychology and Social Practice" is another place where he endorses technocracy.[21] Dewey argues that the teacher has a psychological theory, like it or not. "Teachers tell you that a child is careless or inattentive in the same final way in which they would tell you that a piece of paper is white." But, insists Dewey, "it is only through some recognition of attention as a mechanism, some awareness of the interplay of sensations, images and motor impulses which constitute it as an objective fact that the teacher can deal effectively with attention as a function" [MW1:139]. Dewey's point is exactly that unless teachers have an understanding of the student as a psychosocial being, all their efforts are bound to be misdirected, ineffective, even destructive. It is only by understanding the psychological "mechanisms" of attention, memory, cognition and judgement, and the social "mechanisms" implicated in *all* experience and behavior that the teacher can cultivate the powers of the student.[22] This is for Dewey a research program to be satisfied. We are, he says, discussing the question of the role of psychological science in education only because "we have as yet made so little headway" [MW1:144].[23]

Dewey's use of the term "mechanisms" here is notable and suggests how far he is from a regularity determinist view. This is made even clearer in a 1918 essay entitled "A New Social Science," one of the few places where Dewey explicitly discusses social science (the *Logic* is the other notable place). Dewey argues against the idea, inherited from Comte and Spencer—and still current—that "the existing social order is a product of natural laws which are expounded in a rational, a scientific, way" [MW11:89]. Dewey insists that World War I should finally have exposed this idea as myth. "The war has revealed that our existing social situation is in effect the result of a convergence of a large number of independently generated historic incidents" [MW11:90]. Indeed, "any science which pretends to be more than a description of the particular forces which are at work and a descriptive tracing of the particular consequences which they produce, which pretends to discover basic principles to which social things conform, and inherent laws which 'explain' them, is, I repeat, sheer mythology" [MW11:90].

Dewey acknowledged radical contingency in the universe, a universe which was both "precarious and stable." There were uniformities—a consequence of "selective biases" and there were plenty of surprises, a consequence of the open systematic character of the world. But such a metaphysic calls for a historical and concrete social science. The "description of particular forces" at work are the analogue of the "selective biases" discoverable by physical science. The "particular consequences" that they produce are not guaranteed in advance because the relations of such "mechanisms" are complex and historically contingent. There are no "general laws" under which we can subsume and thereby explain wars, revolutions, or, for that matter, hurricanes or the genesis of a species.

Dewey concludes this brief but rich essay by remarking that "there is . . . an immense amount of empirical subject-matter contained within the confines of existing social sciences. The only trouble is that it has been 'framed up' and betrayed by its mythical and apologetic setting" [MW11:91]. He does not, unfortunately, elaborate on this idea.

Dewey on Experimentation

Dewey's views on experimentation certainly did not help clarify his position. I noted that, for Dewey, one could not understand anything without "experimental operations, involving technique." There is, of course, a paradigm, characteristic of the laboratory, but how far can this be extended? A long way it seems.[24] Thus, he insists that "there is no ground whatever upon which a logical line can be drawn between the operations and techniques of experimentation in the natural sciences and the same operations and techniques employed for distinctively practical ends" [LW12:434]. But what counts here as the "same operations and techniques"? This text continues with what may be his most general definition:

"Experimentation is a form of doing and making. Application of conceptions and hypotheses to existential matters through the medium of doing and making is an intrinsic constituent of scientific method" [LW12:434].[25]

Dewey did not, I think, have a clear understanding of the laboratory experiment as it is actually practiced in the successful sciences and this allowed him to give the idea a very extended sense. Only sometimes does he suggest that the main use of an experiment is to test a well-articulated theory. In this realist view, the idea, roughly, is to deduce what the theory entails and then to establish experimental closure to see if what was "predicted" by theory under closure does, in fact, obtain.[26]

But if we think of an experiment in this sense, as a situation in which a theory of a "mechanism" is to be tested, then, as is very plain, this is never possible in social science—putting it at a distinct disadvantage. This is not, however, what Dewey seems to have in mind when he speaks of experimenting in social science.

In the *Logic*, he remarks that "every measure of policy put into operation is, *logically*, and *should* be actually, of the nature of an experiment" [LW12:502; see also LW12:486]. Insofar as we should make the effort to see as clearly as we can what consequences obtained *after* a policy was introduced, there is good sense to this. We know, for example, that people didn't stop drinking alcoholic beverages when prohibition was enforced. But this is a test of a *policy* not of a theory of social behavior, exactly because, as Dewey clearly recognized, there are always a host of connected and interacting processes involved which conjointly produced the actual outcomes. In this case, as we now know, "demand" for alcohol was satisfied by *illegal* producers and distributors so that, if anything, the policy served to create criminals—including law enforcement officers—and to deprive the society of any effective control of the production and distribution of alcohol.[27]

In his 1931 "Social Science and Social Control," alluded to earlier, Dewey did indeed sound technicist. He there offered that "The Five Year Plan of Russia . . . whether noble or the reverse, has many of the traits of a social experiment, for it is an attempt to obtain certain specified social results by the use of specified definite measures, exercised under conditions of considerable, if not complete, control" [LW6:65]. This is, in my mind, so much nonsense. Despite totalitarian methods of "control," the outcomes were, as they must be, conjoint products of a myriad of interacting activities of which some, at least, were directly contradictory to the intentions of the planners. Here "experiment" and "control" get Dewey into unnecessary difficulty.

The example raises, as well, the question of the relation of democracy to social scientific knowledge. For the technocrats, one "controls" the conditions and gets "predictable results." More, because "experts" have knowledge that the "masses" lack, democracy must give way.

Social Science and Democracy

It is easy enough to establish that World War I had a tremendous impact on Dewey and that one of the consequences was his readiness to believe that the war had brought forward "the more conscious and extensive use of science for communal purposes." It had "made it customary to utilize the collective knowledge and skill of scientific experts in all lines, organizing them for community ends" [MW11:99]. The warfare state, remarkably, had laid the foundations for the Nationalist Liberalism which became the political agenda of Dewey's associates as *The New Republic*.[28] But when Walter Lippmann, already persuaded of a technocratic version of social control, published his *Phantom Public* in 1925, Dewey finally came to grips with the problem of scientific knowledge and democracy.

In *The Public and Its Problems* (1927), Dewey agreed that there were a host of "technical" questions which could be answered by "experts": "sanitation, public health, healthful and adequate housing, transportation, planning of cities, regulation and distribution of immigrants, selection and management of personnel, right methods of instruction and preparation of competent teachers, scientific adjustment of taxation, efficient management of funds and so on" [LW2:313]. But the idea that such knowledge was sufficient was profoundly in error. Those who hold to such views "ignore forces which have to be composed and resolved before technical and specialized action can come into play" [LW2:313]. The problem is deep. "It is in the first instance an intellectual problem: the search for conditions under which the Great Society may become the Great Community" [LW2:327]. The public is lost, eclipsed, inchoate, bewildered, caught in a drift which it cannot grasp and therefore cannot overcome. Lippmann (and later C. W. Mills) was not wrong in diagnosing that the American public was a mass, but he was wrong in thinking that social scientists should now rule. Dewey was clear that such "experts" lacked the knowledge that was needed. Indeed, "the prime condition of a democratically organized public is a kind of knowledge and insight which does not yet exist" [LW2:339]. Citizens needed to understand what was happening and why. Some technical knowledge was needed, to be sure, but in the absence of a widely shared understanding of the "forces" at work, no democratic public could emerge.

Dewey is clearly correct in this analysis, but he is not as radical as he might be in assigning the causes of this. I put aside here the problems of *distributing* "the kind of knowledge which does not yet exist," for example, problems of the corporate control of mass communication, and concentrate here on the role of the social sciences themselves. In particular, while he acknowledges the limits of the special sciences in generating such knowledge, he does not seem to see that they contribute mightily to the mystification of what needs to be known. Instead of illuminating and emancipating, too much contemporary social science obscures and misleads.

Dewey gets his hands on some of the reasons for this. He notes that the "backwardness of social knowledge is marked in its division into independent and insulated branches of learning" [LW2:342].[29] But this is more than a "mark" of its "backwardness." It *guarantees* backwardness. It is not merely, as he says, that there is lacking "continuous cross-fertilization," but that fragmentation prevents us from grasping causes and connections. Thus we are told that poverty is a "psychological" or "cultural" problem. People lose initiative, lack ambition, look for the easy way. The sociologist assumes that this is "fact" (it is not!) and then tries to explain it. We are told the cause is "the breakdown of the family" or "welfare dependency." Moreover, our sociologist can, without risk, ignore an economic or historical analysis. She or he can, for example, altogether ignore the lack of decent-paying jobs and the reasons for this. That can be left to the economists who tell us that markets are self-correcting and that, accordingly, a political analysis which calls for state intervention is self-defeating.

Dewey notes also that specialized knowledge aims to be "abstract," which practically means that "it is not conceived in terms of its bearing upon human life" [LW2:342]. Plainly, the commitment to value-neutrality requires this. The upshot, of course, is not value-neutrality, but as Veblen insisted, scientific legitimation of "usages and conventions that have by habit become embedded in the received scheme of use and wont, and so have been found to be good and right." Social science happily conspires in persuading us that the poor have only themselves to blame.

He argues forcefully that what counts as "news" in our daily papers is rendered completely unintelligible in terms of its connections but fails to argue that this tendency is reinforced by "fact-gathering" social science. He is correct that "a genuine social science would manifest its reality in the daily press, while learned books and articles supply and polish tools of inquiry," but of course, it is precisely because "we" are not journalists but "social scientists" that we write jargonized "learned" books and articles [LW2:348]. As Lynd said, we are either "scholars" or "technicians"—working for whoever will pay the bill.

Finally, for all Dewey's interest in education, he makes no mention of the disastrous consequences of current patterns of education in the social sciences. Instead of cultivating what Mills called "the sociological imagination," we offer students textbooks that guarantee disciplinary fragmentation, empty abstractions, and uncritical thought. Instead of seeking causes and insisting on making connections, we require "disciplinary" integrity. Instead of raising questions about "habits embedded in the received scheme of things," we seek "relations of variables."

Dewey was surely on the right track when he observed as early as his essay on Renan (above, note 13) some reasons for these patterns of ideology and disinformation. He then wrote that we do not yet appreciate "the dead weight of intrenched class interest which resists all attempt of science to take practical form and become a 'social motor' " [EW4:17]. I conclude by saying that we still do not—itself a function of the failure of the present practices of the social sciences.

Notes

1. See Bernard Crick, *The American Science of Politics: Its Origins and Conditions* (Berkeley: University of California Press, 1959), and most recently, see Dorothy Ross, *The Origins of American Social Science* (Cambridge: Cambridge University Press, 1991).

2. Like Crick, Ross is not one of those who celebrates academic social science in the United States. She argues that it is "scientistic." "[Scientism] was the result of a long-standing commitment perennially deferred, an effort to make good on the positivist claim that only natural science provided certain knowledge and conferred the power of prediction and control. With science now defined by its method, scientism demanded that the requirements of natural scientific method dominate the practice of social science." *Origins*, 390.

    While I very much agree with Ross as regards outcomes, her explanation is different than the one I offered in my *History and Philosophy of the Social Science* (Oxford: Basil Blackwell, 1987). Moreover, she seems wrongly to assume that the positivists provide a generally correct understanding of natural science. For her, scientism arises only when the social sciences are constituted in its terms. Ross seems to favor interpretative models "available in history and cultural anthropology" or "the generalizing and interpretative model offered by Max Weber" (p. 473). I argued in my 1987 book that there was a third realist alternative. It allows us to incorporate the historical and hermeneutic and also to give a proper social science an emancipatory role. I shall suggest that Dewey seems to have stumbled toward a fourth alternative, neither positivist, realist, nor "interpretative."

3. Thorstein Veblen, *The Higher Learning in America: A Memorandum on the Conduct of Universities by Businessmen* (New York: Sagamore, 1957), 132, 136. This was written before World War I and published in 1918. It remains a wonderful account. Indeed, things have changed little. Dewey and Veblen agreed on much but it is hard to discern how the influences ran. Both had struggled with the views of Peirce.

4. See Robert B. Westbrook, *John Dewey and American Democracy* (Ithaca, N.Y.: Cornell University Press, 1991), and Alan Ryan, *John Dewey and the High Tide of American Liberalism* (New York: Norton, 1995). Westbrook and Ryan get Dewey's views on democracy and politics right. It is a bit surprising that Ryan pays so little attention to issues in the theory of science, given his interests. Ryan finds Dewey's *Logic: The Theory of Inquiry* "somewhat baffling" (p. 309). This is remarkable (though not unusual) since this is the place where Dewey makes his most fundamental assault on the conventional wisdom.

5. I think also that his influence was minimal even though many parties, often conflicting, were fond of drawing on him to suit their purposes. Early Chicago school sociology has some Deweyan marks, but it too moved toward positivism. See Lester R. Kurtz, *Evaluating Chicago Sociology* (Chicago: University of Chicago Press, 1984). G. H. Mead, of course, was the direct influence on symbolic interactionism, and Mead's relations to Dewey remains unclear. Symbolic interactionism, in any case, was always a minor competitor to mainstream social science. Perhaps C. W. Mills, for all his unhappiness with Dewey—for many of the right reasons—is the most Deweyan social scientist. It may be thought that American psychology was influenced by Dewey, but unfortunately, this was surely not the case. While arguing this would require another paper, for some hints, see below.

6. The most comprehensive comparative overview of the emergence of modern social science is P. Wagner, B. Wittrock, and R. Whiteley, eds., *Discourses on Society: The Shaping of the Social Science Disciplines*, Sociology of Sciences Yearbook (Dordrecht: Kluwer, 1991).

7. See my account, *A History and Philosophy of the Social Sciences*, chap. 11, and Ross, *Origins*, chap. 3.

8. Auguste Comte who articulated this vision and gave us the term "positivism" also gave us a perfectly usable definition of "positivism." First, science must rid itself of both "theological" and "metaphysical" explanations, explanations in terms of either supernatural entities or "occult forces." Second, scientific laws are defined as "invariant relations of succession and resem-

blance." "Causes" as unwitnessable powers are rejected. Third, explanation proceeds by subsuming the particular under the universal: what we today call the covering-law model of explanation. These features are shared by a long list of philosopher/physicists writing at the end of the nineteenth century, a list that includes Wilhelm Ostwald, Ernst Mach, Pierre Duhem, and Karl Pearson. They are found also in Vienna positivism, more recent neopositivisms and, more generally, in antirealist empiricisms. See my *History and Philosophy of the Social Sciences*, esp. pp. 184–90 and chap. 12.

9. See Ralph W. Sleeper, *The Necessity of Pragmatism* (New Haven: Yale University Press, 1986), esp. chap. 6, and Thomas Burke, *Dewey's New Logic* (Chicago: University of Chicago Press, 1994).

10. For a useful account of Dewey's theory of inquiry as epistemology, see H. S. Thayer, "Objects of Knowledge," in John J. Stuhr, ed., *Philosophy and the Reconstruction of Culture* (Albany: State University of New York Press, 1993). I have sketched Dewey's approach as a naturalized epistemology in "Naturalizing Epistemology: Reconstructing Philosophy," in Stuhr, *Philosophy and the Reconstruction of Culture.*

11. See Stephen Steinberg, *Turning Back* (Boston: Beacon Press, 1995), and Herbert Gans, *The War against the Poor* (New York: Basic Books, 1995), for review and criticism of the contribution of recent mainstream social science to this impoverishment.

12. In 1929, Herbert Hoover assembled a distinguished group of social scientists "to examine the feasibility of a national survey of social trends . . . to undertake the researches and to make . . . a complete impartial examination of the facts." This was funded by the Rockefeller Foundation with support from the Social Science Research Council (SSRC), one of Merriam's inspirations. Four years of work by hundreds of social scientists filled sixteen hundred pages of quantitative research. The document called "The Ogburn Report" after its director, William F. Ogburn of Columbia, may be taken to signal the full maturation of American-style social science. See Dean R. Gerstein, *Fifty Years of Discovery* (Washington, D.C.: National Academy Press, 1986), p. 1.

13. For example, in his 1893 review of Ernest Renan's *The Future of Science,* "Renan's Loss of Faith in Science," Dewey agreed with Renan's view that "faith in the social career of science, of a wide distribution of intelligence as the basis of a scientifically controlled democracy, has all but vanished" [EW4:16]. "The forty years since Renan wrote have not done much to add the human spirit and the human interpretation of the results of science; they have rather gone to increase its technical and remote character." Dewey adds an insightful explanation for this: "Furthermore, Renan does not seem to have realized sufficiently the dead weight of class interest which resists all attempts of science to take practical form and become a 'social motor' " [EW4:17]. These charges recur through Dewey's very long life. See, e.g., "The Revolt against Science" (1945) [LW15:188–91].

14. Larry A. Hickman, *John Dewey's Pragmatic Technology* (Bloomington: Indiana University Press, 1990).

15. Ibid., p. 1.

16. Ibid., p. 15.

17. It is not altogether clear what Dewey has in mind here. He may suppose with Bacon that the scientific revolution of the seventeenth century was indebted to incorporation of techniques derived from the workshops of craftsmen. But it has been shown that Baconianism contributed little to the development of the classical sciences: physics and astronomy. As Kuhn notes (in agreement with Koyre and Butterfield) the scientific revolution was not a consequence of new experimental techniques, but of "new ways of looking at old phenomena." Baconian experiments did, later, give rise to a large number of newer scientific fields which had their roots in the crafts and in alchemy. See Kuhn, *The Structure of Scientific Revolution*, 2d ed. (Chicago: University of Chicago Press, 1977). See also *Later Works* 12:388–89.

18. Having abandoned the quest for foundations, Dewey had to justify science as a mode of fixing belief "pragmatically." For some discussion, see my "Naturalizing Epistemology: Reconstructing Philosophy," in Stuhr, ed., *Philosophy*.

19. See Rom Harré, *Varieties of Realism* (Oxford: Basil Blackwell, 1987).

20. He writes that "scientific inquiry proceeds by introducing qualifications. The amount of arsenic taken has to be specified. . . . The conditions of the system into which it is taken have to be determined. . . . The presence or absence of 'counteracting conditions' has to be taken into account" [LW12:446–47].

21. Ross, *Origins*, p. 253.

22. Dewey very early on insisted that all behavior and experience was social, but he did not say much about what this meant or entailed. Mead did better. There are still many problems. For some alternative conceptions, see John Greenwood, ed., *The Mark of the Social* (Lanham, Md.: Rowman and Littlefield, 1997).

23. It may be thought that here, at least, Dewey did have influence. But, I would insist, the direction to which Dewey was pointing is precisely the direction that "scientific psychology" did *not* take. Writing in 1929, Boring summarized the situation:

> By 1900 the characteristics of American psychology were well defined. It inherited its physical body from German experimentalism, but it got its mind from Darwin. American psychology was to deal with the mind in use. . . . Thorndike brought the animals into the formal laboratory . . . then went over to the study of school-children and the mental tests increased. Hall helped here too with his pioneering in educational psychology. . . . Then Watson touched a match to the mass, there was an explosion and behaviorism was left.

E. G. Boring, *A History of Experimental Psychology*, 2d ed. (New York: Appleton-Century-Crofts, 1929), p. 106.

The idea of "the mind in use" *sounds* Deweyan as does the appeal to Darwin. But Thorndike's animal psychology was not inspired by an interest in discovering the mechanisms of cognition and judgement. On the contrary, like his work in educational psychology, it was inspired by interest in prediction and control. From this point of view, "the law of effect" (like Skinner's later operant conditioning) was quite sufficient. The lessons of Dewey's remarkable 1896 essay, "The Reflex Arc Concept in Psychology," were lost.

Similarly, Lewis Terman's 1906 complaint that "the most serious problem confronting psychology is that of connecting itself to life" *sounds* Deweyan, but this should provoke the question: *How* to connect psychology to life? Dewey would not have agreed that "it was the method of tests that has brought psychology down from the clouds and made it useful to men; that has transformed the 'science of trivialities' into the 'science of human engineering' " (quoted by Franz Samuelson, "Putting Psychology on the Map: Ideology and Intelligence Testing," in A. R. Buss, ed., *Psychology in a Social Context* [New York: Irvington, 1979], 106).

24. In some places, he suggests that a mind experiment may be quite sufficient; in others he seems at least to deny this. For example: "Experimental operations change existing conditions. Reasoning, as such, can provide means for effecting the change of conditions but by itself cannot effect it. Only execution of existential operations directed by an idea in which ratiocination terminates can bring about the reordering of environing conditions required to produce a settled and unified situation" [LW12:121].

25. See also *Later Works* 12:458. It is clear that all inquiry requires experimentation for Dewey. He says also that there are at least three needs satisfied by experimentation: the institution of data, the elimination of material that is irrelevant to the problem at hand, and the generation of new existential materials. He generally seems to have in mind something much like the "methods" that Mill had provided in his *Logic* [LW12:190]. But sometimes, experiment seems to be exploratory in its aim [LW12:317], close indeed to the Baconian idea of "twisting the tail of the lion."

26. For a systematic discussion of "experiment," see Roy Bhaskar, *A Realist Theory of Science*, 2d ed. (Atlantic Highlands, N.J.: Humanities Press, 1978).

27. The bearing of this historical experience on drug policy should not be ignored.

28. See *War and Democracy*, chap. 13.

29. See also *Logic* [LW12:501–502].

4 John Dewey's Philosophy as Education

James W. Garrison

> Since growth is the characteristic of life, education is all one with growing; it has no end beyond itself.[1]

John Dewey was perhaps the most important philosopher of education ever to write in English. But since many educators tend to think of the philosophy of education as an application drawn from the results of more serious philosophical study, they have also tended to relegate Dewey to the periphery of the philosophical pantheon.

Perhaps we should stop trying to understand Dewey as a philosopher of education at all. It might be better to think of him as answering the three great questions of human existence: What is life? How should we live? What does life mean? Any complete philosophy must strive to answer these questions. This essay is an attempt to demonstrate how Dewey's philosophy *as* education accomplishes this.

Philosophy as Education

"If we are willing to conceive education as the process of forming fundamental dispositions, intellectual and emotional, toward nature and fellow-man," Dewey wrote, "philosophy may even be defined *as the general theory of education*. Unless a philosophy is to remain symbolic . . . its auditing of past experience and its program of values must take effect in conduct."[2]

By "fundamental dispositions" Dewey meant beliefs, which he took to be an important category of habits. Habits embody predispositions to act that express emotion. When habits are organized into an interpenetrating system, they constitute character. Habits consolidate the thoughts, feelings, and actions that constitute human conduct. Although it is possible for practical purposes to draw functional distinctions among these aspects of human conduct, Dewey thought that the idea that they are ultimately or absolutely separable from one another is the result of a deceptive and untenable form of dualism.

Intelligent conduct requires inquiry into the values that guide and constrain our habits of action. As Dewey put it, "the most far-reaching question of all criticism [is] the relationship between existence and value, or as the problem is often put, between the real and ideal."[3] Since he thought of philosophy as a type of criticism, he also thought of philosophy *as* education. Philosophy as education involves the critical acquisition of habits of conduct, controlled by the ideal values that nurture human growth.

It is well known that "philosophy" means "love of wisdom," from the Greek *philein* (to love) and *sophia* (wisdom). Dewey understood wisdom not as "systematic and proved knowledge of fact and truth, but [as] a conviction about moral values. . . . [It] refers not to the constitution of things already in existence . . . but to a desired future which our desires, when translated into articulate conviction, may help bring into existence."[4] Wisdom thus concerns the relation between what actually exists and what our ideals reveal as possibly valuable. The way things actually are may not be the way they ought to be.

Dewey thought that habits of intelligent conduct, based on a program of values determined by reflective inquiry and criticism, produce wisdom that goes beyond knowledge of the actual to embrace moral possibilities. Seen in this light, philosophy as education is a holistic vision of human growth and flourishing. The aim of education, Dewey argued, was to enable people to *continue* their education. He considered growth the greatest good, since it answers the existential question: What is the meaning of life? For Dewey, the meaning of life is to create and enrich the meanings of life. Reflection about how this occurs, how human growth can be cultivated, is philosophy as education. We grow from the seed of action.

The Seeds of Dewey's Philosophy as Education: The Unity of the Act

What is life? Dewey's answer is that "life is a self-renewing process through action upon the environment" [MW191:4]. Human life renews itself in two ways. The first requires biological reproduction, the second cultural reproduction. If cultures did not reproduce their accumulation of learning, the achievements of millennia would vanish in one generation.

The propagation of children leads to one kind of immortality, the propagation of learning to another. We begin with biological survival, growth, and reproduction.

Human beings must act. If nothing else, we must breathe. Before long we must eat and drink. To reproduce, we must find a mate. Philosophy as education begins modestly with the unity of the act: *"The mode of behavior* [activity] *is the primary thing, and . . . the idea* [object or objective] *and the emotional excitation are constituted at one and the same time; . . . indeed, they represent the tension of stimulus and response within the coordination which makes up the mode of behavior."*[5] Thoughts and feelings emerge simultaneously through our efforts to coordinate our behavior within the soil and sunshine of our physical and social environments. Dewey worked to develop the implications of this crucial insight throughout his long career.

To survive and delight in our existence we must constantly seek to coordinate our behavior with the conditions of our environment: "Life goes on in an environment; not merely *in* it but because of it, through interaction with it. . . . The career and destiny of a living being are bound up with its interchanges with its environment . . . in the most intimate way."[6] We transubstantiate food into ideas, feelings, feces, and ideals worth dying for. Living creatures cannot be sharply distinguished from their environing conditions. For Dewey human nature is a part of nature in its wider sense. We live *through* the environment. As he saw it, "a living organism and its life processes involve a world or nature temporally and spatially 'external' to itself but 'internal' to its functions."[7] Food, drink, and other people are a part of who we are functionally.

It is therefore essential, Dewey insisted, that we recognize the initial unity of trans-action between human nature and the rest of nature. Only later, upon analysis and abstraction, can we discriminate between organism and environment; and we can do so then only for practical purposes. If we were wise, we would see that caring for our physical and social environment is part of caring for ourselves.

Experience for Dewey is simply what occurs when we carry out transactions with our environment. Many philosophers and educators have misunderstood what Dewey meant by experience, and especially what he meant by educational experience. They have assumed that he accepted the modern theory of experience associated with the "sensationalism" of British empiricism or the "sense data" of twentieth-century logical positivism. But Dewey had something else in mind. He thought it unfortunate, for example, that modern theories of experience no longer carry the sense of doing (*poiein* or *praxis*) and being done to (*pathos*) that the concept had borne from the time of the ancient Greeks, and that it had become instead exclusively identified with what is intellectual or cognitive. The modern stance, which Dewey labeled "intellectualism," assumes that knowledge is our primary relation to reality. If we appreciate the unity of the act, however, it is easy to see that knowledge is only one phase of experience. The error of modern epistemology is precisely its assumption of a split between the mind and the world. The only difference between its empiricist and rationalist (or idealistic) varieties is whether the world or the "mind" makes the larger contribution to knowledge.

According to Dewey, two ingredients are necessary for educational experience: interaction (or more exactly, transaction) and continuity. Transaction between us and our environment *is* experience, and experience determines "a situation." Dewey insisted that we "live *in* these situations. . . . The conceptions of *situation* and of *interaction* are inseparable from each other. An experience is always what it is because of a transaction taking place between an individual and what, at the time, constitutes his environment. . . . The environment . . . is whatever conditions interact with personal needs, desires, purposes, and capacities to create the experience which is had."[8]

Situations have a certain quality that we feel even before we engage them cognitively. Initially we grasp the qualities of a situation only intuitively. Intuition controls the determinations of relevant distinctions as they are themselves determined by selective attention. We employ the discursive tools of rational thought only after we have intuited the quality of a situation, and after we have attended to what most interests us in it. "Intuition," Dewey observed, "precedes conception and goes deeper."[9] Emotions drive selective attention. In any situation our internal needs, desires, and purposes determine what we attend to. Intuitions may fail us because feelings such as anger or depression induce us to attend to the wrong aspects of a situation. In failing to grasp our situation properly we respond poorly. If our initial intuitions fail us, it does not matter if subsequent reasoning is flawless. Actions remain uncoordinated. Intelligent action requires both refined feeling and rigorous reasoning in order to establish continuity.

Educational experiences exemplify continuity and growth. Experience inscribes itself upon the body as habits, and every experience modifies these habits. Once modified, our habits alter how we anticipate, recognize, and respond to future experiences: "It covers the formation of attitudes . . . that are emotional and intellectual. . . . The principle of continuity of experience means that every experience both takes up something from those which have gone before and modifies in some way the quality of those which come after. . . . Growth, . . . not only physically but intellectually and morally, is one exemplification of the principle of continuity."[10]

Interaction, or more exactly *trans*action, is meaningless in itself. We learn and grow by establishing continuities. To illustrate this point, Dewey uses the example of a child sticking his finger into a flame. The child first acts (*poiein*) and then suffers (*pathos*) the painful consequences. Unless thought connects the doing and the being done to, unless the activity is continued into the consequences and reflected back into a change made within the child, no learning takes place. If the child makes a backward and forward connection between what he did and what he suffered as a consequence, then the sticking of the finger into flame comes to *mean* a burn.

Dewey draws two conclusions from this example. First, experience is primordially an active-passive concern and not primarily cognitive. Second, the measure of the value of an experience lies in the perception of connections or continuities.[11] Within the unity of the act, cognitive meanings emerge through reflection on precognitive activities and feelings. We learn when we establish connections between what we do and what we suffer as a consequence of our effort to coordinate our activity. This is continuity. Learning requires the reconstruction of our habits, the development of our character, and growth. It is the consequence of establishing continuities within experience.

Growth for Dewey has a rhythmic pattern that moves from equilibrium, to disequilibrium, to the restoration of equilibrium. The child touching the flame provides a good example. Dewey thought that "living may be regarded as a continual rhythm of disequilibrations and recoveries of equilibrium. . . . The state of disturbed equilibration constitutes *need*. The movement towards its restoration is search and exploration [inquiry]. The recovery is fulfilment or satisfaction."[12]

This is the rhythm of life and growth. Initially we are in a state of harmony, then something disrupts our habitual ways of functioning within our environment. This disruption leads to a state of disharmony wherein we experience feelings of need ranging from vague anxiety to terror, while cognitively we experience doubt and uncertainty about how to act. There is no unity to our action. We feel emotional anxiety, but have no idea of what to do. If we can frame an idea (hypothesis, object, or objective) that would restore harmonious functioning, we can translate these feelings into a specific desire for and interest in securing the valued object. This interest extends to any means that we think might help us secure the valued object, or what Dewey preferred to call an "end-in-view." This is the core of Dewey's position regarding internal motivation. It is also crucial to an understanding of his theory of inquiry. I shall take up Dewey's theory of inquiry later. First, however, I should say something more about his treatment of interests, motivation, and aims.

Dewey explained motivation and interest in terms of what he took to be the essential unity of the self and its acts. This unity rests in turn on the unity of the act. Our actions express an existing self (its habits and character), and their consequences are active in the formation of future selves. Unless we grasp the importance of this unity, we will be tempted to think of motivation as something external, acting upon an individual and inducing her to do something. Motivation means redirecting the action of the self, not causing it. Motivation thus unifies the interests that form the core of the self with the objects (and objectives) that alter the direction of activity.

Interests and motives are transactional for Dewey; he thereby avoided the subject/object dualism typical of most modern epistemology and pedagogy. "Any concrete case of the union of the self in action with an object and end is called an interest. . . . A motive . . . *is* the movement of the self as a whole, a movement in which desire is integrated with an object so completely as to be chosen as a compelling end [or value]."[13] Objects or values move people, but only because the object as a moving force and the self are both within the larger unity of the whole situation. In reflection it is sometimes useful to separate self from motive and object, but it is essential that we do not allow useful distinctions to harden into dysfunctional dualisms.

We are participants in life, and not just spectators. Unlike spectators, participants have care and concern for the future; they are therefore inclined to act so as to assure the best possible consequences. The self is bound up with the possibilities within objects and situations. Words such as "interest" and "motivation" indicate the importance of foresight and desire to act so as to secure the best possible result. When our concerns, interests, and motivations connect with foresight, we have already begun to use intelligence to secure a better future.

We may now understand what Dewey meant by the function of aims in education: "An educational aim must be founded upon the intrinsic activities and needs . . . (and acquired habits) of the given individual."[14] Educational aims must connect organically with the lived situation of the unique individual student.

Many "progressive" educators have erroneously claimed that Dewey demanded a "student-centered" education. In his view, however, the act of teaching must coordinate teacher, student, and subject matter. Dewey insisted that the teacher must always connect the subject matter with the student's present needs and abilities, and he thought educational method performed this function.

Dewey admonished his readers that educational aims must be capable of translation into methods that fit the activities of those receiving instruction and that they must foster the kind of environments required to liberate and to organize *their* capacities. Indoctrination and dogmatism in education have their origin in the violation of this principle. This occurs, for example, when parents and teachers confuse their own aims with those of their children. It occurs in cases of state-mandated testing, legislated learning, and teacher proof curricula.

A further dimension of Dewey's view is that "we never educate directly, but indirectly by means of the environment. . . . We design environments" [MW9:22–23]. Education does not necessarily require teachers. Sometimes it simply involves the design of better learning environments. In any situation educational methods must coordinate subject matter with the student's needs, interests, and capacities. This is why knowledge of subject matter alone does not make a good educator.

"Method," for Dewey, "means that arrangement of subject matter which makes it most effective in use. Never is method something outside of the material. . . . Method . . . is the effective direction of subject matter to desired results" [MW9:172]. The educator's task is thus to arrange the subject matter so as to make it most accessible to each student.

Dewey distinguished two kinds of method. The "logical" method of a subject matter is the structure it takes as it is used by experts or specialists when the desired result is to make further discoveries. To the nonexpert student, this perfected product of previous inquiries is often a barrier to learning because it does not connect with his or her present needs, interests, and abilities. The "chronological," the "psychological," or, as we usually call it, the "developmental" method begins with the prior experience of the learner. It organizes the subject matter so as to coordinate it with each student's needs, interests, and abilities. If the subject matter cannot connect to the students' present state of knowledge, needs, and interests, then it has no pedagogical value for the individual student on that occasion. Educational value is not intrinsic to the subject matter. The value of any given subject matter depends on its contribution to the growth of the learner. Educators and the public at large must learn that there is no one best method of education. There is no one best way to grow.

The Stem of Philosophy as Education: Growth through Inquiry and Conversation

How should we live? Dewey's answer is that we should live intelligently, freely, and creatively. In this section I shall examine what this means.

Dewey was greatly influenced by the work of Charles Darwin. He believed that Darwin had overthrown not only the old conception of fixed species, but the notion of fixed form, identity, or essence (the Greek *eidos*) as well, and had thereby established change rather than stability as the measure of reality. As Dewey saw it, Darwin's great lesson was that we must abandon the notion of fixed, eternal, and indubitable identities and essences.

"Nature," according to Dewey, "is viewed as consisting of events rather than substances," and "every existence is an event."[15] Events are diachronic rather than synchronic. We cannot immediately know their meaning, truth, or value. In Dewey's transactional metaphysics every event is a mixture of the actual and the potential. The actual in one event realizes the potential in the other (and conversely). This is especially true of the relationships between human events such as those between teachers and students.

Existence exhibits a union of the relatively stable and the relatively contingent. Although everything is continually changing, "the rate of change of some things is so slow, or so rhythmic, that these changes have all the advantages of stability in dealing with more transitory and irregular happenings" [LW1:64]. The human task, therefore, after Darwin, is to create relative stability of meaning within a world of unstable events.

Human life itself is a natural event. Even though as much as 99 percent of all species that have ever lived are now extinct, the human *eidos* is currently a relatively stable form. Since human nature is a part of nature, human activities such as thinking, inquiry, and reflection are natural activities. The goal of such activities is not only to increase the potential for survival, but to enrich the meanings of existence. The development of intelligent attitudes and ideas, including good habits of inquiry, was in Dewey's view one of the most important aims of education.

Within the unity of the act our task is to coordinate our behavior in ways that relieve feelings of unease and cognitive doubt and enhance prosperity and growth. The rhythm of nonhuman life proceeds unconsciously from equilibrium to disequilibrium, and thence either to the restoration of equilibrium or to debilitation and death. But among human beings, intelligence intervenes. Since inquiry is a primary tool of intelligence, a major goal of education should be the improvement of skills of inquiry, including an enhanced ability to communicate.

Dewey thought it marvelous that "existence in general must be such as to be *capable* of taking on [intelligent] logical form. . . . But," he continued, "the operations which constitute controlled inquiry are necessary in order to give actuality to these capacities or potentialities."[16] Giving actuality to potentiality is an artistic activity that Dewey identified as *techne*. *Techne* for the ancient Greeks meant skill, knowledge of making, or know-how. It was the form of knowledge associated with *poiesis*. *Poiesis* meant art, production, or simply making. Creation, making meaning, therefore, *is* poetry. Dewey thought that harmonious forms of all kinds, including natural laws, essences (*eidos*), and identities, are the consequence of artistic creation. Some of these are so formal that we express them as mathematical formulas. Science itself was in Dewey's view a cultural artifact or instrument whose product is truth or warranted assertion.

Natural laws, essences, and truths are created products of inquiry; they do not exist in nature antecedent to inquiry. We create essences and identities to serve our functional needs, interests, and purposes in transforming disequilibrium into equilibrium. They are the means for securing our teleological interests and aims. Such constructions emerge as the event we call Homo sapiens carries out transactions with other events. Things, essences, and identities may endure, but in a changing universe nothing is eternal. Things and people are continuously open to further reconstruction as needs, interests, and purposes change. To think otherwise is to commit what Dewey called "*the* philosophic fallacy," that is, the "conversion of eventual functions into antecedent existence" [LW1:34]. Logical essences, for Dewey, are the eventual results of inquiry; they are not antecedently existing metaphysical events.

Inquiry begins in doubt and concludes when the stimulus of doubt is removed. Dewey acknowledged that we normally use the terms "belief" and "knowledge" to designate the outcome of inquiry. But because he rejected the notion of truth as establishing a correspondence between propositions and some antecedently existing state of affairs, and because he acknowledged the fallibility of truth claims, he preferred the phrase "warranted assertibility."

Dewey's definition of inquiry has a richly aesthetic component: "*Inquiry is the controlled or directed transformation of an indeterminate situation into one that is so determinate in its constituent distinctions and relations as to convert the elements of the original situation into a unified whole*" [LW12:108; emphasis in text]. Intelligent inquiry serves to artistically trans-form an unstable, distressful, or confusing situation into a beautiful and harmonious form that is relatively stable.

Human beings are Homo poeticus, or meaning makers. Artistic creation and aesthetic appreciation are crucial to the education of any being that lives not by fang or claw, but by its capacity to create meaning: "Men's fundamental attitudes toward the world are fixed by the scope and qualities of the activities in which they partake. The ideal of interest is exemplified in the artistic attitude. Art is neither merely internal nor merely external, merely mental nor merely physical. Like every mode of action, it brings about changes in the world."[17] Forms, artistic artifacts, emerge whenever we achieve a relatively stable equilibrium. We create these forms. Enduring forms are essences, things, and identities. Intelligent action for Dewey is thus emergent and creative. Rational action is not separate from creative action. He therefore rejected the "museum" conception of art associated with eccentric fancy and emotional indulgences and argued instead for an art that transforms things, thus making them more significant for self and society.

The artistic dimension of human growth and flourishing is a crucial aspect of Dewey's philosophy as education. "Genuine art grows out of the work of the artisan. . . . In the ideal school the art work might be considered to be that of the shops, passed through the alembic of library and museum into action again."[18]

Dewey identified the communication of meaning as a form of art, and therefore as of immense educational importance. Language is thoroughly social: "Meanings do not come into being without language, and language implies two selves involved in a conjoint or shared undertaking" [LW1:226]. Meanings *emerge* when, through the reciprocal coordination of behavior, we render something common between two or more centers of action.

For Dewey, linguistic meaning stands midway between metaphysical existence (events) and the logical essences that result from inquiry. "There is a natural bridge," he writes, "that joins the gap between existence and essence; namely communication, language, discourse."[19] We ex-press essences from existence much as we do the "essence" of grapes in the *process* of making wine. We begin by wringing meaning out of existence as the wine press wrings out the juice of the grape. Language acts like the wine press in the larger process that eventually yields the "essence of the grape" (wine). Once meanings emerge we may then further refine them into logical essences, which are the products of inquiry: "Essence . . . is but a pronounced instance of meaning. . . . Essence is never existence, and yet it is the essence, the distilled import, of existence. . . . In it, feeling and understanding are one" [LW1:144]. Different processes of distillation yield different essences; that is why there were no eternal essences or meanings, but only relatively stable ones.

Language and communication are activities of mind: unless we have a clear idea of what it means to have a mind, we have no idea of what it is we are attempting to educate. For Dewey there is no antecedently existent essence of mind or self. Dewey insisted that mind *emerges* when language supervenes upon social beings with sufficient levels of biological complexity: "Through speech a person dramatically identifies himself with potential acts and deeds; he plays many roles, not in successive stages of life but in a contemporaneously enacted drama. Thus mind emerges" [LW1:135]. To hold that mind exists before participation in the sociolinguistic practices of a culture is to commit the philosophic fallacy. In Dewey's theory of emergence, to have a mind means to be capable of possessing and responding to meanings. Meanings themselves are sociolinguistic artifacts. To acquire a mind means to become able to participate productively in the discourse practices of a culture.

Dewey entirely rejected the dominant Western theory of the mind. This dualistic theory assumes a noncorporeal mental realm that exhibits innate faculties of reason and free will. In this view, innate rationality is eternal and immutable, and therefore superior to the body, which suffers change. Further, our essential identity as "rational animals" is unaltered by the consequences of our acts. Free will governs the passions and gives us the power to execute the decisions of reason. Finally, in this view, we are social atoms because our essential identity is prior to and independent of social interaction. We enter into social contracts and form unions of all kinds, such as marriage and political associations.

John Dewey's Philosophy as Education 73

This last notion—that we are social atoms—has led to one of the most absurd features of modern epistemology, namely, the purported problem of whether we can know that there are minds other than our own. But this type of solipsism never tempted Dewey, and he thought of freedom and rationality as emergent functions of education, not as mental faculties. He also rejected all forms of mind-body dualism.

Dewey replaced the mental functions postulated by Western faculty psychology with the embodied dispositions to act already discussed and that he termed "habits." He maintained that "habits formed in process of exercising biological aptitudes are the sole agents of observation, recollection, foresight and judgment: a mind or consciousness or soul in general which performs these operations is a myth."[20] He conceded that we have innate impulses, by which he meant neurophysiological proclivities such as tropisms. Although such impulses are too diffuse to call coordinated responses or meanings, they do give us the power to act. Learned habits of response channel and refine our innate affective impulses. They are modifications of our neurophysiological system acquired from prior experiences as participants in the customs of some sociocultural tradition and in our natural biological environment. They allow us to respond systematically to subsequent situations that resemble the ones that shaped the original habit.

We can only understand the habits that coordinate our behavior in terms of their larger environmental situation or context. Because they involve coordinated responses to our habitats, Dewey thought that habits are the means of coordinating self and environment. In order to grow, we must integrate lesser functions into ever expanding and ever more discriminating webs of habitual functioning. Inquiry aids effective integration by reconstructing and refining our habits of response.

Learning is a pattern of habit formation in which new habits are conditioned by the consequences of past and present activities. "Concrete habits do all the perceiving, recognizing, imagining, recalling, judging, conceiving and reasoning that is done. . . . Yet habit does not, of itself, know, for it does not of itself stop to think, observe or remember" [MW14:124].

Dewey rejected the traditional notion of "the metaphysical freedom of will." He characterized freedom instead in terms of three naturalistic elements: efficiency in action, capacity to vary plans, and the power of desire and choice to be factors in events [MW14:209]. Regarding efficacy in action, he distinguished between negative freedom (freedom *from* constraint) and positive freedom (freedom *for* something). Negative freedom is all that many people ever seek; yet it is only desirable as a prelude to positive action oriented toward some end-in-view. Positive freedom requires immense discipline; it is the discipline of craft, or *techne*. Effective action is a central aim of education. This is why training in the arts and occupations is an essential component of Dewey's curriculum: it gives us the know-how to accomplish the ends we desire.

What Dewey has to say about deliberation destroys the conventional splits between creative and rational thought and between reason and passion. "Deliberation [inquiry] is a dramatic rehearsal (in imagination) of various competing possible lines of action. It starts from the blocking of efficient overt [habitual] action, due to . . . conflict" [MW14:132]. Imagination determines beforehand the consequences of acting on an idea that might restore equilibrium. Dewey thus stresses the importance of creative imagination in the determination of possible consequences and the importance of determining meanings before overt action is undertaken.

"More 'passions,' not fewer," Dewey boldly proclaimed, "is the answer. . . . Rationality . . . is not a force to evoke against impulse and habit. It is the attainment of a working harmony among diverse desires" [MW14:136]. Within the unity of the act we achieve rationality when we restore harmony to some conflicted situation. Feelings of peace and cessation of doubt mark the close of inquiry. Since human nature is part of wider nature, and since there is no sharp line of separation between ourselves and our environment, our habits and feelings are part of the working harmony that closes inquiry. Sometimes the portion of a situation that requires transformation is *our* interests and aims.

Education should free intelligence in ways that reconstruct physical and social environments, including the selves which are among their constituent parts. Intelligence is as much about creative imagination and passion as it is about cognition. This means that the education of *eros* (passionate desire for what is valuable) and the development of a creative imagination capable of envisioning future possibilities are every bit as important as acquiring a mastery of facts and the principles of logic. And this cannot be done in the absence of a thorough critique of existing social customs.

Dewey emphasized the social dimensions of habits. They are detachable neither from their social nor their physical habitats. "Customs persist," he wrote, "because individuals form their personal habits under conditions set by prior customs. An individual usually acquires the morality as he inherits the speech of his social group" [MW14:43]. Conduct is always social; that is why it is not *merely* a physiological process. To acknowledge oneself as controlled by habits and conditioned by social customs is simply to recognize that one's values, beliefs, interests, and perceptions are largely predetermined by scripts and plot lines that constitute the social context, including the dominant cultural texts, of the historical epoch into which one is born. If we become aware of the environmental conditions, especially the social conditions, that influence our habits of conduct, we can then recreate ourselves by reconstructing our environment. To care for ourselves we must care for our world, and to care for our world we must care for ourselves. Social critique and care for others is the key to personal freedom and self-creation.

Understanding education as a social function allows us to comprehend Dewey's claim that "an occupation is a continuous activity having a purpose. Education *through* occupations consequently combines within itself more of the factors conducive to learning than any other method."[21] Customs persist in the occupations of a culture. We have already seen that what Dewey meant by "mind" is a participatory response to meaning in social affairs. Occupations structure the habitual responses that gather around our fundamental relations to the world in which we live. Doing the deeds prescribed by some cultural occupation conditions habits that unify thought, feeling, and action. Occupational education therefore means much more than simply training *for* the trades. The occupation of teacher, for example, is a social function that is oriented toward the inculcation in the young of good social practices, that is, of the activities that occupy members of the society.

Occupations have moral content. They are cultural practices that secure some culturally valued end. The individual practitioner must acquire the virtues of the practice as well as the know-how (*techne*) required to bring into existence the goods (both moral and material) of the practice. Furthermore these cultural practices require cooperation through communication. Proper occupational practice requires critical comprehension of the goods of the practice, possession of the virtues of the practice, a sense of duty and devotion, and cooperation with others. Occupational education thus involves much more than the teaching of rules: it is moral education based on care, concern, and commitment. It is more about who we are, and our habits of doing, thinking, and feeling, than about what we publicly proclaim.

Education is crucial for cultural reproduction. It takes an entire society to educate a child, and good community requires good communication. Consequently, good communication is crucial to good education. "The aim of education is to enable individuals to continue their education . . . [and] the object and reward of learning is continued capacity for growth. Now this idea cannot be applied to *all* the members of a society except where intercourse of man with man is mutual, and except where there is adequate provision for the reconstruction of social habits and institutions by means of wide stimulation arising from equitably distributed interests. And this means a democratic society" [MW9:107]. Dewey thought education a paramount social function because it socializes the student to all the other social functions. That is why education is inevitably political, and why it is inherently controversial.

But controversy need not entail stalemate. Since the interests of the constituent groups within a society inevitably overlap, there is always the possibility of cooperation. Dewey offered two criteria for evaluating a given society. First, how many and varied are the interests and purposes that are consciously shared? Second, how free and fully engaged is the interplay with other forms of association? Oppressive societies eliminate diverse interests in favor of the special interests of the powerful few. Such societies are maladaptive because they are unable to respond adequately to environmental change. Diversity provides alternatives and thereby enhances freedom.

It is essential that individuals and groups with diverse interests enter into free and equitable intercourse. By doing so they discover shared interests and novel ways of approaching common problems. It is important that all modes of life be subjected to honest evaluation, even though many of them may ultimately be rejected as unsatisfactory or inappropriate. When social inquiry of this sort is lacking, prevailing purposes and protected privileges become institutionalized. In such societies, intransigence and inability to adapt to changing circumstances lead to decay. Isolationism diminishes freedom because it reduces the capacity to imagine alternative possibilities for free choice and action. Each of us needs to draw on the experiences and insights of others different from us if we are to continue to grow.

Dewey's two criteria for evaluating a society are also his criteria for evaluating the degree to which it has embraced democratic faith and practice. "The first signifies not only more numerous and more varied points of shared common interest, but greater reliance upon the recognition of mutual interests as a factor in social control. The second means not only freer interaction between social groups . . . but change in social habit—its continuous readjustment through meeting the new situations produced by varied intercourse" [MW9:92]. Dewey's criteria sanction growth as the all-inclusive ideal of any society. Good societies grow by cultivating the growth of good individuals who actively promote the good of others in the community. Democratic ideals, and the means to their realization, are moral, economic, and educational, as well as political.

Poetry and Prophecy:
The Flowering and Fruit of Philosophy as Education

Communication and habits of conduct conditioned through participation in the occupations of a culture and refined by habits of inquiry are the stem of Dewey's philosophy as education. Where should we then look for the flowers and fruits of communal living? "Of all affairs," Dewey wrote, "communication is the most wonderful. . . . The fruit of communication [is] participation . . . a wonder by the side of which transubstantiation pales. When communication occurs, all natural events are subject to reconsideration and revision; they are re-adapted to meet the requirements of conversations, whether it be public discourse or that preliminary discourse termed thinking. Events turn into objects, things with a meaning."[22] The fruit of democratic participation transcends even transubstantiation because it involves what Dewey called "ethereal things."

Dewey borrowed this phrase from the poet John Keats, for whom it meant that we should look "upon the Sun, the Moon, the Stars, and the Earth and its contents as material to form greater things, that is ethereal things—greater things than the Creator himself made."[23] Dewey thought that we are creative participants in an unfinished and unfinishable creation, and not spectators observing a completed cosmos. Artistic creativity is, happily, an unavoidable condition of life. To satisfy our needs, desires, interests and ends-in-view, we must continually transform ourselves as well as our environment.

Dewey recalled two of Keats's most famous lines: "Beauty is truth, truth beauty—that is all / Ye know on earth, and all ye need to know." This is not the truth function of a proposition. Keats and Dewey were, I suggest, thinking within the Greek tradition of *aletheia*, which we can translate only roughly as "truth."

Aletheia means "disclosure" or "unconcealment." Perhaps an even better rendering is "revelation." Dewey focuses our attention on this notion in order to remind us that there is a truth in imagination as it functions to reveal possibilities. He reminds us that "only imaginative vision elicits the possibilities that are interwoven within the texture of the actual. The first stirrings of dissatisfaction and the first intimations of a better future are always found in works of art" [LW10:348]. We transcend the constraints of our actual situation by imagining possibilities and then working to create them. Poetic creation is part of criticism and practical wisdom.

Dewey also draws our attention to Matthew Arnold's dictum that "poetry is criticism of life," but he wonders how this is so. He concludes that it is "by disclosure, through imaginative vision addressed to imaginative experience (not to set judgment) of possibilities that contrast with actual conditions" [LW10:349]. Imaginative vision was thus for Dewey the most penetrating form of criticism. Although it is useful to ascertain the truth values of propositions, including statements about values and duties, the most powerful form of criticism goes beyond knowledge of actual conditions to an exploration of possibilities. When habits fail us, the only alternative to caprice is reflection: "Reflection cannot be limited to the selection of one end out of a number which are suggested by conditions. Thinking has to operate creatively to form new ends."[24] Values (ends-in-view) are not merely something we discover. If we are to live well, we must create them.

Poetry is for Dewey creative, generous, and reflectively communicative. It is therefore pedagogically supreme: "Poetry teaches as friends and life teach, by being, and not by express intent. . . . It is by way of communication that art becomes the incomparable organ of instruction, but the way is so remote from that usually associated with the idea of education . . . that we are repelled by any suggestion of teaching and learning in connection with art. But our revolt is in fact a reflection upon education that proceeds by methods so literal as to exclude the imagination and one not touching the desires and emotions of men."[25] His high regard for democratic conversation and the freedom that is produced by means of creative reflection led Dewey to assign to the arts (in the sense of *techne* and *poiesis*) a central role within education. Dewey's treatment of pedagogical poetry recalls a lesson taught to Socrates in Plato's *Symposium* by the prophet Diotima.

Diotima teaches Socrates that "there is more than one kind of poetry in the true sense of the word—that is to say, calling something into existence that was not there before, so that every kind of artistic creation [*poiesis*] is poetry, and every artist a poet."[26] Creation, production, calling some possibility into existence, or making meaning, *is* poetry. Words written or recited with meter are but a small aspect of poetry in its fullest sense. In the sense of calling possibilities into existence, all art is poetic *technē*. Dewey puts this clearly enough in *Art as Experience:*

> Imagination is the chief instrument of the good. . . . The ideal factors in every moral outlook and human loyalty are imaginative. . . . Hence it is that art is more moral than moralities. . . . The moral prophets of humanity have always been poets even though they spoke in free verse or by parable. Uniformly, however, their vision of possibilities has soon been converted into a proclamation of facts that already exist and hardened into semi-political institutions. Their imaginative presentation of ideals that should command thought and desire have been treated as rules of policy. Art has been the means of keeping alive the sense of purposes that outrun evidence and of meanings that transcend indurated habit.[27]

Wisdom lies beyond knowledge of the actual. That is why moral prophets must also be poets. But schools are semipolitical institutions whose curricula and policies sometimes incorporate the gospel of greed and other false prophesies. Democratic educators must therefore also be moral prophets and poets. One of their most important tools in this endeavor is the arts.

The aim of education is growth. To live, the student must learn to conduct successful transactions with his or her environment. To grow, the student must create novel forms of recognition and response, which he or she must then refine in ways that make them more discriminating and in ways that integrate them into his or her experience.

There are two types of world in which artistic creativity and growth could not occur. In a perfectly harmonious, eternally stable, and completed cosmos, we would need nothing. Without need or desire there would be nothing to motivate inquiry, action, or creation. Such a world would be deathless only because it would be lifeless. Heaven, as it is sometimes conceived, might be just such an existential horror. Conversely, in an entirely disharmonious world where everything was perpetually unstable, nothing could come to fruition: need would be permanent. Such a world would be deathless only because nothing could ever be born into it.

Only in a world that is both stable and precarious—our world—is inquiry both possible and necessary. Only a living world can feature both growth and death. Dewey arrived at his philosophy of art, his theory of inquiry, and his metaphysics as a result of his profound understanding of our living, changing world, and as a result of his faith that the conditions for growth can be fostered, and life thereby improved. His philosophy is holistic: it is philosophy as education.

Notes

1. *Democracy and Education* [MW9:58].

2. MW9:338. See also MW9:341.

3. *Experience and Nature* [LW1:310].

4. "Philosophy and Democracy" [MW11:44].

5. "The Theory of Emotions" [EW4:174].

6. *Art as Experience* [LW10:19].

7. *Experience and Nature* [LW1:212, see also 215].

8. *Experience and Education* [LW13:25].

9. "Qualitative Thought" [LW5:249].

10. *Experience and Education* [LW13:18–19].

11. *Democracy and Education* [MW9:146–47].

12. *Logic: The Theory of Inquiry* [LW12:34].

13. *Ethics* [LW7:290–91].

14. *Democracy and Education* [MW9:114].

15. *Experience and Nature* [LW1:5 and 63].

16. *Logic: The Theory of Inquiry* [LW12:387].

17. *Democracy and Education* [MW9:142].

18. *The School and Society* [MW1:53].

19. *Experience and Nature* [LW1:133].

20. *Human Nature and Conduct* [MW14:123].

21. *Democracy and Education* [MW9:319].

22. *Experience and Nature* [LW1:132].

23. *Art as Experience* [LW10:38].

24. *Ethics* [LW7:185].

25. *Art as Experience* [LW10:349–50].

26. Plato, *Symposium*, in *The Collected Dialogues of Plato*, ed. Edith Hamilton and Huntington Cairns, trans. Michael Joyce (Princeton, N.J.: Princeton University Press, 1985), 205b.

27. *Art as Experience* [LW10:350].

5 Dewey's Social and Political Philosophy

John J. Stuhr

Has Dewey's Philosophy a Future?

John Dewey was born in 1859 and died in 1952. Because his long life reached from the American Civil War through World War II, it should be obvious that the world he inhabited changed immensely during his lifetime. In this same vein, it should be equally obvious that our own world today is itself very different from Dewey's world. He lived an increasingly long time ago, and much has changed.

Dewey certainly would have recognized this fact. His pragmatic philosophy emphasized precariousness, disturbance and instability, sweeping social change and technological transformation, genuine novelty, and real beginnings and endings. He criticized earlier philosophers and many of his contemporaries for failing to recognize that ideas, theories, and philosophies are products of definite times, places, problems, and persons, and, as such, have meaning and value only in relation to definite situations. As life conditions change, Dewey argued, our ideas must change in order to have critical relevance. He reminded us that we must be careful not to become prisoners of outdated theories and worldviews. Like Emerson, James, and many other American philosophers, Dewey believed that each age must invent its own ideas and write its own books.

From this perspective—Dewey's own perspective—certain questions arise: Given the reality of change, why study the philosophy of John Dewey any longer? In the twenty-first century, what would be the relevance or possible point of doing so? Does the philosophy of John Dewey, an important chapter in the history of philosophy, have a future? How is Dewey's pragmatism the least bit pragmatic anymore (if it ever was)? In short, what is the significance and value of Dewey's philosophy today?

Dewey himself frequently asked questions like this, and his answers are instructive. In his 1917 essay "The Need for a Recovery of Philosophy," he outlined several possible futures for American philosophy. Most of these options were dismal and empty: "I believe that philosophy in America will be lost between chewing a historic cud long since reduced to woody fibre, or an apologetics for lost causes (lost to natural science), or a scholastic, schematic formalism, unless it can somehow bring to consciousness America's own needs and its own implicit principle of successful action" [MW10:47]. This worried prediction about philosophy now seems pretty much on target. Most professional philosophers today are historians, apologists, and scholarly formalists. Ironically, pragmatist philosophers are no exception. They often busy themselves by chewing the historic cud of Dewey's pragmatism and professionally reducing it to the woody fiber that frequently fills scholarly journals, conferences, and books such as this one.

As a result, if it is to have a future or really be pragmatic, there is today a need for *a recovery of Dewey's philosophy*. What sort of recovery? It must be more than theoretical; a few more big books on Dewey's contributions to philosophy and a few more shelves of dissertations on topics not yet exhausted by previous Dewey scholars won't suffice. Instead, the recovery must be practical. It must take place in our lives—in our actions and not just in our thoughts. Above all, this amounts to a recovery of Dewey's social and political philosophy and a renewal of its spirit of meliorism. It is this spirit—more than any particular doctrine or thesis about democracy, liberalism, freedom, community, individualism, or social intelligence— that constitutes the key to Dewey's philosophy and the source of its greatest possible relevance today. This meliorism—William James's "strenuous mood" writ large in social and political terms—demands hard work on behalf of what may be possible. As Dewey pointed out: "Faith in the power of intelligence to imagine a future which is the projection of the desirable in the present, and to invent the instrumentalities of its realization, is our salvation. And it is a faith which must be nurtured and made articulate: surely a sufficiently large task for our philosophy" [MW10:48].

Perhaps this social meliorism is too hard, too demanding, too large a task for philosophy and too large a task for us. Dewey himself frequently expressed worries like this, and again his responses are insightful. In his 1949 essay, "Has Philosophy a Future?" he emphasized three points. First, he outlined professional philosophy's well-worn path of retreat from life, social relevance, and action. One branch of this path leads to cultural marginalization and remoteness through almost exclusive devotion to the study of past systems (like much study of Dewey's philosophy today): "As a matter of scholarship, the outcome is often admirable, but since the study is not conducted in order to discover the light these past systems shed upon what philosophy should now engage in, its outcome is a matter of history rather than of philosophy" [LW16:361]. A second branch of this same path winds through the search for abstract and pure and certain and eternal: "This movement, in spite of or rather because of its devotion to acquisition of merely technical skill, results in forms that are useful only in producing more forms, of the same empty type" [LW16:362]. In both its historical and formal branches, this path, Dewey concluded, is "an expression of a growing sense that past systems are irrelevant to the present human state combined with a defeatism that has not the courage to search out a philosophy that shall be relevant" [LW16:362]. Any effective recovery of Dewey's philosophy must clear a new, different path.

Second, he pointed out that any recovery of a genuinely pragmatic philosophy cannot be conducted in isolation from other, often greater, cultural forces and changes. Instead, it must go hand in hand with a larger reconstruction of culture, a "reconstruction of institutions that will have to go on for an indefinitely long time" and one in which philosophy "can have only a share in the work of reconstruction that has to be carried on" [LW16:367]. Although it may disappoint some philosophers, this means that any recovery of Dewey's philosophy cannot be accomplished by philosophers alone. If philosophy is to be concerned with more than the so-called "problems of philosophers," it must not consist of, or confine itself to, the activities of philosophers.

And, third, and most importantly, Dewey noted that this recovery of philosophy requires a cultural climate unfavorable to old traditions and old ways of thinking—a particular climate of belief, "conditions so widely extended that they are no longer matters of book knowledge or the exclusive property of an intellectual class." In another 1949 essay on the same topic, "Philosophy's Future in Our Scientific Age: Never Was Its Role More Crucial," he wrote: "Without such a cultural climate even the most important undertakings are born out of due season; they fade and die" [LW16:380]. The recovery in practice of Dewey's pragmatic social meliorism, then, has cultural prerequisites.

Is Dewey's pragmatism fated to fade and die? Is it already faded or dead? Does our present cultural climate support the recovery in action of his philosophy? Calling for courage and commitment in the face of this strenuous agenda, Dewey's own judgment was sober yet characteristically melioristic. At present we have no genuine culture, he wrote. We still have to achieve it, and we cannot do so by a "shrinking classicism" that "requires only the accidents of a learned education, the possession of leisure and a reasonably apt memory for some phrases, and a facile pen for others." Instead, Dewey concluded: "To transmute a society built on an industry which is not yet humanized into a society which wields its knowledge and industrial power in behalf of a democratic culture requires the courage of an inspired imagination" [MW10:198].

Democracy and Community

Dewey's philosophy was a sustained effort to help forge a democratic culture. His most important social and political writings, clearly connected to his theories of experience, inquiry, and education, appeared relatively late in his career in books such as *Liberalism and Social Action, Individualism: Old and New, The Public and Its Problems,* and *Freedom and Culture.* However, in the widest sense, all of Dewey's philosophy—a comprehensive account of experience, inquiry and logic, education, morality, religion, and art—simply *is* social and political philosophy. For Dewey, social and political philosophy—and not metaphysics or epistemology—is First Philosophy.

It is impossible to understand or imaginatively expand Dewey's thought except in this context. It is in this context, after all, that Dewey defined all philosophy as criticism, as discriminating judgment and appraisal of values [LW1:298]. It is in this context that he, like George Herbert Mead, claimed that the self is irreducibly social in nature and argued that the social is the largest, most inclusive ontological category [LW3:41]. And it is in this context that Dewey called on philosophers to stop disguising their social and political concerns in metaphysical abstractions: The philosophical "problems" bound up with creating dualisms and then trying to unify them—artificial problems that promote the remoteness of philosophy from the real world and its real lives—need to be replaced by social and political analysis of the conditions in which dualisms "occur as *distinctions,* and of the special uses served by the distinctions" [LW16:248].

Philosophy, then, must examine the real needs of social life in global America, must direct imagination and inquiry to social problems, tendencies, working forces, and possibilities for improvement. The reason for this is simple: A democratic society and form of life does not arise or perpetuate itself automatically. It demands persistent social inquiry, imaginative vision, and courageous action. This imperative to renew and deepen our democratic heritage is strikingly captured in "Creative Democracy—The

Task Before Us," an address that Dewey read at a dinner in his honor in New York in 1939. Claiming that we now face a moral rather than physical frontier and now must grapple with wasted resources that are human rather than material, Dewey argued that

> we now have to re-create by deliberate and determined endeavor the kind of democracy which in its origin one hundred and fifty years ago was largely the product of a fortunate combination of men and circumstances. We have lived for a long time upon the heritage that came to us. ... The present state of the world is more than a reminder to us that we have now to put forth every energy of our own to prove worthy of our heritage. It is a challenge to do for the critical and complex conditions of today what the men of an earlier day did for simpler conditions. [LW14:225]

These demands, Dewey stresses, are demands on individuals—on you and me—because democracy fundamentally is a way of life and not simply a form of government.[1] As a way of life, democracy exists in the attitudes and values and meanings of individuals in their interactions with one another. To view democracy simply as a form of government is to think about democracy in what Dewey calls an "external way" and to believe mistakenly that democracy can be defended by military or civil means external to the character of individuals: "we can escape from this external way of thinking only as we realize in thought and act that democracy is a personal way of individual life; that it signifies the possession and continual use of certain attitudes, forming personal character and determining desire and purpose in all the relations of life" [LW14:226].

By contrast, to view democracy in an internal way, in its "generic social sense" [LW2:327], is to expand this notion to the full and harmonious development of individual and society. Dewey wrote: "From the standpoint of the individual, it consists in having a responsible share according to capacity in forming and directing the activities of the groups to which one belongs and in participating according to need in the values which the groups sustain. From the standpoint of the groups, it demands liberation of the potentialities of members of a group in harmony with the interests and goods which are in common" [LW2:327–28]. In this light, Dewey identified democracy as a way of life with the life of genuine community: "Wherever there is conjoint activity whose consequences are appreciated as good by all singular persons who take part in it, and where the realization of the good is such as to effect an energetic desire and effort to sustain it in being just because it is a good shared by all, there is in so far a community" [LW2:328].

Understood in this way, democracy is meliorism; it is action informed by faith in the possibilities of human nature and human life. Democracy as a way of life is controlled by a working faith in the possibilities that may result from intelligent judgment and action. Dewey was aware that faith in this ideal might appear utopian, but he saw no alternative:

> For what is the faith of democracy in the role of consultation, of conference, of persuasion, of discussion, in formation of public opinion, which in the long run is self-corrective, except faith in the capacity of the intelligence of the common man to respond with common sense to the free play of facts and ideas which are secured by effective communication? I am willing to leave to upholders of totalitarian states of the right and the left the view that faith in the capacities of intelligence is utopian. [LW14:227]

This point is fundamental for understanding Dewey: our task is to move from a society with a democratic government to one with a democratic way of life, to move from what Dewey called a Great Society to a Great Community. We have not yet made this move or put into practice Dewey's insights, in part because the weight of tradition and habit is so great. Still, this move requires us to think differently—a reconstruction in philosophy and our traditional ways of thinking—and to live differently—a reconstruction in our individual habits and our social practices and institutions. Because it requires great change on both fronts, Dewey argued that democracy is radical: *"The end of democracy is a radical end. For it is an end that has not been adequately realized in any country at any time"* [LW11:299]. The recovery of this social and political philosophy is at least as radical today as it was when Dewey first articulated it.

Liberalism

Can a liberal politics advance these radical changes? If not, Dewey answered, there is nothing really liberal about liberalism: "A democratic liberalism that does not recognize these things in thought and action is not awake to its own meaning and to what that meaning demands" [LW11:299]. Accordingly the need to reconstruct thought, Dewey believed, was nowhere greater or more clear than in the case of liberalism. Liberalism, of course, is a term that means many things to many people: Many of its current critics today associate it with big government, high taxes, and ineffective social programs that undercut individual initiative and responsibility; many of its contemporary champions link it to concern with equal opportunity and social inclusiveness, the protection of the public interest, and the advancement of collective social goals. By contrast, Dewey understood liberalism in terms of the central values that he identified as its core commitments. More specifically, Dewey understood liberalism to be social and political theory and action committed to the three key values of individualism, freedom, and social life guided by intelligence (rather than, for instance, ignorance, mere authority, or violence). Anyone genuinely committed to these values is a liberal as Dewey defines the term. Given Dewey's unusually broad definition, it is important to realize that a great many people on the political right, left, and center—a great many people who disagree with one another on many issues—all alike are committed to liberalism in Dewey's sense. It is in this context that Dewey observed that the only real alternatives to liberalism are mindless political drift and violent radicalism.

Despite their shared commitments to individualism, freedom, and intelligence, Dewey clearly recognized that different liberals have stood for, and worked for, different goals at different times in the past. As a result, liberalism must be understood historically. As expressed by thinkers such as John Locke, Thomas Jefferson, and Adam Smith, early liberalism was committed to the innate individuality of all persons and to their self-evident individual rights to life, liberty, and the pursuit of property and happiness. The effective exercise of these individual rights required freedom from interference by others. Therefore, these liberals were committed to the institution of governments to protect these rights and to the belief that governments which infringe on these rights are illegitimate and should be overthrown. Thus, this early liberalism, Dewey argued, understands individualism as something ready-made and automatically possessed by all members of society, understands freedom as the absence of interference from others, and understands intelligence as the innate capacity to grasp supposedly self-evident moral truths and economic laws. Early liberalism, Dewey summarized, was highly individualistic "in the sense in which individualism is opposed to organized social action" and regards the individual as having moral primacy and authority over the state:

> It defined the individual in terms of liberties of thought and action already possessed by him in some mysterious ready-made fashion, and

which it was the sole business of the state to safeguard. Reason was also made an inherent endowment of the individual, expressed in men's moral relations to one another, but not sustained and developed because of these relations. It followed that the great enemy of individual liberty was thought to be government because of its tendency to encroach upon the innate liberties of individuals. [LW11:7]

This view of individual, society, and government was not shared by later liberals. Philosophers such as Hume, Bentham, and Mill were skeptical of so-called "self-evident" truths. They argued that self-evident beliefs are not directly justified or self-justified in any logical sense; rather, they simply are unquestionably obvious or evident (to those who hold them) in a psychological sense. Because these philosophers denied that any belief comes somehow prepackaged with its own justification, they claimed that all actions and institutions must be judged by their consequences (rather than their origins). Still other writers, also dedicated to freedom, individualism, and intelligence, developed less individualistic or atomistic accounts of human nature. Romantics such as Coleridge, Wordsworth, Carlyle, and Ruskin, for example, emphasized the organic, holistic, interconnected character of society. As a result, many more recent liberals have adopted a more utilitarian and communal approach toward government and organized, collective social action.

However, these various strands of liberalism, as Dewey noted, are incompatible. Their theoretical differences lead to differences in practice and to different social agendas. As a result, liberalism became and today remains confused, wavering, and internally divided. It has arrived at an impasse: Unable to advance democracy as a way of life, liberalism now seems impotent. Analyzing this paralysis, Dewey criticized those persons who cling to the old notion of liberalism that understands organized social action as an enemy of individual initiative, liberty, and effort: "In the name of liberalism, they are jealous of every extension of governmental activity. . . . Wittingly or unwittingly, they still provide the intellectual system of apologetics for the existing economic regime, which they strangely, it would seem ironically, uphold as a regime of individual liberty for all." In contrast, Dewey argued that liberalism now requires commitment to "the principle that organized society must use its powers to establish the conditions under which the mass of individuals can possess actual as distinct from merely legal liberty" [LW11:21].

As a result of this inner split or division between liberals, the beliefs and methods of liberalism have proven ineffective in the face of contemporary problems. The underlying cause of this crisis in liberalism is the failure of liberals to reconstruct, in theory and in practice, the enduring values of liberalism—individualism, freedom, and intelligence—so as to bring them into harmony with, and critical relevance to, contemporary social conditions. This means that the specific meaning of these basic values must change continuously as social conditions change. This means that liberals, like philosophers more generally, must have a historic sense of their own liberalism. Liberalism, if it is to avoid the revenge of history and be pragmatic, must become genealogical.[2] The absence of this genealogical self-understanding, Dewey observed, blinded earlier "liberals to the fact that their own special interpretations of liberty, individuality and intelligence were themselves historically conditioned, and were relevant to their own time. They put forward their ideas as immutable truths good at all times and places; they had no idea of historic relativity, either in general or in its application to themselves. . . . The tragedy is that although these liberals were the sworn foes of political absolutism, they were themselves absolutists in the social creed they formulated" [LW11:26].

The key point to grasp here is that this historical blindness has resulted not simply in incoherent social and political theories, but that it has resulted in self-contradictory social and political practices. Recent liberals have not simply failed to advance the causes of individualism, freedom, and intelligence; worse, guided by outdated interpretations of these values, they have acted in ways that actually now oppose freedom, individualism, and intelligence. In short, traditional liberal theory itself now functions as a major obstacle to the realization of liberal values in social life.

As a result, change is needed. In this light, Dewey called for a "renascent liberalism" and proposed a three-step general strategy to achieve it. To be effective, renascent liberalism first must develop historical perspective. That is, it must note the actual social conditions that give rise to liberal theory—in both its past and present forms. Second, and on this basis, renascent liberalism must reconstruct traditional liberal values. That is, it must develop the meaning of individualism, freedom, and intelligence in light of current social realities. Third, renascent liberalism must use this conceptual reconstruction to inform and guide the active reconstruction of social institutions, practices, and relations. That is, it must involve action—must translate new theory into new practice.

Dewey addressed each of these points. First, to provide liberalism with historical perspective, he highlighted sweeping social changes that have taken place since traditional, early liberalism was first formulated. As a result of science and technology, these include new material possibilities. However, this potential plenty and material security is often treated as an end—materialism as the good life—rather than a means—material abundance as a means to a more fully human social life and potential plenty. Conditions have changed, but old habits of thought and action remain. Dewey emphasized the force of these old habits that "pathetically" bind us: "the habits of desire and effort that were bred in the age of scarcity do not readily subordinate themselves. . . . Even now when there is a vision of an age of abundance and when the vision is supported by hard fact, it is material security as an end that appeals to most rather than the way of living which this security makes possible" [LW11:43].

As a result, despite potential material security, social life now is marked by massive insecurity. But this insecurity is not so much the result of nature as the consequence of human institutions, practices, and social relations. Claiming that this change in the nature and cause of insecurity "marks one of the greatest revolutions that has taken place in all human history," Dewey argued that insecurity is "not now the motive to work and sacrifice but to despair" [LW11:43]. Here is Dewey's radicalism: "Force, rather than intelligence, is built into the procedures of the existing social system. . . . That the control of the means of production by the few in legal possession operates as a standing agency of coercion of the many, may need emphasis in statement, but is surely evident to one who is willing to observe and honestly report the existing scene" [LW11:45–46]. This coercion by concentrated and organized property interests leaves the individual isolated and helpless: "Concentration and corporate organization are the rule." But it also leaves individuals unable to perceive the need for radical change, unable to imagine and take seriously alternatives, unable to escape from habitual old ideas about individualism, freedom, and intelligence: "But that society itself should see to it that a cooperative industrial order be instituted, one that is consonant with the realities of production enforced by an era of machinery and power, is so novel an idea to the general mind that its mere suggestion is hailed with abusive epithets—sometimes with imprisonment" [LW11:44].

Individualism, Freedom, and Intelligence

The second step in Dewey's strategy for a renascent liberalism is the reconstruction of our notions of individualism, freedom, and social intelligence. His sustained, detailed reconstruction of the meaning of individualism begins with an analysis of individualism and its nearly total submergence in our society today. Our lives, Dewey argued, now are marked by economic insecurity, political apathy broken by confused spasms of concern, deep decline in the roles of religion and family as integrative and directive forces in persons' lives, growing social conformity, crime and disregard for other persons and our environment, and increasing but unsuccessful efforts to solve social problems externally through legislation rather than internally through the formation of character and shared activities and values. Collectively, these developments indicate that the loyalties and relations that in the past gave rise to, sustained, directed, and unified individuals' outlooks and lives have virtually disappeared. However, new loyalties that might play a similar function today have not been forged. The result is what Dewey calls the "lost individual"—confused, bewildered, unanchored persons without stable allegiances and unifying commitments. Dewey observed that "it would be difficult to find in history an epoch as lacking in solid and assured objects of belief and approved ends of action as is the present" in which "individuals vibrate between a past that is intellectually too empty to give stability and a present that is too diversely crowded and chaotic to afford balance or direction to ideas and emotion" [LW5:68].

This point is crucial: Individuality is a social product, a result of social relationships, a consequence of publicly acknowledged and stable social functions. We are born as separate (and, in this sense, individual) organisms, but we are not born individuals. Individuality is not a given fact about human beings, something static, guaranteed and (in Dewey's phrase) "ready-made." Instead, individuality, if and whenever it occurs, is an achievement, the result of an irreducibly social development process. In the absence of appropriate social conditions, individuality is impossible. Just as not all societies are genuine communities, so too not all human beings are genuine individuals.

This point is missed by all those who think that individuality is simply a matter of being different at all costs from everyone else—of driving a different car, listening to different music, having a different haircut or different clothes, and acting differently. Dewey allows us to see that by itself all this has nothing to do with genuine individuality and everything to do with mindless conformity: Whether one does something just because others do it, or avoids something just because others do it, the actions of others uncritically direct one's life. Dewey's point is missed also by those who think that individuality is simply a matter of personal self-sufficiency or what Dewey calls "rugged" or, more accurately, "ragged" individualism. Dewey makes clear that this image is a fiction: Human beings in our complex world are involved in countless social interdependencies from education to food production, from communication and transportation systems to the care of our shared environment and our personal health, and from friends and neighbors to the military, corporations, and geographically distant peoples. This recognition that individuality is a social product is missed as well by those who think that individuality is something innate, a guaranteed birthright of every different human organism, something that each one of us necessarily has. Dewey shows us otherwise: Individual self action presupposes an individual self, and this individuality, when it occurs, is a matter of the social development of a self, not a primordial trait inherited by all and maintained only by those few who can escape to private Walden ponds.

Dewey's distinction between being a genuine individual and just being a separate organism parallels and is informed by the distinction between the self and the body, made forcefully by philosopher and sociologist George Herbert Mead, Dewey's friend and colleague at Chicago. The self, Mead observed, is essentially and irreducibly a social structure that arises in social experience. Accordingly, it is important to distinguish the self—a social category—from the body (without a self)—a biological or physiological category: "The body can be there and can operate in a very intelligent fashion without there being a self involved in the experience. The self has the characteristic that it is an object to itself, and that characteristic distinguishes it from other objects and from the body." This defining characteristic of the self, Mead claimed, is created indirectly and from the standpoints of others in the same social groups: The self "enters his own experience as a self or individual, not directly or immediately, not by becoming a subject to himself, but only in so far as he first becomes an object to himself just as other individuals are objects to him or his experience; and he becomes an object to himself only by taking the attitudes of other individuals toward himself within a social environment or context of experience and behavior in which both he and they are involved."[3]

The social development of this self is the development of individuality, and, for Dewey, this process is one with the development of democracy as a way of life. And this individuality, then, is not reverse-conformity, self-sufficiency, or a necessary, natural human quality. Instead, for Dewey, individuality, like community, is a process of growth. It is self-realization, the continuous development of one's potentialities. Seen in this way as self-actualization, individuality is fragile. It does not happen naturally or automatically, but rather requires the presence of those conditions which make possible continuing growth. If a renascent liberalism is committed to a new individualism, then it must be committed to the development and attainment of those social conditions upon which real individuality (like real community) depends.

Freedom, Dewey argued, is the presence of, and participation in, these conditions necessary for the self-realization of individuals. This means that our understanding of the traditional liberal value of freedom, like that of individualism, must be reconstructed. This has important implications for social action and makes clear the need for a reconstruction of the goals of liberalism. Dewey made this point repeatedly and at length. In his 1928 "Philosophies of Freedom," he argued that the central error of traditional liberalism is its belief that "all that is required on the side of institutions and laws is to eliminate the obstructions they offer to the 'free' play of the natural equipment of individuals." This liberated some few persons to take advantage of new social and economic conditions, but it enslaved many other persons to the newly freed powers of the few. Dewey concluded: "The notion that men are equally free to act if only the same legal arrangements apply equally to all—irrespective of differences in education, in command of capital, and the control of the social environment which is furnished by the institution of property—is a pure absurdity, as facts have demonstrated. . . . The only possible conclusion, both intellectually and practically, is that the attainment of freedom conceived as power to act in accord with choice depends upon positive and constructive changes in social arrangements" [LW3:100–101].

In this light, Dewey argued that the creation of real individuality (and community) today is stymied by the hold of an earlier, outdated individualism defined in terms of private enterprise and private profit. Dewey's sobering analysis in *Individualism: Old and New* rings true in our consumer culture today: "It is not too much to say that the whole significance of the older individualism has now shrunk to a pecuniary scale and measure. The virtues that are supposed to attend rugged individualism may be vocally proclaimed, but it takes no great insight to see that what is cherished is measured by its connection with those activities that make for success in business conducted for personal gain. Hence the irony of the gospel of 'individualism' in business conjoined with suppression of individuality in thought and speech" [LW5:84–85].

Dewey's point is even more radical than it may seem at first because he did not argue that we simply need to redistribute income or extend economic initiatives and opportunities to those who are poorest. Instead, Dewey claimed that we need nothing less than the formation of a new psychological and moral type of individual—a new individualism, a new human nature. Dewey never pretended to have a crystal ball and offered no detailed blueprint for this new individualism: "Indeed, I do not see how it can be described until more progress has been made in its production." Our outdated individualism that enlists technology and social organization in the service of private material gain is the greatest obstacle to this progress, Dewey believed, and he often wondered about our unwillingness to even try to surmount it: "I sometimes wonder if those who are conscious of present ills but who direct their blows of criticism at everything except this obstacle are not stirred by motives which they unconsciously prefer to keep below consciousness" [LW5:89].

An economy, a government, or a society, then, is not fully free unless it makes available to its members the prerequisites of their growth—both their growth as individuals and the growth of the social groups through which they live. It is not easy to do this; it requires imagination, criticism, experimentation—in short, intelligence. What sort of intelligence? The nature of intelligence, Dewey argued, is not at all what earlier liberalism has held it to be. It is not an innate faculty or some sixth sense for perceiving supposedly fixed, universal, self-evident truths—truths antecedent to action. Instead, for a renascent liberalism, intelligence must be understood in terms of inquiry, experimental action, and its results. Dewey analyzed how the actual links (to which we frequently pay lip service) between democracy and education—the regular and broad use of intelligence—are undermined and opposed by the authority of custom, superstition, and old beliefs.

The interdependence of democracy and education, however, is opposed also by propaganda, institutionalized violence, and new forms of manipulation that threaten individualism and freedom. Dewey argued at length throughout his life against this paralysis of democracy in which sensationalism and credulity, force and coercion, and private manipulation of public opinion substitute for shared intelligence. Superficial, temporary conformity of opinion, Dewey thought, masquerades as genuine communication. Created by means external to the judgment of individuals, this mass credulity takes us from one intellectual fashion to the next according to "the dominant suggestions of the day": "We think and feel alike—but only for a month or a season. Then comes some other sensational event or personage to exercise a hypnotizing uniformity of response" [LW5:82]. To urge social change through a process of intelligence, Dewey argued, is to champion real change; to advocate social change through force, by contrast, is to promote business as usual. It is force—coercion and violence—rather than intelligence, he claimed, that drives our social system. This leaves no room for Enlightenment hopes or simple-minded optimism, Dewey concluded. Instead of dispelling ignorance and superstition, the progress of science and its technological application

> has resulted in business corporations possessed of extensive legal rights and immunities; and, as is commonplace, has created a vast and intricate set of new problems. It has put at the disposal of dictators means of controlling opinion and sentiment of a potency which reduces to a mere shadow all previous agencies at the command of despotic rulers. For negative censorship it has substituted means of propaganda of ideas and alleged information on a scale that reaches every individual, reiterated day after day by every organ of publicity and communication, old and new. In consequence, for practically the first time in human history, totalitarian states exist claiming to rest upon the active consent of the governed. While despotic governments are as old as political history, this particular phenomenon is as startlingly unexpected as it is powerful. [LW13:156]

Dewey offered a powerful alternative, but one that he admitted was not very seductive. Democratic ends, he argued, require democratic means for their realization: "Our first defense is to realize that democracy can be served only by the slow day by day adoption and contagious diffusion in every phase of our common life of methods that are identical with the ends to be reached and that recourse to monistic, wholesale, absolutist procedures is a betrayal of human freedom no matter in what guise it presents itself" [LW13:187]. In this spirit, Dewey avoided political prophecy and refused to tell others *what* to believe—only that belief should rest on the basis of careful judgment and public access to the results of free inquiry.

Moreover, Dewey's renascent liberalism requires social action in order to ensure that the results of this free inquiry inform social policies and that communication pervades social life. In the absence of this communication, our great society cannot become a great community. To produce a full and rich democratic culture—a genuine community—we must foster shared and intelligent communication. To do so is to execute our democratic ideals directly in our lives. The processes of inquiry must be expanded and its results must be disseminated and made available for public use. From Dewey's perspective, this has always been the promise of democracy in America. Democracy, Dewey wrote, "is a name for a life of free and enriching communion. It had its seer in Walt Whitman. It will have its consummation when free social inquiry is indissolubly wedded to the art of full and moving communication. . . . We lie, as Emerson said, in the lap of an immense intelligence. But that intelligence is dormant and its communications are broken, inarticulate and faint until it possesses the local community as its medium" [LW2:350, 372].

Has Dewey's Philosophy a Future—Again?

Dewey often pointed out that he was not interested in making philosophy pragmatic, but rather in making practice intelligent. From this perspective, of course, it does not matter much whether Dewey's philosophy has a future. The important question is whether our future will be one of democratic community marked by individuality, freedom, and shared intelligence.

I don't know. I do know that Dewey's vision of a democratic way of life remains largely unrealized today. Intelligence does not possess the local community as its medium. Our society is anything but a great community. The lost individual has not been refound—in fact, search and rescue efforts seem to have been abandoned. The ideals and methods that Dewey advocated are very distant.

They are so distant that some thinkers have concluded that Dewey's social and political philosophy is absolutely unrealizable, merely utopian, just an idle dream or pleasant vision of a secular heaven on earth. In its place, some philosophers have broken apart Dewey's unification of the public and the private, the community and the individual, society and the self; they have turned away from his commitments to democracy and pluralism; they have renounced his radical criticisms of American life and his determination that we do better. In doing so, they have offered two alternatives.

In the first alternative, at the theoretical level of the individual, this dualism leads to narratives of private perfection and vocabularies of self-creation as independent of social arrangements and practices. At the practical level, this dualism leads to countless efforts to lead the good life in private by avoiding society and its mounting problems. The "cash-value" of this dualistic theory is everywhere evident—from private home gyms and private entertainment centers to private security systems, private schools, and private gated neighborhoods and villages. While Dewey searched for the public, these theorists of the private self aren't even bothering to look. In terms of society, at the theoretical level this dualism leads either to an "it doesn't get any better than this" complacency and conservativism about American government and culture, or to political fundamentalism, extremism, and the security and guarantees of absolutism in our otherwise pluralistic society.

In the second alternative, efforts to reconstruct critically individual life or social institutions and practices are abandoned happily. Our vices are declared virtues, and a materialistic philosophy—Dewey sometimes called it the outlook of the "business mind"—is set forth as harmonious with our materialistic, business culture. On this view, being human is equated with having possessions, the good life is equated with material wealth, and the good society is identified in terms of high gross national product or high gross national consumption. Here the search for the public is replaced by the search for the nearest shopping mall, stack of mail-order catalogs, or quick access to new electronic "virtual" marketplaces.

The shallowness of these views, as Dewey knew well, cannot be demonstrated by mere argument alone. Moreover, the shallowness of these ways of life cannot even be experienced by those who cannot or will not inquire into them, critically imagine alternatives, and work hard to realize those alternatives. Dewey's social and political philosophy demands that we cast aside old ways of thinking and old social arrangements that prevent just this sort of criticism and imagination. We now face new roadblocks—some of which Dewey never even imagined, much less addressed. The path that stretches out ahead, however, remains the same. It is the path that Dewey traveled: "The task is to go on, and not backward, until the method of intelligence and experimental control is the rule in social relations and social direction" [LW11:64]. And it is a long path, a path without end: "the only ultimate result is the result that is attained today, tomorrow, the next day, and day after day, in the succession of years and generations. . . . At the end as at the beginning the democratic method is as fundamentally simple and as immensely difficult as is the energetic, unflagging, unceasing creation of an ever-present new road upon which we can walk together" [LW 13:188].

Whether or not we have the melioristic faith and courage to continue on this path is up to us—you and me, here and now. This challenge has always been the core of pragmatism, and it is Dewey's most enduring message.

Notes

1. See my "Democracy as a Way of Life," *Philosophy and the Reconstruction of Culture: Pragmatic Essays after Dewey,* ed. John J. Stuhr (Albany: State University of New York Press, 1993), pp. 37–57.

2. See Part III, "Community," of my *Genealogical Pragmatism: Philosophy, Experience, and Community* (Albany: State University of New York Press, 1997).

3. George Herbert Mead, *Mind, Self, and Society: From the Standpoint of a Social Behaviorist* (Chicago: University of Chicago Press, 1934), pp. 136–37.

6 Dewey's Ethics: Morality as Experience

Gregory F. Pappas

John Dewey's ethics is perhaps the most original—and the most underappreciated—area of his entire philosophy.[1] Like the rest of his work, it has an organic structure. This means that his treatment of a particular moral issue cannot be understood in isolation from his larger moral project. And each thread of that larger moral project is in turn interwoven within the still larger fabric of his whole philosophy. Dewey's ethics, therefore, cannot be judged or appreciated from the standpoint of assumptions that are foreign to his wider philosophy.[2]

Unlike many contemporary approaches to ethics, the one that Dewey constructed does not rest on a set of postulates and arguments that are recognizable as an ethical "system." Instead his work exhibits criticisms based on hypotheses about our moral experience as it is inspired by commitments that we sometimes leave unstated. When reading Dewey, therefore, it is important to resist the philosophical habit of trying to find a "system." A better approach is to become acquainted with his moral vision.

But this task is complicated by the fact that Dewey did not consolidate his ideas about ethics in any single work. He scattered his ideas throughout his many books and essays. In some cases he even presented them in a paragraph or two placed almost parenthetically in the midst of a passage devoted to another philosophical topic. The few books in which Dewey focused explicitly on ethics were textbooks and syllabi, written primarily for classroom work. They were therefore not intended to be systematic theoretical formulations.

Dewey's ideas about ethics, just as his ideas about other subjects, underwent gradual but continual reconstruction during the seventy-one years that constituted his public career.[3] Although these modifications are important, they are not substantial or drastic enough to support a sharp distinction between an "early" and a "later" Dewey. It is probably more accurate to say that Dewey developed his views about moral experience early in his career, and that he then tended to revise his thinking as the implications of his views became apparent, and as he felt the need to present his case in fuller detail or wider scope.[4] The works that best represent Dewey's mature treatment of ethics are *Democracy and Education* (1916), *Reconstruction in Philosophy* (1920), *Human Nature and Conduct* (1922), "Three Independent Factors in Morals" (1930), and *Ethics* (1932).[5]

It is fair to say that the intellectual resources contained in these texts have never been fully exploited. They are, however, receiving more and more attention. As this trend continues, it will become clear that Dewey's work is poised to make a solid contribution to a number of current ethical debates, such as those that concern feminist ethics, virtue ethics, and cognitive science.[6] Although it would be impossible in this brief essay to present Dewey's ideas about ethics in a comprehensive manner, it is possible to outline their most distinctive features. They include:

(1) a critical stand on the limits, nature, problems, and function of the type of inquiry that takes our moral experience as its subject matter (a metatheory);

(2) a treatment of the generic traits and components of moral experience (a descriptive ethics);

(3) a constructive, though not explicitly articulated, proposal regarding how we should live, and how we can improve our appreciation of morally problematic situations (a normative ethics).

First, a word about how these features are related. The metatheoretical, the descriptive, and the normative facets of Dewey's ethics are found intertwined throughout his writings. They support one another and what Dewey regarded as his larger inquiry, namely, an investigation of the conditions and instrumentalities required to ameliorate concrete, existential, lived experience. Unlike many other ethical theories, Dewey's theoretical inquiries, whether metatheoretical, descriptive, or normative, were never presented as an end in themselves. They invariably emerged from concrete, experienced, problematic situations. Once formulated, they were applied and checked against those situations in order to ascertain whether they could be improved.

Dewey's concern with ethics arose out of his perception that individuals and institutions had not been able to find viable alternatives to the moral absolutism offered by custom and authority, on the one side, and the subjectivistic views supported by moral philosophers, on the other. He thought that such ethical theories, as well as the economic and political institutions that depend upon and perpetuate them, have tended to encourage habits and attitudes that impoverish moral life. He thought that many of the conditions of contemporary life have exacerbated this situation; they have tended to produce undesirable and unaesthetic types of experiences that prevent men and women from having fruitful moral experiences.

The main problem with many ethical theories and the institutions that support them, Dewey argued, is that they tend to distrust the capacity of human intelligence to find innovative ways of coming to terms with experienced problems. Such theories and institutions thus assume a profound dualism—a split between what they take to be dignified, autonomous moral theory, on the one side, and what they take to be common, contingent, everyday experience, on the other. Dewey charged that the major theories so far advanced by moral philosophers, including subjectivism, rationalism, and transcendentalism, have been constructed squarely on top of this dangerous fault line. He thought that in their efforts to achieve incontrovertible theories and indubitable foundations they had abandoned any effort to come to terms with experience as it is actually felt and lived.

The three aspects of Dewey's ethics just mentioned—the metatheoretical, the descriptive, and the normative—were thus in his view not ends in themselves, but just different uses of philosophy as criticism and different types of instruments to be used to liberate and improve actual moral practice. I shall briefly consider his use of each of them.

Moral Theory and Practice

Dewey mounts a devastating and systematic critique of contemporary moral theory as a part of his proposal of a new starting point. His empirical approach begins and ends with moral experience as it is experienced,[7] and not as it exhibits any special relation to the methods or subject matter of any particular science.[8] If we are to begin and end with "primary experience" in ethics then we have to begin with the primitive situations of life where moral experiences are had [LW1:15–16]. Moral subject matter, in this sense, is always experienced as a part of a "situation," and we are always in some situation or other. A philosopher can of course "step back" from unique life situations as they are experienced into a second, *reflective* situation and then design theories about moral life. But it is important to remember, because many philosophers tend to forget it, that it is always the unique, lived situation that is the context of moral experience.[9] In our moral life it is always a specific "felt" trouble, question, or confusion that initiates moral inquiry and that makes the moral qualities of alternative courses of action the focus of our awareness.

Although there is no area of our experience that is exclusively or essentially moral, we can identify and characterize those situations that we experience as *predominantly* moral. They have the pervasive quality of demanding that we deliberate about conflicting moral demands.[10]

Failure to acknowledge the situation-bound nature of moral deliberation and moral inquiry is a failure to be sufficiently empirical. Dewey was highly critical of moral theories that begin by treating their favored categories and distinctions as complete in themselves apart from any context. Such categories are treated as though they are antecedent and just need to be applied to concrete situations in which moral agents have to decide what they ought to do. This tendency to absolutize or universalize in ethics by providing theories of "the good" constitutes, in Dewey's view, a failure to see that any meaningful quest for "the good" is always tied to a particular inquiry within the unique context of a morally problematic situation. The dualisms, or splits, that have plagued most moral theories (self versus act, character versus conduct, and fact versus value, to name but a few)[11] are also a result of the failure to begin with experience rather than with theory. Instead of starting empirically then, with the "integrated unity" and "unanalyzed totality" found in a lived situation, modern moral philosophy begins antiempirically, with ontological gaps.

Although Dewey anticipated many of the recent criticisms against normative ethical theories, he also reaffirmed the importance of moral theory. He developed a position that lies between the extremes of divorcing ethical theory completely from moral practice, on one side, and the pretensions of some normative ethical theories to dictate our moral conduct, on the other.[12] Dewey thought that the purpose of disclosing the limitations of moral theory is to determine the functions it might be able to perform. "Theory having learned what it cannot do, is made responsible for the better performance of what needs to be done" [MW 4:45].

For Dewey, moral theory is developed from the particular facts and the deliberation that are the features of a particular moral situation. Moral philosophy is thus a function of the moral life, and not the reverse. Moral theory thus involves refined and secondary products of moral deliberation, but these products are not absolute. They are instrumentalities that assist or illuminate daily effort and give intelligent direction to the affairs of primary moral experience. When theory is conceived as something within practice, and not just imposed on it from the outside, it takes on the responsibility of being a part of the available means for the intelligent amelioration of practice.

If moral theory is *in* and *for* our moral life, then one cannot determine what an adequate ethical theory will be without considering what kind of moral theory works better within our actual moral lives. This point may seem obvious, but it has been overlooked by many contemporary moral philosophers. Dewey's criticism of normative rule-oriented theories, and of nonempirical ethics in general, is based on the fact that such theories do not really assist our moral practice. Ethical theory even becomes an obstacle to moral practice once it presumes to replace individual and contextual reflection with fixed rules and mechanical decision procedures. One of Dewey's great insights was that our moral lives are such that what is and is not important cannot be determined beforehand, and that theoretical rules most often function as little more than blinders. No matter how good the rules might be, they are not universally applicable. Every action is undertaken in a particular situation that has its own unique conditions. In any case, a rule-bounded morality results in a kind of casuistry that would "destroy the grace and play of life by making conduct mechanical" [EW3:155]. In other words, it encourages a nonaesthetic way of living morally.

Dewey diagnosed the quest for fixed rules and ideals in morality as a counterpart to the general quest for certainty that characterizes modern epistemology [MW14:166]. Just as epistemologists have assumed that without certainty there is no knowledge, ethicists have tended to assume that "absence of immutably fixed and universally applicable ready-made principles is equivalent to moral chaos" [MW14:164]. This either-or dilemma can take different forms: Either there is an absolute standard of value or we cannot judge or measure any value; either there is a "uniform and unchanging code of morals" or morals are "all conventional and of no validity" [LW7:283]. The debates between absolutists and relativists, and between objectivists and subjectivists, are usually based on accepting the terms of this dilemma.

Dewey's response to this either-or dilemma was that his rejection of rules does not entail that moral agents should ignore altogether the moral precepts that they have inherited. That is, Dewey's situation ethics is not the view that one has to face each situation passively and "empty handed." There is a choice between "throwing away rules previously developed and sticking obstinately by them" [MW14:165]. What is needed is to take rules as principles.[13] There are principles because there are stabilities in experience. Situations are unique but they are also similar in many respects. This makes it possible for experience to be intellectually cumulative, that is, for general ideas to develop. Principles are "general" moral ideas in the sense of proposing generic conditions and relations to be met under circumstances of a certain kind. They are general maxims of frequent validity, but their validity ultimately depends upon their applicability to a situation: they alone have no normative force. We can rely on principles because we can learn, and we can learn because there is continuity in experience.[14] "Principles are empirical generalizations from the ways in which previous judgments of conduct have practically worked out" [MW14:165]. They are instrumentalities and hypotheses for inquiry, that is, "methods by which the net value of past experience is rendered available for present scrutiny of new perplexities" [MW14:166]. Without principles we lack the knowledge that serves as a background that could help us in particular situations.

The possibility of living by principles signifies the possibility of taking seriously the moral principles we have inherited from our families, culture, and personal history without giving up the kind of flexibility entailed by Dewey's situation ethics. Flexibility in our moral lives is needed not because of human limitations with respect to an antecedent moral truth, but because of the reality of change and novelty, that is, because "life is a moving affair in which old moral truth ceases to apply" [MW14:164]. Dewey thought it was possible and commendable to educate children to become committed to some valuable traditional moral principles and at the same time prepare them to be able to modify and apply these principles to complex and changing conditions.

Dewey's opposition to rules, fixed ends, and universal standards is based on his conclusion that there is a better method. To find the guidance for rectifying a particular situation, it is necessary to give up looking for a universal theoretical formula and get on to the difficult task of studying "the needs and alternative possibilities lying within a unique and localized situation" [MW14:196]. Dewey thus advocated an approach to moral decision-making that may be termed "situational."[15] The flexibility and "anti-theoretical" character of his view does not, however, entail less work, intelligence, or responsibility than fixed-theory approaches. On the contrary, Dewey argued that his view "does not destroy responsibility; it only *locates* it [my emphasis]" [MW12:173]. It implies that the work of intelligence cannot be accomplished once and for all. We cannot rely solely upon the theoretical use of intelligence to construct rules that will obviate the need to make hard decisions. A situation ethics of the sort that Dewey advances demands that we try a "fresh" and wholehearted use of intelligence each time that there is a new situation that requires amelioration.

For Dewey, ethical theory can aid moral practice only indirectly, not in the direct way that has been assumed by most of contemporary philosophy. Dewey therefore proposed that the use of intelligence in moral theorizing should be redirected from its accepted function. He favored an ethics that treats theory neither as a cookbook, nor a remote calculus, but as a tool of criticism. His ethics refuses to set down inflexible rules; it is instead a method for generating and testing hypotheses about the conditions for living a richer moral life.

One of the most important of these conditions is what has been called "character." From Dewey's standpoint, moral philosophy has had the tendency either to overestimate or to underestimate the importance of character. Underestimation is usually a result of denying the participatory role in moral experience. Overestimation is usually a result either of assuming that the direction of moral experience is totally within our control or of making character an end in itself. Character and habits occupy a central place in Dewey's ethics, but they do not (as some other approaches argue) thereby occupy a place of ontological or epistemological primacy. Character and habits are central to moral reflection, and to ethical theory, simply because they are among the most controllable factors of moral experience. To a great measure, habits determine "how" we will interact with particular situations.

Theory of Our Moral Life

Dewey argued that there is no area of our experience that has suffered more from distortion and misleading conceptions than our moral experience.[16] And among the most troublesome misconceptions has been the reification of morality into something that is separate from ordinary experience. Morality has thus been isolated and honored as something "spiritual." It has been cut off from lived experience and placed in an extraexperiential or subjective realm of its own. This understanding of morality, which has dominated western culture, has been fostered in large part by the dualisms, such as the fracture that opposes "fact" to "values," that have been assumed and nurtured by traditional philosophy. As a part of his goal of reconstructing traditional philosophy, Dewey attempted to heal these conceptual fissures. Just as he objected to the "museum conception of art," that isolates the arts from lived experience, Dewey warned against separating morality from relationships in the workplace, from the technical-scientific use of intelligence, and from the "material" orientation of the business world [LW10:12]. If Dewey sometimes seems almost to conflate morals with science, industry, or politics, it is because he wanted to "bring morals to earth, and if they still aspire to heaven it is to the heaven of this earth" [MW14:16].

This persistent separation of morals from experience is one of the ways in which men and women seek to escape responsibility for their actions. If morality is perceived as something external to the material-natural realm of industrial and economic relations, or something that is just sometimes added to them, then the instrumentalities of technology, science, and business are not properly perceived as tools that can be taken up and used to improve unsatisfactory moral conditions. This is a costly mistake; it diverts intelligence from the concrete situations where moral demands are encountered. If the continuity between morals and the rest of experience were acknowledged, however, then a fuller range of resources would become available for moral action.

Moral theorists have contributed in several ways to this alienation of morality from lived experience. The tendency in the history of moral theory has been to replace the authority of custom with moral absolutes, or to try to reduce the subject matter of morality to mathematical and legalistic calculations. These are signs of resistance to the view that morality *is* experience. Moral philosophers have consistently sought to prove that there exist, independently of the "phenomenal" changes that occur in the world, special moral precepts that are universal, fixed, certain, and unchanging. But in Dewey's view, change, conflict, contingency, uncertainty, and struggle are at the very heart of moral experience. This is not to say that he was a pessimist. But he did think that he had presented a more honest assessment of our potential to ameliorate existing conditions. He thought that amelioration requires the recognition that even our most stable moral principles will have to be revised over time.

In order to recover morality from "other-worldly" views, on the one hand, and subjectivist views on the other, Dewey had to engage in a critical redescription of moral experience. He worked through the one-sidedness and vicious abstractions of past moral philosophizing in an attempt to construct a view that was more adequate to actual moral experience. He thought that traditional ethics had become bankrupt because it had discussed moral notions "in isolation from the concrete facts of the interactions of human beings with one another" [MW14:219]. Because traditional ethics begins with an isolated subject or self that has a purely cognitive apprehension of moral truths, it begins with an abstraction. But this abstraction ignores the social (transactional) and affective (qualitative) character of moral experience. Dewey's ethics thus points to dimensions of moral life that tend to be overlooked and undervalued in much of modern ethical thought. He rejects their intellectualist, passive, and possessive views of our moral life in favor of a conception of morality as a social, creative, imaginative-emotional, hypothetical, and experimental effort to ameliorate situations and to bring new goods into existence.

Dewey characterized the generic elements and phases of our moral life as a process. In his view, the "rhythm" of our moral life is one of disruptions followed by reunions and then by phases of "confident, straightforward, organized" activity [MW14:127]. These "breaks" in the "flow" are problems that often call for moral decisions. The process of moving from the inception of these problems to their resolution does not constitute all of what counts as our moral life, but it is one of its most intense and important phases.

There are three predominant stages in Dewey's model of moral inquiry. First, the agent finds herself in a morally problematic situation. Second, the agent engages in a process of moral deliberation. Finally, she arrives at a judgment that results in a choice. It is in light of this process that Dewey provided novel and provocative reconstructions of the traditional notions of character, moral deliberation, value judgments, principles, and moral problems. In contrast with the usual rationalistic-sterile account of moral deliberation, for example, Dewey describes moral deliberation as an experimental, emotional, and imaginative process.[17] Moral deliberation results in a moral judgment—a decision to act in one way or another. But judgments are not static. They continue throughout the entire deliberative process, and they are transformed as deliberation proceeds. Within this process, Dewey distinguishes between the direct judgments of value ("valuing") and the reflective judgments ("valuations").[18]

For Dewey the opposition between objectivism and subjectivism in value theory was evidence that "it is a common occurrence in the history of theories that an error at one extreme calls out a complementary error at the other extreme" [LW13:240]. The subjectivist starts with the assumption of isolated desires as sources of valuation. There is therefore nothing to test values, and no possibility of intellectual control: they are rendered arbitrary.[19] This evokes a contrary theory, one in which values are "ends-in-themselves" or outside of experience. "This theory, in its endeavor to escape from the frying pan of disordered valuations, jumps into the fire of absolutism" [LW3:241]. From Dewey's standpoint, these two views, in spite of the opposition to one another, exhibit the same error: they both assume the "same fundamental postulate of the isolation of valuation from concrete empirical situations" [LW13:241]. Without the qualitative context of a situation there is no basis in experience for control, guidance, and experimentation in regard to values; we must either go outside of experience for a standard or make values subjective. Subjectivism troubled Dewey because it made criticism, appreciation, and cultivation in matters of value arbitrary or absurd. But for Dewey "educated interest or taste is, ultimately, supreme, the *unum necessarium*, in morals" [LW2:76]. And "The saying '*De gustibus, non disputandum*' . . . is either just a maxim of politeness or a stupid saying" [LW2:95].

Subjectivist views take value as identical with being enjoyed or desired. They reduce theory of value to a psychological theory about desire and liking. These views "admit a human factor in values . . . which interpret[s] it in such a way that the result is sceptical denial of the possibility of any genuine judgments about them" [LW15:63]. Dewey argued against the reduction of value situations to mere liking or enjoyment. Valuings are about things in the world and not mere reports of our "internal" emotional state. As he said "We do not enjoy enjoyments, but persons, scenes, deeds, works of art, friends, conversations with them" [LW15:80]. Valuing "judgments" are reports of qualities found in a particular situation as "objective" attributes of acts and persons in a particular situation as manifestations of nature[20] and not "subjective" projections.[21] Valuing judgments can turn problematic, and then be subjected to "objective" criticism (i.e., valuation) without having to appeal to anything outside of experience. Inquiry into relations and conditions is just as applicable to valuings as it is to scientific subject matter. To be sure, value judgments differ from other judgments in their subject matter and in the usual importance they have in directing conduct, but there is nothing inherent in the nature of values that precludes them from the general method of inquiry. Hence, intelligent-objective criticism of existing values is possible even if it is always relative to what is available in the particular situation, and not from a "God's eye point of view."

Perhaps the more significant way in which subjectivism has affected ethics is in the concerns that have made the issues of moral realism and objectivity meaningful. When the qualitative content of experience is taken as an "internal" phenomenon with no guarantee that it corresponds to anything in the "outer" natural world, moral objectivity becomes a philosophical problem and subjectivism becomes an alternative to moral realism. Subjectivism in this sense denies that moral qualities or traits are part of reality. It holds instead that they somehow have their origin in the subject. This view was supported by modern science, which discovered the instrumental value of stripping nature of its immediate qualities for the purposes of experimental control. For Dewey, however, moral qualities, traits, or values are experienced. Insofar as they are experienced and when they are experienced, they *are*.[22] Moral qualities are not "subjective," but part of the world as it is experienced. Moral qualities require an experiencer but they do not "belong" to consciousness. They are found in situations and reveal aspects of nature. Dewey was defending just this type of moral realism when he wrote:

> Instead of presenting that kind of mechanistic naturalism that is bound to deny the "reality" of the qualities which are the raw material of the values with which morals is concerned, I have repeatedly insisted that our theory of Nature be framed on the basis of giving full credence to these qualities just as they present themselves [LW14:63].
> If experience actually presents aesthetic and moral traits, then these traits may also be supposed to reach down into nature, and to testify to something that belongs to nature as truly as does the mechanical structure attributed to it in physical science. . . . [E]sthetic and moral experience reveal traits of real things as truly as does intellectual experience. [LW1:13–14, 27]

In *The Quest for Certainty*, Dewey claims that his philosophy of experience is comparable to a "Copernican revolution" in philosophy. His ethics is thus a shift from an "old center" to a "new center" [LW4:232]. The "old center" is the dualistic model that underlies character-centered and act-centered moralities, namely, that of a self as an outside beholder "complete within itself" that has to act in an external world of other people and things. In Dewey's ethics, the "new centers" are contextual situations of concrete transactions where both character and conduct are mutually implicated. Character and conduct are thus for Dewey features of an ongoing unity that can only be defined by their interrelation and mutual dependence within the process of reconstructing unique and particular situations.[23]

In Dewey's ethics, the self is not a substance but an organization of habits that is relatively stable and enduring. The self changes, therefore, as habits are modified. Because we are selves in a process of continuous formation, what we do at any point in time is not a creation ex nihilo. Instead, what we do depends on the history of the self. In deciding what to do, we rely on the habitual tendencies, projections, and desires that constitute our character as it was formed, at least in part, from previous experience. Although having a good character does not guarantee that we will always do the right act, it does increase our chances. The good habits we bring to a situation are among the means by which we are enabled to discover and do what is right. It is only by doing what we ought to do, however, that we can improve our habits.

This is not circular reasoning, but simply the recognition that being good and doing good are mutually dependent within any moral life that is both growing and educative. The most important moral "learning" that a person can acquire in a situation is not information (or rules), but the indirect cultivation of the habits that tend to affect the quality of future situations. This is to say that although the moral decisions we make depend on our characters, they also affect the habits that are carried forward by a growing self. The reconstruction of situations and the reconstruction of the self are not things that can be separated.

In Dewey's ethics, the moral self is an integral part of the process of reconstructing morally problematic situations. Therefore, the self affects, and is affected by, what goes on while transactions take place in a particular situation. This establishes a very important, organic relation between the quality of what we do and of the character we bring to a situation. A growing educative moral life requires both improvements of the habits that will determine the quality of present experience as well as of the present experiences that will determine the quality of our habits.[24]

To take situations as the starting point of ethical theory does not entail a narrow or scaled-down view of moral experience. On the contrary, Dewey thought that much of the reductionism and oversimplification of the subject matter of contemporary moral theory has been caused by failing to consider the complexity and richness of our moral experiences as they are had in unique situations.[25] In "Three Independent Factors in Morals,"[26] Dewey argued that the history of moral philosophy is characterized by one-sidedness because philosophers have abstracted one factor or feature of situations which are experienced as morally problematic and then made that factor supreme or exclusive. "Whatever may be the differences which separate moral theories," he wrote, "all [philosophers] postulate one single principle as an explanation of moral life" [LW5:280]. Hence, moral theories have been classified according to whether they take good (teleological-consequentialist), virtue (virtue ethics), or duty (deontological theories) as their central category or source of moral justification. As Dewey points out, however, good, virtue, and duty are all irreducible features found intertwined in moral situations. Dewey's pluralistic ethics is a promising alternative to the narrow, reductionistic views that have dominated the history of moral philosophy.

Dewey's view of moral experience is a "metaphysics" of morals in the sense that Dewey is willing to use this term "metaphysics" as a general description of the generic traits of existence.[27] This type of inquiry gave Dewey the resources he needed to criticize other ethical theories and to reconstruct a more robust notion of moral intelligence.[28] Moreover, a metaphysics of morals can provide a basic orientation and guide for conduct. As Dewey said, "The more sure one is that the world which encompasses human life is of such and such a character (no matter what his definition), the more one is committed to try to direct the conduct of life, that of others as well as of himself, upon the basis of the character assigned to the world" [LW1:309].

Dewey's Moral Normative Vision

Dewey did not have a theory about the "good life." This notion is in fact antithetical to the pluralistic and contextualist thrust of his moral philosophy. Nevertheless, his ethics is unintelligible apart from some normative commitments and hypotheses about the conditions and instrumentalities for a better moral life that are central to his moral vision.

The Situation as the End of Morality.

Dewey insisted that it is essential for the reconstruction of moral philosophy that we stop seeking ends or standards that are over and above particular situations. In his view, the "end" of morality lies within each particular situation. There is no moral task over and above the amelioration of each concrete and specific morally problematic situation. Dewey's ethics entails nothing less than a complete transformation of the "center of gravity" of morality. Most traditional ethical theories treat situations as mere means to something else, for example, the good life, the maximization of future pleasure, or the acquisition of a virtuous character.

For Dewey, however, there is no ultimate and overarching end that defines and makes meaningful all moral activity. But "while there is not a single end, there also are not as many as there are specific situations that require amelioration" [MW12:175]. In other words, each concrete morally problematic situation presents a unique moral task with its own immanent end and meaning, even if its resolution happens to produce wonderful instrumentalities for further experiences. "If the need and deficiencies of a specific situation indicate improvement of health as the end and good," Dewey wrote, "then for that situation health is the ultimate and supreme good. It is no means to something else. It is a final and intrinsic value" [MW12:180].

Dewey often complained about "how much of distraction and dissipation in life, and how much of its hard and narrow rigidity is the outcome of men's failure to realize that each situation has its own unique end and that the whole personality should be concerned with it"[29] [MW12:176]. The moral tasks of responding to irreducible moral demands, judging, and deciding what I ought to do are always related to the unique context of a situation. What is sought in moral inquiry, therefore, is the very action among its alternatives that is "called for" by the situation, that is, the very action that answers better to the particular experienced problem in the light of the context as it presents itself.[30] To find this out requires an intelligent, open, sensitive, and full consideration of the situation in its uniqueness.

Moral Intelligence and the Situation as the Means of Morality.

The suggestion that we try a "fresh" and wholehearted use of intelligence each time a situation requires amelioration, instead of appealing to external authority or to ready-made rules, assumes a positive trust in the possibilities and instrumentalities available in a situation.[31] Stated another way, Dewey's ethics holds that the situation is not only the end but also the "means" of moral endeavor. Hence, a morally problematic situation can achieve its "end" through its own means. Dewey suggests that we need to consider a situation on its own merits, and that in deciding what to do the situation is the only place where we need to "look" for guidance and instrumentalities. The situation itself gives the qualitative indications of when an act is "morally called for" or when it is irrelevant. This is an instance of Dewey's faith in experience,[32] and this commitment is central to his philosophical vision.

This is the idea that we do not have to look for guidance outside of experience because experience contains the resources for its own transformation. To be sure, principles, ideals, and habits are instrumentalities that are available to a moral agent in such a situation. In order to transform a morally problematic situation into one that is determinate, however, these tools become a part of the concrete qualitative complexity of the situation.

Because the moral agent is also an integral part of the transactions that make up a situation, one of the resources that experience has for its own transformation is the character of the moral agent. This is why character and habit are important in Dewey's ethics. Whether and to what extent a situation can guide us in its reconstruction depends in part on how and to what extent we participate in it. Even though what is right or wrong in a particular situation is determined *in* and *by* its particular context, not all characters are equally prepared for moral tasks. It is not that the moral agent remains passive before a problematic particular context, receiving guidance from it in a way that is automatic or inevitable. Situations do not hand ready-made answers to the moral agent. A high level of involvement on the part of the moral agent is called for. He or she must exhibit the dispositions and the energy called for by a situation. This would include the sensitivity to read it properly and a willingness to take part in its transformation. Hence, Dewey's contextualism advances a view about how moral agents as participants should confront moral situations. It demands the participation of the whole character of a moral agent in a moral situation. Moral anarchy and chaos are not avoided by fixing moral rules, but by the proper cultivation of character. The kind of character we should become is thus for Dewey a more important consideration than what decision procedure we should adopt.

In the final analysis, that part of Dewey's ethics that might be treated as a virtue ethics is complementary to his situation ethics. He holds that the most important instrumentalities for morality, the "cardinal" virtues if you like, are the traits of character that make it possible to determine what morality requires *here* and *now*. Dewey's situation ethics exhibits a positive-normative position in the sense that it undertakes judgments about what kinds of habits will serve as virtues, that is, as instruments for the development of better moral lives. Such virtues include sensitivity, conscientiousness, sympathy, and open-mindedness. These are the habits he identified with moral "intelligence."

To give each situation the attention and care that it deserves is the first imperative of Dewey's moral philosophy. This particularist thrust is not incompatible with some of the general concerns exhibited by virtue ethics.[33] As should by now be obvious, moral ideals and character have an important place in Dewey's ethics. But he is able to incorporate these elements without postulating abstract notions that are antecedent to concrete situations. He treats ideals as means to the amelioration of a situation. And he treats virtues as habits that come into play within the context of situations and not as a priori or abstract models of human flourishing. Dewey's hypothesis was that the moral task of ameliorating the concrete, specific situations that present themselves in moral experience must be undertaken in ways that are "intelligent," "aesthetic," and "democratic."

The Intelligent, Aesthetic, and Democratic Way of Life

The broadest possible characterization of Dewey's normative vision is that he advocated a moral life that is "intelligent," "aesthetic," and "democratic." These three adjectives characterize mutually dependent aspects of a single moral vision.

To say that a moral life is "intelligent" is merely to indicate that it can educate itself and ameliorate its problems through its own resources. What Dewey called "experimental intelligence," involves those habits of inquiry by means of which hypotheses are tested and by means of which working connections are found between old habits, customs, institutions, and beliefs and new conditions.[34] With respect to moral life, "intelligence" refers to a way of appropriating a moral tradition. Dewey contrasts intelligence with the practice of guiding our lives by authority, custom, coercive force, imitation, caprice, or drift.

To say that a moral life is "aesthetic" is to point to its qualitative and inherently meaningful mode of engagement. The "aesthetic" qualifies "how" moral reconstruction is undertaken. Dewey contrasts what is aesthetic with the mechanical, the fragmentary, the nonintegrated, and all other nonmeaningful forms of engagement. Dewey thus invites us to drop legalistic-absolutistic models of moral conduct and to look instead to art as the paradigm of an activity that can steer between living aimlessly and living rigidly or mechanically. To engage a situation intelligently is to engage it aesthetically. It is in this way that "moral life is protected from falling into formalism and rigid repetition. It is rendered flexible, vital, growing" [MW12:180]. Dewey envisions an aesthetic moral life as one that achieves a balance between "work" and "play" and that therefore integrates what might otherwise seem to be incompatible generic traits of our moral experience.

To say that a moral life is "democratic" is to emphasize that it involves a certain way of interacting with others in the world, a certain kind of community, and a certain kind of communication. Dewey understood democracy as a form of moral association in which a certain way of life is instituted in the relations and interactions of its citizens. "[I]t is primarily a mode of associated living, of conjoint communicated experience" [MW9:93]. Although Dewey never provided more than a vague notion of what this broad ideal means in terms of habits, kinds of relationships, and kinds of communication, it is nevertheless clear that his notion of democracy was an outgrowth of his ideas about moral experience.[35] What Dewey sometimes referred to as "the democratic way of life" involved "intelligent" and "aesthetic" communities. Democracy was for him a moral-social ideal that encourages the kinds of environing conditions and ongoing interactions that maximize the potentialities for everyday experience to regulate and reconstruct itself.

In sum, although Dewey's moral theory does not provide set answers to moral problems, he hoped that his ethics would encourage us to explore the possibilities inherent in moral experience as it presents itself instead of seeking transcendental or absolutist solutions. Dewey wanted to provide an ethics that was faithful to the "spirit" of morality, and that puts the "center of moral gravity" inside the concrete process of living. The moral life that Dewey envisions is one that relies on experience for direction, illumination, inspiration, and motivation. A moral life that is aesthetic, intelligent, and democratic is preferable to morality conceived as the rigid observance of fixed and ready-made rules or ideals. This is the kind of moral life that can maintain its own integrity without the support and guidance of fixed and external foundations. This is the kind of moral life that promises to be the most fruitful general form of engagement in experience. This is the moral life that is lived *in* the context of a situation, *by* means of the resources found within the situation, and *for* the situation.

Notes

1. This is not Dewey's fault. It is a consequence of the poor state of philosophical reflection on Dewey's ethics. As Ralph Sleeper has said, "attacks from the

outside are less serious impediments to the development of a new program of inquiry than the misinterpretations and misapplications from *within* by those who profess the espousal of the program." Ralph W. Sleeper, "Dewey's Metaphysical Perspective: A Note on White, Geiger, and the Problem of Obligation," *The Journal of Philosophy* 57 (1960): 101.

2. For articles that point out instances of this mistake in interpretation see: Ralph W. Sleeper, "Dewey's Metaphysical Perspective," 100–115; James Gouinlock, "Dewey's Theory of Moral Deliberation," *Ethics* 88 (1978): 218–28; and Robert L. Holmes, "The Development of John Dewey's Ethical Thought," *Monist* 48 (1964): 392–406.

3. Dewey's philosophical work spanned the period from 1882 to 1953. In his first writings on morality (1887) Dewey was an absolute idealist, but by his 1908 *Ethics*, there is almost no residuum of his early idealism.

4. For the history of the changes in Dewey's early work, see Darnell Rucker's and Herbert W. Schneider's essays in *Guide to the Works of John Dewey*, ed. Jo Ann Boydston (Carbondale: Southern Illinois University Press, 1970), pp. 99–130. For the changes from Dewey's early period to his middle period (1908), see Jennifer Welchman, *Dewey's Ethical Thought* (Ithaca, N.Y.: Cornell University Press, 1995). For the changes from Dewey's 1908 *Ethics* to his revised 1932 edition, see the introduction to the 1932 *Ethics* [LW7] by Abraham Edel and Elizabeth Flower. In general, what distinguishes Dewey's later ethical writings from his early writings is a more acute awareness of the complexity of the particular, of the indeterminacies and elements of novelty in situations, and of the social and instrumental nature of our character. Dewey's early ethical writings were more "psychological" or self-oriented in the sense that ethical concepts were generally interpreted in terms of inner-individual processes and tensions. In Dewey's mature ethical philosophy there is more of a direct focus on a situation as the field of moral experience constituted by transactions. The moral agent is conceived as a participator in a network of relations in situations. The function of intelligence in moral experience is defined in terms of habits and the reconstruction of particular situations. Moral situations are characterized as involving choice among irreconcilable demands.

5. Dewey did not write a book about ethics comparable to his three books *Logic, Experience and Nature*, and *Art as Experience*. It would have been fitting for him to write one more revision of his 1932 *Ethics*, not as a textbook, but as a more comprehensive, updated, elaborated rendition of his moral thought.

6. For the relation with feminism and virtue ethics, see my "Open-mindedness and Courage: Complementary Virtues of Pragmatism," in *Transactions of the Charles S. Peirce Society* (forthcoming), and "Dewey and Feminism: The Affective and Relationships in Dewey's Ethics," *Hypatia* 8, 2 (Spring 1993): 78–95. For Dewey and cognitive science, see Mark Johnson, *Moral Imagina-*

tion (Chicago: University of Chicago Press, 1993). For a general considera-
tion of Dewey and some recent ethical theories, see James Gouinlock,
"Dewey and Contemporary Moral Philosophy" in *Philosophy and the Recon-
struction of Culture*, ed. John Stuhr (Albany: State University of New York
Press, 1993), pp. 79–96, and idem, *Rediscovering the Moral Life* (New York:
Prometheus Books, 1993).

7.   For the issue of experience as method, read "The Postulate of Immediate
Empiricism" [MW5] and the first chapter of *Experience and Nature* [LW1].

8.   Dewey's insistence on making ethics empirical is part of his general attempt
to base philosophy in experience. But this requires an understanding of
his kind of empiricism. Although Dewey might have shared the twentieth-
century preoccupation with the possibility of an empirically grounded ethics, he cannot be identified with any sort of "naturalistic" reduction of
moral judgments to scientific statements. This would neglect the radical nature of his empiricism. A radical empiricism in ethics discloses the continuities and shared methods between science and our moral practice but it is
also sensitive to differences, and to the irreducibly unique nature of moral
experience. In fact, it could be argued that it was precisely because Dewey
avoided the scientific readings of our moral experience that he was able to
provide one of the most thoroughgoing empiricist ethics of the twentieth
century.

9.   In ethics one cannot assume concreteness or empirical grounding simply because one begins with language (e.g., a conceptual analysis of moral terms)
or because one takes seriously the historical and communal context of morality. Dewey identified empiricism with taking context seriously, but not
just any contextualism in ethics is thereby empirical. The importance of
moral language and historical traditions is not denied, but in Dewey's work
they are understood as features of situations as the primary context in
which we live our lives.

10.   When a felt moral perplexity controls and pervades the development of the
situation as a whole, we can designate the situation as a moral one.

11.   These dichotomies have in turn generated all kinds of false dilemmas and
debates, such as egoism versus altruism, subjectivism versus objectivism,
and "ethics of character" versus "ethics of act."

12.   The key to seeing this alternative lies in understanding the nature of the relation between theory and practice. The conception of moral theory as
somehow outside the context of moral practice is the source of recent skepticism against theory. Bernard Williams, for example, criticizes the history of
moral philosophy for its futile attempt to find an "Archimedean point."
Bernard Williams, *Ethics and the Limits of Philosophy* (Cambridge, Mass.:
Harvard University Press, 1985), p. 29. Williams asserts the Deweyan thesis
that the starting point of moral theory is within moral practice. "They [ethi-
cal theories] still have to start from somewhere, and the only starting point
left is ethical experience itself" (p. 93). But he says very little about what this

means and where it should take us. Although Williams makes a compelling argument about the "limits" of ethical philosophy, he leaves us in the dark as to what a conception of ethics within practice (or that starts from "*here*") allows us to do. It is here that Dewey is a step ahead.

13.   Principles, as Dewey uses the term, are not fixed or universal maxims that prescribe and determine what an agent ought to do. Principles are instead inherited instrumentalities for analyzing individual and unique situations. He is willing, for example, to accept and adopt the "golden rule," but only as part of the tools of analysis that might be needed to decide in a particular situation what I should consider as relevant. Dewey explained, "the Golden Rule gives me absolutely no knowledge, of itself, of what I should do. The question of what in this case I should do in order to do as I would be done by has still to be resolved, though the Golden Rule be a thousand times my maxim. . . . [The Golden Rule] is a most marvellous tool of analysis; it helps me hew straight and fine in clearing out this jungle of relations of practice" [EW3:100–101].

14.   The possibility of converting rules which are offered as absolute into principles is grounded in Dewey's view of experience. The choice between the fixity of moral rules and moral chaos of the either-or dilemma assumes that experience is either a fixed block or a spontaneous flux. This ignores the fact that an alternative to fixity in habits or principles is change as a continuity of growth. "Only an uncritical vagueness will assume that the sole alternative to fixed generality is absence of continuity" [MW14:168]. The either-or dilemma ignores the principle of continuity. For habits to change they do not have to move from rigid repetition to nonentity (or abrupt change), for there is continuity in the development of a habit. "While a flexible habit does not secure in its operation bare recurrence nor absolute assurance neither does it plunge us into the hopeless confusion of the absolutely different. To insist upon change and the new is to insist upon alteration *of* the old" [MW14:168].

15.   A similar kind of contextualism has been held by Aristotle, W. D. Ross, and Joseph Fletcher. But the contextualism in these thinkers is only operative at the level of making particular moral judgments. Their ethical views assume at some other level fixed moral truths. Dewey's contextualism is more radical, however, since it is a thoroughgoing contextualism according to which no general rule or principle can escape the relativity to context. Dewey does not cling to any moral absolute. The term "situation ethics" was already employed by Fletcher in *Situation Ethics* for his own flawed theory, but it obviously fits Dewey's view better.

16.   Many things are associated with morality that have very little to do with concrete moral situations. It is customary to associate it with "a body of proverbial saws and maxims instilled in us from early childhood" [LW5:398]. Dewey complained that "what passes for 'ethics' oscillates between sermonizing, moralizing of an edifying emotional type, and somewhat remote dialectics on abstract theoretical points" [LW5:398–99]. But if "morality" is about

the concrete moral situations that we face in everyday life, then the philosopher's abstract maxims are more removed from this subject matter than writers (in literature) who, by indirect imaginative means, point to these kinds of situations. Dewey said, "it must be admitted that those who have worked it most successfully have done so indirectly. They have approached the mine not as moralists but as novelists, dramatists, poets, or as reformers, philanthropists, statesmen. The contributions which they have made have found their way, however, into common life rather than into moral theory" [LW5:399].

17. Dewey's early concerns to reconcile ethics with experimental science led him to investigate the ways in which scientific inquiry and moral inquiry can share a way of forming and justifying judgments (i.e., a general method). For an interpretation that emphasizes this, see Jennifer Welchman, *Dewey's Ethical Thought* (Ithaca, N.Y.: Cornell University Press, 1995). On the other hand, Dewey's description of moral deliberation as a transformation into a unified consummatory experience, as well as his emphasis on the importance of the imagination and the emotions in this process, suggests an aesthetic model. For this view, see Steven A. Fesmire, "Dramatic Rehearsal and the Moral Artist: A Deweyan Theory of Moral Understanding," *Transactions of the Charles S. Peirce Society* 31, 3 (1995), and Thomas M. Alexander, "John Dewey and the Moral Imagination," *Transactions of the Charles S. Peirce Society* 29, 3 (1993). An adequate understanding of Dewey's overall philosophy would indicate that both of these qualifications (aesthetic and scientific) are not mutually exclusive. We do not have to choose between an aesthetic view of Dewey's ethics and a scientific one. Dewey used science and art as metaphors by which to understand moral experience, but he avoided a reduction of morality either to art or science. Secondary sources that stress one or the other of metaphoric tools often fail to make this clear.

18. For Dewey's theory of value in light of his views on experience and nature, see James Gouinlock, *John Dewey's Philosophy of Value* (New York: Humanities Press, 1972).

19. One version of subjectivism that Dewey attacked was emotivism. This is the view that "so-called 'values' are but emotional epithets or mere ejaculations" [LW13:191].

20. For a recent article defending this Deweyan naturalism, see John Teehan, "In Defense of a Naturalism," *Journal of Speculative Philosophy* 10, 29 (1996): 79–89.

21. This is perfectly compatible with the hypothesis that such judgments (i.e., the having of a certain quality) depend (as a condition) on bringing to a situation certain character traits, for the qualitative is a result of a transaction of a human being (as an organism) and its environment in a situation.

22. This follows from Dewey's "postulate of immediate empiricism." This is the hypothesis that "things—anything, everything, in the ordinary or non-

technical use of the term 'thing'—are what they are experienced as" [MW3:158].

23.   The distinction between character and conduct, just as the distinction between experiencing subject and experienced object, is a discrimination by reflection from primary experience. The distinction between character and conduct is based for example on the distinction between "what" one does and "why" or "how" one does it. Dewey used this distinction in *Middle Works* 5:10–12. "What" occurs in moral experience is a choice of conduct that arises out of deliberation that is responding to moral demands (forces) in the context of an evolving morally problematic situation. This could be distinguished from "why" in terms of motives and beliefs, or "how" in terms of what habits (as ways of interacting) we bring forth to a situation. These are functional distinctions that can be extremely important (effective) in the effort to improve primary moral experience and not different domains of our moral experience.

24.   A nongrowing moral life is one in which neither habits nor present experiences affect each other in significant ways. This might be because habits are not flexible or open enough to be affected by present experiences, or because present experiences are not significant enough to affect habits. Notice how in Dewey claims of improvement and growth are not dependent on any particular fixed conception of human good or flourishing. If there is such a conception, it is a very general notion of a moral life that is educative, i.e., that guides and enriches itself by its own resources.

25.   Ethical theorists have been more concerned with theoretical coherence and simplicity than with adequacy to the rich and concrete context from which distinctions are abstracted.

26.   Dewey's article "Three Independent Factors in Morals" is a centerpiece of his moral thought. The tripartite description of our moral experience of this essay explains why Dewey discussed good, duty, and virtue in separate chapters of his 1932 *Ethics*. Without this essay one misses important support for the situational and pluralistic thrust of his moral philosophy, which is not evident in his discussions about value in general. Dewey's faith in the instrumentalities of experience was tempered by the honest realization that the most intense moments of our moral life are tragic in the sense that there is an irreducible, and sometimes irresolvable, conflict between positive moral demands or values. This view is quite different from, and has different consequences than, the general view of our moral life as merely a struggle between good and evil.

27.   For Dewey metaphysical-descriptive conclusions play an important instrumental function in philosophy as criticism. "Any theory that detects and defines these traits is therefore but a ground-map of the province of criticism, establishing base lines to be employed in more intricate triangulations" [LW1:309]. Here we can distinguish between the most general

"ground map" of the generic traits of existence from a more specific map of the general features of our moral experience.

28.   A more robust notion of moral intelligence would not suffer from the traditional dualisms that have plagued ethical theories, such as "social versus individual" and "emotional versus intellectual."

29.   Dewey complained that in morals and in education the abstract future and not "the active process of transforming the existent situation" is usually the significant thing. Even when he said that "growth itself is the only moral 'end' " [MW12:181], he explicitly qualified it: " . . . growing, or the continuous reconstruction of experience, is the only end" [MW12:185]. "The end is no longer a terminus or limit to be reached. *It is the active process of transforming the existent situation*" (emphasis added) [MW12:181]. If there is a generic end it is the very *process* of ameliorating, reconstructing, transforming a present morally problematic situation; it is not an acquisition of or approximation to something that supersedes each situation and all moral action. By "growth" Dewey sometimes meant the kind of continuity and interaction of experience that allows the improvement of our character. This is an important aspect of his ethics because growth is one of our most reliable means to confront future situations and enrich present experience. It is not, however, the end of morality.

30.   One implication of the "situation as the end of morality" is that, no matter how much Dewey may have stressed the importance of consequences in moral deliberation, he was not a consequentialist. In arriving at a conclusion, consequences may enter into consideration, but the moral act does not derive its rightness from producing a certain proportion of some consequences over others. It derives its rightness from being the act "called for" by consideration of the situation as a whole.

31.   "Intelligence" as habits are part of the resources that are present in a situation.

32.   I could have instead said that Dewey had a faith in nature or that this is what makes Dewey a naturalist. For Dewey, experience is continuous with and a part of nature, and any claim about experience is therefore a claim about nature. Dewey's undermining of the split between experience and nature can be found in *Experience and Nature*. It is true that the term *experience* gave Dewey a lot of trouble because of its ambiguity and associations. But I am not convinced that *nature* is any better in this respect. This is especially true today when what is associated with "naturalism" are views that have a truncated scientistic understanding of the natural. My use of the term *faith* might also be considered as problematic. For Dewey's and James's understanding of this notion, and how different it might be from the traditional one, see my "William James and the Logic of Faith," *Transactions of the Charles S. Peirce Society* 28, 4 (Fall 1992): 781–808.

33.   Dewey's ethics does not fall, however, into the vice of contemporary virtue theorists: deemphasizing particular acts for the sake of long-term disposi-

tions. On the other hand, his contextualism avoids the atomistic view of acts, the legalistic form of morality, and the neglect of the self and communal context that characterizes many modern act-centered views. In Dewey there is no inconsistency in holding an ethics with a strong character orientation and a commitment to particular situations.

34.   Dewey is explicit about the fact that the notion of "intelligence" that he is continually trying to refurbish is a normative notion, a regulative notion of what should be and not a description of a faculty that we all possess. "The choice of intelligence as the preferred method of action implies, like every choice, a definite *moral* outlook. The scope of this choice is so inclusive that the moral implication outlines, when followed out, an entire ethical and social philosophy" [LW8:101].

35.   The importance that ethics had in Dewey's lifelong preoccupation with democracy should be obvious since Dewey repeatedly referred to democracy as a *moral* ideal. However, Dewey's views on democracy are often segregated by his commentators and critics as politics or social thought apart from his moral thought.

7 Dewey's Philosophy of Religious Experience

Steven C. Rockefeller

Throughout his career Dewey aspired to create a comprehensive philosophical vision, and integral to his thinking at each of the major stages in the evolution of his philosophy is a theory of religious experience, including a well-developed concept of the nature and significance of religious faith. A knowledge of his theory of religious experience is necessary for a complete understanding of his psychology, ethics, social theory, and aesthetics. An appreciation of Dewey's personal religious faith clarifies his deepest concerns and objectives as a philosopher, educator, and social reformer. In addition, Dewey's reflections on the religious dimension of experience and his liberal reconstruction of the meaning of religious faith in a democratic technological culture are an important contribution to twentieth-century religious thought.

In an autobiographical essay, Dewey described how early in his career he arrived at the conviction "that any genuinely sound religious experience could and should adapt itself to whatever beliefs one found oneself intellectually entitled to hold."[1] He added: "I have enough faith in the depth of the religious tendencies of men to believe that they will adapt themselves to any required intellectual change." This standpoint was "a half-conscious sense" at first, explained Dewey, but even as a young philosopher he was reluctant to affirm religious beliefs that were not consistent with his own independent philosophical reflections and the scientific examination of experience. As a college and graduate student he learned to respect the scientific method, and early on he accepted Darwinian evolutionary theory under the influence of writers such as Thomas Henry Huxley and Herbert Spencer.

Dewey was raised in the Protestant Christian tradition, and he remained an active member of the Congregational Church until he was thirty-five. At the beginning of his philosophical career he embraced a form of neo-Hegelian idealism that made it possible to interpret religious experience with reference to certain Christian theological beliefs, and he worked out his own liberal synthesis of science, philosophy, and Christian theology. As he moved during the 1890s from absolute idealism to his own new brand of empirical naturalism, humanism, and experimentalism (instrumentalism or pragmatism), he found himself forced to abandon his neo-Hegelian Christian theology. As a consequence he terminated his membership in the church when he moved from the University of Michigan to the University of Chicago in 1894. In the years that followed, he developed a new appreciative empirical and naturalistic understanding of religious experience.

As a religious liberal Dewey was not only concerned to overcome the problematical split in modern culture between religion and science; he also sought to overcome the split between the sacred and the secular, religious life and everyday life. Dewey endeavored to achieve this objective by exploring the deeper moral and religious meaning of the creative forces shaping American culture and by identifying the moral and religious life with the democratic way of life guided by the experimental method of truth, which he viewed as all part of the evolving world of nature.

Dewey believed that his naturalistic and humanistic philosophy had carried to its logical conclusion the liberal reconstruction of religious values started in the late eighteenth and early nineteenth centuries by philosophers and theologians seeking to reconcile religion with reason and modern culture. His thinking on these issues was worked out over a period of roughly six decades in a great variety of books and essays. He never published a comprehensive statement of his views on religion and religious experience, and consequently commentators and critics often do not fully understand his position. There are important continuities as well as differences between his early and later thinking, and his outlook can best be understood by considering the evolution of his thought.

I

John Dewey was born in 1859 and raised in Burlington, Vermont, a thriving town situated on the shores of Lake Champlain. His childhood was a healthy and happy one in many respects, but it had its darker sides. The Civil War caused his father to be separated from his family for almost six years, and his mother was overzealous in her efforts to save her three sons from sin and to instill in them strong feelings of attachment to Christ. Young John was a sensitive and conscientious child, and his mother's intense religious concerns had a negative effect. He encountered a liberal theological approach at the First Congregational Church where he attended Sunday school and services, but his early experience with religion was a major factor in contributing to some difficult adolescent emotional problems.

Late in his career Dewey described the adolescent crisis through which he passed as "an inward laceration." He recalled being painfully oppressed by "the sense of divisions and separations that were . . . borne in upon me as a consequence of a heritage of New England culture, divisions by way of isolation of self from the world, of soul from body, of nature from God." This experience filled young Dewey with "an intense emotional craving . . . for unification." The unity he sought involved several interrelated dimensions, including integration of personality, achievement of a satisfying social adjustment, and realization of a sense of unity with the larger world and the divine. During his junior year in college Dewey's craving for unification caused his deepest intellectual interests to become centered on the idea of organic unity, which he first encountered in T. H. Huxley's description of the human organism in a physiology textbook. Huxley's account left Dewey with "a sense of interdependence and interrelated unity that . . . created a kind of type or model of a view of things to which material in any field ought to conform." He writes that "I was led to desire a world and a life that would have the same properties as had the human organism in the picture of it derived from study of Huxley's treatment" [LW5:147–48, 153].

In Dewey's craving for unification and his fascination with the idea of organic unity lie one of the principal keys to understanding both his philosophical and his religious development. His search for a unified vision of the world as a whole led him into philosophy. His quest for unity explains why he was drawn to Hegel and philosophical idealism at the beginning of his career. It is also a fundamental reason for his lifelong hostility to all dualisms and his deep concern to discover and build connections, continuities, and community. As a young man Dewey viewed his quest for unity as all one with a religious quest for God, the unity of the ideal and the real. Long after he abandoned belief in Congregational theism and the God of Hegelian idealism, he continued to view the religious life as a quest for the ideal and for unification of the ideal and the real in everyday life. He also retained the conviction that experiences that have a profoundly unifying effect on the self and the relation of self and world are religious in quality.

Of special significance for his religious development, during his years at the University of Vermont, Dewey fell under the influence of the James Marsh tradition of Vermont Transcendentalism. Marsh was a Congregational minister and philosopher who had taught during the 1820s and 1830s at the University of Vermont, where he eventually became president. In 1829 he edited the first American edition of Samuel Taylor Coleridge's *Aids to Reflection*, introducing the volume with an enthusiastic essay endorsing Coleridge's blend of seventeenth-century Cambridge Platonism, Kant, and German idealism. The book helped to inspire the movement of New England transcendentalism in the 1830s, and Dewey as a college student in the 1870s found in Marsh's edition his "spiritual emancipation" because it enabled him to be both "liberal and pious." After writing *A Common Faith* over fifty years later, Dewey commented that Coleridge and Marsh had had a lasting influence in shaping his thinking regarding the nature of faith and religious experience.[2] It is also noteworthy that the poetry of Wordsworth inspired in young Dewey a mystical sense of unity with the world that remained important to him over the years.[3]

II

At Johns Hopkins University where he went for graduate training, Dewey enthusiastically immersed himself in the findings of the new psychology in the lecture hall and laboratory of G. Stanley Hall, who had been a student of William James at Harvard and Wilhelm Wundt and Hermann von Helmholtz in Germany. However, the major influence on Dewey at Johns Hopkins was the neo-Hegelian philosopher George Sylvester Morris. Having studied with F. A. Trendelenberg in Germany, translated Friedrich Ueberweg's *History of Philosophy*, and authored books on Kant and British empiricism, Morris was probably the best trained and most accomplished scholar in America in the field of western philosophy and Hegelian idealism. In Morris's lectures, Hegel's philosophy, and in the writings of the British neo-Hegelians T. H. Green and John and Edward Caird, Dewey found the vision of a unified world for which he was searching. Dewey writes that "Hegel's synthesis of subject and object, matter and spirit, the divine and the human . . . operated as an immense release, a liberation."[4] What especially attracted young Dewey to the Hegelian worldview was the way Hegel used the idea of organic unity, demonstrating "in a great variety of fields of experience, the supreme reality of this principle of a living unity maintaining itself through the medium of differences and distinctions."[5]

Inspired by the concept of organic unity and Hegel, Dewey was led at the outset of his career to adopt the view that reality is one, not two. His early philosophical idealism was a move away from traditional religious supernaturalism and theism as well as a rejection of mechanistic materialism. Young Dewey embraced a one world hypothesis and a Hegelian panentheism that imagined God to be immanent in the world as the unifying life and spirit of the world and human society. God is the ideal, the divine reason, and also the organic unity of the world in the form of the unity of the ideal and the real. Furthermore, even though in some of his earliest essays Dewey hints that God, who is the eternal absolute consciousness, is in some sense transcendent, his idealist philosophy imagines the reality of God as forever expressed and realized in and through the world of nature and human history. Building on his understanding of the organic relation of God and the world and of God and humanity, Dewey also affirmed the interconnection of spirit and matter, soul and body, and means and ends. For example, he viewed means and ends as interdependent and explained that ends are constituted by the means necessary to their realization.

During his first few years at the University of Michigan where he secured his first teaching position, Dewey devoted much of his time and energy to writing a *Psychology* (1887), in which he tried to organize the findings of the new psychology within the framework of neo-Hegelian philosophical categories. It was a bold but problematical attempt to integrate absolutism and experimentalism. It contains a religious vision that he continued to reconstruct in radical ways but never completely abandoned. Dewey's objective was a theory of self-realization and perfection of personality that explains how the individual unites the actual self with the ideal self. He defines the self as will, an active process of self-determination, and explains that the chief end of the self is to realize itself, that is, to realize the ideal self, which is the formal and final cause of the self. Dewey's early psychology makes the further assumption that the ideal self is nothing less than the perfect personality of God. Accordingly, the process of individual self-realization is described as a process by which the divine is reproduced in the human and the individual self is unified with the universal self.

Dewey goes on to explain that the ideal personality, which combines truth, beauty, and goodness, is reproduced in the individual in and through science, philosophy, art, moral action, and religion. His theory is based on the idea that self-realization requires the active relation of subject and object, a process whereby the self identifies itself with and finds itself in the objects with which it enters relationship. Self-realization takes the form of relations to intellectual and aesthetic objects and to persons and God. As the self expands and deepens its intellectual, aesthetic, social, and religious experience, it identifies itself ever more fully with its true self. The whole process culminates in moral and religious faith.[6]

The moral life is perfected in an autonomous choice of the supreme ideal as the guide to conduct. Such an act of moral faith is essential to the unification of the self. However, the union of the ideal and the real in the moral life remains partial and incomplete. Dewey also argued that speculative metaphysics can never conclusively prove the ultimate identity of the ideal and the real in the self and the world. The full and complete realization of the unity of the ideal and the real is achieved only in the religious life by an act of faith. According to the *Psychology,* religious experience involves knowledge and feeling, but it is most fundamentally a matter of will involving a person's whole being. Following closely the thinking in John Caird's *Introduction to the Philosophy of Religion* (1880), Dewey explains that in the act of faith the religious will affirms the ultimate identity of the ideal and the real, of God and the world, including the unity of God and the essential being or true self of each and every person. The religious life culminates in religious action, which is moral action inspired by religious faith.

Dewey's *Psychology* also explains that the act of religious faith generates certain religious feelings that give to experience a distinct religious quality. Dewey's theory of the religious feelings is part of a larger theory regarding the qualitative feelings. As the self realizes itself in and through its relationships to truth, beauty, persons, and God, it is the function of feeling to register and express the meaning and value for the self of its various relationships. In the religious life, the qualitative feelings awakened by faith and relationship to God are feelings of dependence, peace, and joy. Dewey further explains that faith leads to a complete adjustment of the self in its relation to the world at large. These early ideas about faith, the religious qualitative feelings, and the complete adjustment of the self are one source of Dewey's later thought regarding religious experience.

In the *Psychology* Dewey defended the church as a social institution that promotes the development of the universal consciousness in the individual and inspires love of persons, sympathy, as "the expression of the spiritual unity of mankind," and "the bond of union in society" [EW2:286, 295]. During his ten years at the University of Michigan (1884–94), he participated in the life of the local Congregational church and taught a variety of church-sponsored courses on the Bible, church history, and Christian thought. He also delivered twelve addresses before the Students' Christian Association and contributed essays to the *Andover Review, The Christian Union,* and other publications with church connections. During this period Dewey viewed Jesus as the first person in history to awaken fully to the unity of God and humanity and as the supreme example of an individual who had harmonized his individual mind and will with universal truth.

III

The last two decades of the nineteenth century were a time of considerable social unrest in America that led to the emergence of labor unions, the social gospel, establishment of urban settlement houses, the Populist Party, and the Progressive movement. Responding to the call for social reform and with the urging of a strong-minded young woman named Alice Chipman, who became his wife in 1886, Dewey shifted the focus of his intellectual interests during the late 1880s. At the outset of his career he had tried to idealize the world primarily in and through philosophical speculation and religious faith, but he now made moral action and social transformation his central concern. Much influenced by the writings of T. H. Green in this connection, his neo-Hegelian absolutism became a form of ethical idealism.

This shift in interest led Dewey during his last six years at the University of Michigan (1888–94) to further develop his liberal reconstruction of Christianity and to expand and deepen his vision of the moral ideal. It was at this time that he came to identify the spirit and meaning of Christianity in the modern period with the ethics of democracy and experimental intelligence, resulting in a vision of the social ideal that he continued to refine and develop for the rest of his life. The main lines of Dewey's thinking during this formative period in the development of his moral and religious convictions are set forth in four essays, "The Ethics of Democracy" (1888), "The Value of Historical Christianity" (1889), "Christianity and Democracy" (1892), and "Reconstruction" (1894).

In these essays Dewey associates the essence of Christianity with three interrelated ideals: the absolute value of the individual self, the revelation and incarnation of liberating truth in the individual and society, and the unification of humanity in the kingdom of God. In developing his interpretation as to what these Christian ideals should mean to modern men and women living at the end of the nineteenth century, Dewey tried to formulate what he understood to be "the direct, natural sense" of these teachings. In this regard he points out that it was difficult in the ancient world and during the medieval period for people to grasp the original plain meaning of these ideals. Given the political and industrial organization of society, most people were not respected as persons, but rather were treated as means to ends external to themselves. In addition, the methods for discovering liberating practical truth were limited. The ideal of realizing the kingdom of God, a community of free, fully actualized persons united by mutual love and justice, was an impossibility. As a result the basic ideals of Christianity were "held to be true only in emotion, or at some remote time, or by some supernal means," and Christians came to identify these ideals with a special organization, the church, rather than with society at large.[7]

However, during the modern period the social situation was revolutionized by democracy and economic and technological change. As a result "the organs of grace, the means for lifting up the individual and binding men together in harmony are now found working in all forms of life" [EW4:101]. These new conditions make it possible for the first time for people to understand and realize the direct, natural meaning of Christian teaching. For Dewey this meant identifying the true essence of Christianity in the modern world with the democratic ideal and "the spirit of science as undogmatic reverence for truth in whatever form it presents itself."[8] In and through democracy and the experimental method of truth, individual persons are freed to realize themselves, to discover practical truth, and to build a harmonious just society.

Dewey arrived at these views initially with the aid of his neo-Hegelian understanding of religion and Christianity, which emphasized the immanence of God as both the organic unity of society and the spirit of progressive social evolution through history. Stating a position that became a lifelong conviction, he wrote in 1892: "Every religion has its source in the social and intellectual life of a community or race. Every religion is an expression of the social relations of the community; its rites, its cult, are a recognition of the sacred and divine significance of these relationships" [EW4:3]. As long as the symbols, rites, and beliefs of a religion are expressions of a living civilization, the religion can serve as a source of inspiration and liberation. However, the goal of the religious life is unity with God, and this cannot be achieved by clinging to the religion of a bygone era. What may have been an inspiring expression of living truth for one generation easily becomes an oppressive set of rites and doctrines empty of vital meaning for another.

Dewey further argues that the essence of Christianity is not to be identified with a religion, a fixed cult and creed. It is to be found in the unfolding life of God who is immanent in history, "working *in* and *through* humanity to realize its highest good."

> God is neither a far-away Being, nor a mere philosophic conception by which to explain the world. He is the reality of our ordinary relations with one another in life. He is the bond of the family, the bond of society. He is love, the source of all growth, all sacrifice, and all unity. He has touched history, not from without but has made Himself subjected to all the limitations and sufferings of history; identified Himself absolutely with humanity, so that the life of humanity is henceforward not for some term of years, but forever, the Life of God.[9]

Authentic Christianity comprehends all that is involved from the time of Jesus onward in the awakening of humanity to the divine immanence, the ongoing revelation of liberating truth, and the realization of persons, leading to the progressive establishment of the kingdom of God on earth.

In this view the spiritual and the secular, religious life and social life, are intimately related.

> The healthy religious life knows no separation of the religious from the secular, which has no Sunday or week-day divisions in it, which finds in every daily duty, whether in study or business, or recreation an approach to God as surely and truly as in the retirement of the closet. This frame of mind can never be attained unless we realize that God is in history, is in the social state of life, reconciling men unto Him. [LW17:533]

The individual finds freedom from sin and guilt, the peace and joy of unity with God, and ultimate meaning, not by escaping from the world or by trying to live in the past, but by identifying his or her self with the shared life of the community, which is the life of God, and by working for progressive social change.

In addition, Dewey contends that in America the Christian life is to be identified with the creative life of the democratic community. Inspired especially by the writings of Walt Whitman, Dewey wrote in 1888: "Democracy and the one, the ultimate, ethical ideal of humanity are to my mind synonyms."[10] The democratic ideal had this ethical significance for young

Dewey because he conceived it as a vision of harmony in the midst of diversity that involves the full realization of the principle of organic unity governing the universe. A democracy is founded upon respect for the absolute worth of the individual person and promises freedom and opportunity for the individual. Democracy also means a commitment to equality and community. Furthermore, from Dewey's democratic perspective the well-being of the individual and the community are interdependent and indivisible. The autonomous individual finds self-realization in and through relationships and by contributing to the life of the community according to his or her abilities. For Dewey the democratic ideal is a contemporary expression of the Christian ideal of a kingdom of God on earth. It is the idea of community life itself perfected.

Dewey views the idea of democracy as something much more than a theory of government. Quoting James Russell Lowell, he asserts that democracy is first and foremost " 'a sentiment, a spirit, and not of a form of government, for this is but the outgrowth of the latter and not its cause' " [EW1:240]. As he explained in 1939: "Democracy is a *personal* way of individual life; . . . it signifies the possession and continual use of certain attitudes, forming personal character and determining desire and purpose in all the relations of life."[11] According to Dewey the democratic ideal should govern a person's relations in the family, school, church, and work place as well as in the sphere of government. He was more interested in the dynamics of a truly democratic civil society than he was in the mechanics of democratic government.

Advancing the democratic way of life became Dewey's overarching concern, and throughout his career he worked to identify and clarify the attitudes and values he associated with the democratic ideal. Fundamental to moral democracy is a "faith in the potentialities of human nature," that is, a faith in the capacity of people to lead their own lives and to make intelligent judgments, if proper conditions are provided for their education and development [LW14:226–27]. The democratic ideal means a high degree of social responsibility. "If democracy has a moral and ideal meaning, it is that a social return be demanded from all and that opportunity for development of distinctive capacities be afforded all."[12] Dewey rejected the identification of democracy with an atomistic self-centered individualism as a corruption of its real meaning. He also opposed all those prejudices of gender, class, nationality, race, and religion that erect dividing walls between people and prevent a full rich sharing of experience. He emphasized the values of wide sympathy, free communication, tolerance, amicable cooperation, and a nonviolent approach to problem solving. He put special emphasis on the fundamental role of sympathy as sensitive responsiveness to the sufferings, interests, and rights of others and considered the attitude of sympathy to be essential to the making of sound moral judgments and resolving conflicts.

In attempting to break down the dualism of Christianity and democracy, religious life and secular life, the spiritual and the material, Dewey was especially concerned to point out that the separation of the material and the natural from the spiritual has a demoralizing effect on the common people whose lives are devoted to working everyday in this sphere. Dewey hoped to awaken women and men to a realization that the deeper meaning and joy of life are to be found in the here and now by adopting the democratic spirit and entering wholeheartedly into the concrete situation where one is living and working. In line with this concern, he became a prophetic critic of all forms of social and industrial organization that are empty of vital meaning and dehumanizing for the workers involved.

The most radical implication of Dewey's democratic reconstruction of Christianity finds expression in the idea of industrial democracy, which he first embraced in the late 1880s. His position is clearly stated in *Reconstruction in Philosophy* in 1920: "Democracy has many meanings, but if it has a moral meaning, it is found in resolving that the supreme test of all political institutions and industrial arrangements shall be the contribution they make to the all-around growth of every member of society."[13] From a truly democratic point of view, social institutions exist first and foremost, not as a means for producing things, but as "means of *creating* individuals," that is, as instrumentalities for developing informed, self-motivated, responsible, creative persons [MW12:191]. In this regard Dewey supported the full participation of men and women, according to their capacity, in the formation of institutional goals and the making of decisions that affect them.

In his lecture on "Christianity and Democracy" in 1892, Dewey focused his attention on the idea of revelation, arguing that the essence of Christianity is not a cult and creed, but the ongoing revelation of truth and the incarnation of truth in humanity. Reflecting on the Gospel of John, he declared that: "The only truth Jesus knew of as religious was Truth. There were no special religious truths which He came to teach; on the contrary, his doctrine was that Truth, however named and however divided by man, is one as God is one; that getting hold of truth and living by it is religion." Christianity and democracy are closely related because democracy is an instrument for the ongoing revelation of truth and the incarnation of God, who is truth, in humanity. "Democracy is, as freedom, the freeing of truth. . . . Democracy, as freedom, means the loosening of bonds, the wearing away of restrictions, the breaking down of barriers." As the obstacles to the discovery and communication of truth are overcome in a democratic society, truth is shared and "becomes the Common-wealth, the Republic, the public affair." Dewey concludes that democracy is leading to "the spiritual unification of humanity" since "all that Christ called the Kingdom of God is but the further expression of this freedom of truth" [EW4:4–10].

In other essays like "Reconstruction," Dewey connected the unfolding revelation of practical truth with the experimental method and cooperative scientific research. Following the thinking of philosophers like Hermann Lotze, F. H. Bradley, and Bernard Bosanquet, he arrived in the 1890s at the conviction that the scientific method should be regarded as the sole authority in matters of knowledge. Influenced in part by Auguste Comte and Joseph Ernest Renan, he also took the controversial position that the experimental method, joined with an attitude of wide sympathy, should guide the quest for moral truth as well as the quest for a knowledge of the physical world. By constructing a scientific method of moral valuation Dewey tried to overcome the split between science and moral values. His confidence that science could be harnessed in this way to serve as a practical moral guide was a basic reason for his hope that the emerging new social sciences would promote ongoing progressive social change.

As a mature philosopher who embraced empirical naturalism, Dewey viewed his faith in democracy and his faith in the experimental method as intimately related. In "Creative Democracy—The Task Before Us" (1939), for example, he identified his trust in democracy with a faith in experience, and his faith in experience is closely tied to his faith in the power of intelligence using the experimental method to direct the process of experience. "The task of democracy," states Dewey, "is forever that of creation of a freer and more humane experience in which all share and to which all contribute." He explains that "democracy is belief in the ability of human experience to generate the aims and methods by which further experience will grow in ordered richness. Every other form of moral and social faith rests upon the idea that experience must be subjected at some point or other to some form of external control; to some 'authority' alleged to exist outside the processes of experience." His argument is that "democracy . . . is the sole way of living which believes wholeheartedly in the process of experience as . . . that which is capable of generating the science which is the sole dependable authority for the direction of further experience." Dewey also points out that "since the process of experience is capable of being educative, faith in democracy is all one with faith in experience and education." At different times throughout his career Dewey wrote about having a religious faith in democracy, experience, intelligence, the experimental method, and education, and these values were for him closely interrelated.[14]

IV

After Dewey abandoned neo-Hegelian metaphysics and all traditional forms of Christian theology and terminated his relationship with the church, he continued to be interested in religious experience and to maintain what he regarded as a religious faith in democracy and intelligence. In the light of his own life experience, he retained a firm belief that the democratic way of life could generate the deep sense of meaning and fulfillment that he had associated with the Christian way of life and relationship to God. However, it was not until publication of *The Quest for Certainty* (1929) and *A Common Faith* (1934) that he clearly explained what he meant as an empirical naturalist by the adjective *religious* and by a religious faith. In these volumes he also set forth a concept of piety toward nature and suggested how a naturalist and religious humanist might use God language.

Dewey came to object to the Hegelian idea of an absolute and eternal unity of the ideal and the real for a number of reasons. The empirical evidence is lacking, he claimed, and the idea creates an insoluble problem as to why the world we live in is so unideal. In addition, the notion that the ideal and the real are unified on the level of ultimate reality does nothing to help solve the practical problems of unifying the ideal and the real in human experience except provide consolation in the face of hardship and defeat. As a young man Dewey had wanted consolation and argued that a faith in the unity of the ideal and the real was the only protection against despair and a sense of meaninglessness. However, as a mature thinker, he claimed that a person can outgrow this need. He, therefore, chose to give up completely the quest for certainty and philosophical idealism with its attempts to find a purely theoretical solution to the problem of unifying the ideal and the real, and he embraced an "idealism of action" that is concerned with developing practical methods and strategies for unifying the ideal and real in everyday life.[15] This became the central concern of his new philosophy of empirical naturalism, creative democracy and experimentalism, which he developed during his years at the University of Chicago (1894–1904) and Columbia University (1904–39).

The term *nature* is employed by Dewey in his later thought as a word that refers to everything that is, the universe. He adopted an empirical approach to understanding nature, and his thinking is heavily influenced by the new science, especially evolutionary biology and the new physics. However, by developing his own distinctive understanding of experience and the empirical method, he charted a middle way between a mechanistic materialism and a monistic idealism or between what William James called a tough-minded and a tender-minded worldview. He embraced a form of evolutionary naturalism and process philosophy similar in many respects to the outlook of Alfred North Whitehead. In Dewey's radical process philosophy, change is a fundamental characteristic of all things, and there are no fixed essences or pre-established final causes of the universe, history, or the self. We live in an open evolving world that is a mixture of contingency and necessity, and choice and decision can make a difference. Dewey understood humanity to be an interdependent part of nature, and his view of nature anticipates the kind of ecological outlook that would become widely accepted toward the end of the twentieth century.

As a naturalist Dewey argued that even though the real and the ideal are not one, there is continuity between the real and the ideal, between nature and human values. True ideals, he argued, are real possibilities resident in nature. Like Ludwig Feuerbach, Dewey contended that even though people have frequently projected their ideals onto a transcendent God to ensure their security, ideals have their actual origin in humanity's natural experience of what is good and beautiful in the relations between people and between people and nature. The possibilities of nature become ideals when they are projected by the human imagination as dreams for the future and desirable objectives. Dewey believed that scientific inquiry can deepen and expand the human vision of the ideal. He devoted much of his attention as a philosophical experimentalist to developing a theory of moral valuation that shows how the experimental method can be used to evaluate ideals by exploring conditions and consequences and distinguishing what is truly good from what may only appear to be good. In addition, through experimental inquiry the means and material needed to realize the ideal can be identified, and with effort guided by imaginative vision human beings can make progress toward embodying the ideal in existence. In this sense "nature . . . is idealizable" and "lends itself to operations by which it is perfected" [LW4:240–43].

In his Gifford Lectures published as *The Quest for Certainty,* Dewey explained that a religion consistent with naturalism, democracy, and experimentalism would be "a religion devoted to inspiration and cultivation of the sense of ideal possibilities in the actual," and he described religious faith as "devotion to the ideal" [LW4:244, 248]. However, his thinking was not fully clarified until he published *A Common Faith* in 1934. This slim volume of three essays was written during a time of grave economic and social crisis in defense of the kind of moral and religious outlook that he believed was needed to unite Americans in support of radical democratic social reform.

In *A Common Faith,* Dewey draws a sharp distinction between the religious and religion, further developing the distinction he had made at the University of Michigan between the religious life and religion. He uses the noun *religion* as a strictly collective term to refer to the many diverse institutional religions with their creeds and special practices. He then proceeds to set forth an empirical and naturalistic concept of the religious quality of experience, pointing out that there is no necessary connection between the religious quality of experience and religion or the idea of the supernatural, which is commonly associated with religion. Moreover, he wanted to emancipate the religious from its association with religion and the supernatural, since "religions now prevent, because of their weight of historic encumbrances, the religious quality of experience from coming to consciousness and finding the expression that is appropriate to present conditions, intellectual and moral."[16] His empirical approach to the study of religious experience shows the influence of William James's *The Varieties of Religious Experience* (1902), but Dewey was not interested in exploring and speculating about the kind of extraordinary mystical experiences that had fascinated James. His main objective was to identify the distinctively religious values that may be, and often are, realized in the natural experience and everyday life of ordinary people.

Dewey is careful to point out that his notion of the religious quality of experience does not refer to a special kind of experience that is marked off from aesthetic, scientific, moral, or political experience or from experience as companionship and friendship. The religious quality of experience is not the result of interaction with some distinct uniquely religious object like a supernatural deity or the numinous. In explaining his meaning, he focuses attention on consequences, not causes. Many different kinds of experience may produce an effect or have a function or force that is religious, giving to experience a religious quality. An experience that has a religious effect is one that operates to bring about "a better, deeper and enduring adjustment in life," generating a sense of security and inner peace. Dewey has in mind a unification of self and of self and world that awakens an enduring sense of meaning and value capable of carrying "one through periods of darkness and despair" [LW9:11–13]. In *Art as Experience*, Dewey writes of "a fulfillment that reaches to the depths of our being—one that is an adjustment of our whole being with the conditions of existence."[17] He describes the process of unification as voluntary, but he adds that "an 'adjustment' possesses the will rather than is its express product." It reflects "a change *of* will conceived as the organic plenitude of our being."[18]

With his own experience in mind, Dewey describes some of the many ways in which such a reorientation and transformation of the self may be generated: "It is sometimes brought about by devotion to a cause; sometimes by a passage of poetry that opens a new perspective; sometimes . . . through philosophical reflection" [LW9:11]. Many different things and experiences may acquire religious meaning and value. Dewey notes that devotion to an ideal end or cause is a particularly common source of experiences with a religious effect. In this way "many a person, inquirer, artist, philanthropist, citizen, men and women in the humblest walks of life, have achieved, without presumption and without display, . . . unification of themselves and of their relations to the conditions of existence" [LW9:19]. Dewey emphasizes that the conditions that generate a religious adjustment from an empirical perspective are "conditions of nature and human association." When the conditions are right and a person's life acquires a religious quality, there may be grace at work, but it is natural grace, not supernatural.

As Dewey explains it, human experience acquires a religious quality in a way that is similar in certain respects to the way people find happiness. A person achieves happiness not by aiming at it, but as the unintended side effect of certain relationships or of devotion to some cause or way of life that takes the self out into relation with the larger world beyond itself. The religious quality of experience, like happiness, comes as a spontaneous side effect. In his *Ethics* (1932) Dewey uses the phrase "the final happiness" to refer to the quality of experience that he later associated with the religious quality of experience in *A Common Faith*. The final happiness, he explains, is a spontaneous end product of the growth and expansion of the self that "comes from lively and ever-renewed interest in others and in the conditions and objects which promote their development."[19] This outlook recognizes the religious meaning that can be found in the democratic way of life. It celebrates the religious values that may be realized through scientific research, creative art, the struggle for justice, and human friendship and intimacy. Dewey's thinking on this matter is a naturalistic reconstruction of his early Christian neo-Hegelian view of the way the self realizes the ideal or universal self and finds fulfillment.

In his endeavor to integrate religious life and everyday life, Dewey attempted as a naturalistic humanist something comparable to what Martin Buber sought to achieve within a theological framework in his highly influential book *I and Thou* (1923). Dewey's approach to finding an enduring sense of meaning and value in life in and through relationship and democratic community life is also similar in many respects to the outlook of Viktor Frankl set forth in *Man's Search for Meaning* (1946). Buber, Dewey, and Frankl, each in their own unique way, all taught that religious experience and a sustaining sense of meaning are to be found, not by turning away from and looking outside the world, but by entering deeply into relationship with nature, persons, and the ideals that inspire the moral life, social action, the search for knowledge, and artistic creativity. This reorientation of the spiritual life lies at the heart of Dewey's concern in his reconstruction of the concept of religious experience. One finds variations on this theme in much contemporary liberal religious thought, especially among feminist thinkers and liberation theologians such as Rosemary Radford Ruether. In addition to his empirical and naturalistic approach, what is especially significant about Dewey's thinking on this matter is the manner in which he links religious experience with the democratic life, offering people a way to rediscover the spiritual meaning of democracy and the practical significance of the religious life.

Dewey developed his naturalistic theory of faith in connection with his concept of the religious significance of devotion to the ideal. He defined faith as moral conviction rather than intellectual belief pertaining to matters of fact. "Conviction in the moral sense signifies being conquered, vanquished, in our active nature by an ideal end; it signifies acknowledgment of its rightful claim over our desires and purposes" [LW9:15]. A moral faith in the ideal involves being possessed in the deeper center of one's being by an imaginative vision of ideal possibilities. When a moral faith in the ideal has a religious effect, it may be called a religious faith. A faith in a vision of the ideal has religious power only when the ideal ends involved are so inclusive that they unify the self and self and world [LW9:16, 23]. By inclusive ideal ends Dewey means a comprehensive integrated vision that encompasses the interrelations of self, society, and nature. A religious faith involves a commitment of the whole self to a unified inclusive vision of the ideal.

So defined there can be no fundamental conflict between science and faith. A religious faith, as Dewey conceives it, is committed unalterably only to the "value of the worth of discovering the possibilities of the actual and striving to realize them" [LW4:242]. It is concerned with "creation of a future," not propositions about the past. New scientific discoveries will from time to time cause modifications in a people's moral values and vision of the ideal. However, science cannot alter humanity's capacity to devote itself to a liberating vision of ideal possibilities. Commitment to an idealism of action is the heart of the religious attitude in Dewey's democratic humanism; so described, the religious attitude finds in science a useful instrument, not a rival or enemy.

V

By the mid 1890s God language vanished from Dewey's philosophical writings. However, his correspondence and poetry indicate that he had not completely abandoned the possibility of using God language in a new naturalistic fashion. For example, in 1915 he wrote to a friend that he employed the word *God* as a preferential term "to denote *those* forces which at a given time and place are actually working for the better."[20] He found encouragement for this line of thought in Edward Scribner Ames's *Religion* (1929), and in *A Common Faith* he explained his thinking more fully. He did not insist on the use of God language. However, if a person finds it meaningful to use the word *God*, Dewey wanted to clarify how the language might appropriately be employed in a manner consistent with empirical naturalism and religious humanism.

First of all, Dewey asserts that the words *God* or *the divine* can be used to refer to the object of a religious moral faith, that is, to a unified imaginative vision of ideal possibilities. "The word 'God' means," writes Dewey, "the ideal ends that at a given time and place one acknowledges as having authority over his volition and emotion, the values to which one is supremely devoted, as far as these ends, through imagination, take on unity" [LW9:29]. Dewey points out that to identify God with the ideal does not mean that God is just a fantasy. Authentic ideals "are made out of the hard stuff of the world of physical and social experience," and when they are embodied in character and action they become forces shaping the world [LW9:33–34].

Second, Dewey adds another dimension to his empirical concept of the divine, explaining that the term *God* may be used to comprehend all the natural conditions and social processes that promote the growth of the ideal and further its realization. Reconstructing the neo-Hegelian idea of God as the unity of the ideal and the real, he asserts that God is the "*active relation between ideal and actual*" [LW9:34–35]. Dewey makes it clear that God does not transcend the world and is not a person or a being or some organic unity of all the forces that promote realization of the ideal. The processes that constitute God are unified only in imaginative vision and through human effort. Dewey proposes using the terms *God* and *the divine* simply as a kind of poetic language designed to inspire commitment to the ideal and to focus energy on all those creative forces in nature, the self, and society that contribute to the idealizing of the world. Employed in this fashion, he believed that God language could have significant social as well as religious value.

In defending his radical liberal interpretation of faith and the divine, Dewey argued that the true essence of religious faith in all cultures with a highly developed moral consciousness has always been devotion to a unified vision of the ideal and commitment to the process of uniting ideal ends and actual conditions. He believed that here lies the real heart and highest value of humanity's religious life. He clearly expresses the fundamental spirit of this basic faith when he writes: "Ours is the responsibility of conserving, transmitting, rectifying and expanding the heritage of values we have received that those who come after us may receive it more solid and secure, more widely accessible and more generously shared than we have received it." "Such a faith has always been implicitly the common faith of mankind," declares Dewey, and he adds: "It remains to make it explicit and militant" [LW9:57–58].

Dewey believed that the democratic way of life and the experimentalist's search for knowledge and the ideal are the embodiment of this common faith. Moreover, it was Dewey's hope that humanity would be united beyond all distinctions of gender, class, race, nationality, and religion by a faith in the democratic ideal and experimentalism. In a rapidly changing pluralistic world, he argued that humanity's best and only real chance for freedom, justice, and peace, and for local, national, and global community, lies in such a unifying social faith. As long as people put their faith in traditional religious supernaturalism and theism Dewey was concerned that claims to a knowledge of ultimate and immutable truths would perpetuate dogmatism and violent conflict. He challenged the church and other religious institutions to undertake a naturalistic and democratic reconstruction of their thinking and practice, which he predicted would lead to "a recovery of vitality."[21]

Dewey could be eloquent in celebrating the religious effect, the spiritual rewards, of the democratic way of life in a multicultural world. In many of his writings he states that the heart of the democratic life is free communication and the sharing of experience, for it is shared experience that forms the common understandings and interests that unite people and build community in a democracy. Dewey regarded communication, sharing, and cooperation as "the greatest of human goods," because they generate a deep sense of communion, "the sense of . . . merging in a whole."[22] Borrowing imagery from Wordsworth's "Elegiac Stanzas," Dewey writes in 1920: "When the emotional force, the mystic force one might say, of communication, of the miracle of shared life and shared experience is spontaneously felt, the hardness and crudeness of contemporary life will be bathed in the light that never was on land or sea" [MW12:201]. When Dewey wrote these lines, it was twenty-five years after he had abandoned his neo-Hegelian vision of God immanent in democratic community life, but his deep sense of the ultimate meaning to be found in and through participation in the democratic life remained unchanged.

Dewey's philosophy is primarily concerned with the needs and problems of people, but as an evolutionary naturalist he had a keen sense of the interdependence of humanity and nature. In this regard, he argued that a vital religious faith, which involves a concern to unify the ideal and the real, should include an attitude of piety toward nature. His thinking on this subject is influenced by Schleiermacher's notion of religion as the feeling of dependence, the poetry of Wordsworth and Whitman, and the concept of natural piety found in the philosophy of George Santayana. In explaining his idea of natural piety, Dewey writes that "a religious attitude . . . needs the sense of a connection of man, in the way of both dependence and support, with the enveloping world that the imagination feels is a universe" [LW9:36]. He rejected both a romantic idealization of nature's support for the human endeavor and the gloomy perspective of a despairing atheism. His middle way recognizes that "nature, including humanity, with all its defects and imperfections, may evoke heartfelt piety as the source of ideals, of possibilities, of aspiration in their behalf, and as the eventual abode of all attained goods and excellencies" [LW4:244]. Dewey's piety toward nature grows out of an understanding that in its quest for the ideal humanity should see itself "as a cooperating part of a larger whole" [LW9:18] and that humanity and nature are permanently bound together in a "common career and destiny" [MW4:176].[23] Dewey wrote very little on the subject of conservation, but his concept of natural piety includes respect and care for the earth.

Dewey's natural piety was reinforced and deepened over the years by poetic intuitions and intense aesthetic experiences of a mystical nature that left him with a profound sense of belonging to the larger universe and generated feelings of cosmic trust and inner peace. He explained that every being is both a unique individual and interconnected with its environment, and the efforts of human beings are sustained and supported by the larger universe in and through an infinite number of events and interconnections. In this sense the infinite whole is present in every experience and every experience is of the whole. Mystical intuitions involve an immediate realization and felt appreciation of the presence of the ineffable whole. Such mystical experiences contribute to the religious quality of experience because they generate a sense of oneness, having a unifying effect on the self in relation to the universe. As with devotion to a cause greater than the self, the self finds itself in these experiences by being taken out beyond itself. The essence of sanity, asserted Dewey, is the sense of belonging to the larger whole, and the religious consciousness steadies and deepens this awareness. Dewey did not believe in immortality, but he pointed out that the mystical sense of unity with the infinite whole can reconcile people to the tragic side of life [LW10:196–99].[24] One finds in this aspect of Dewey's thought an enduring influence of the Romantic movement and also elements of the kind of ecological spirituality that a number of environmental philosophers and ecotheologians have emphasized in the 1980s and 1990s.[25]

The publication of Dewey's religious views in the 1930s precipitated an extended lively debate, and the debate has continued. Conservatives and fundamentalists have attacked him for espousing secularism and atheism. Reinhold Niebuhr criticized him for failing to address satisfactorily the problem of evil and for perpetuating an unrealistic liberal optimism. The Protestant Liberal theologian Henry Nelson Wieman applauded Dewey's naturalistic and empirical approach to an understanding of religious experience and God, and American religious empiricists have continued to draw inspiration from Dewey.[26] Many religious humanists, including the leadership of the Ethical Culture Society, founded by Felix Adler, enthusiastically embraced Dewey's general outlook, but his proposal regarding the use of God language was controversial. Some pragmatists and humanists like Sidney Hook, a principal defender of Dewey's philosophy, strongly objected to his acceptance of God language as certain to generate misunderstandings. Others have contended that Dewey's sense of belonging to the universe and cosmic trust imply more from a theological point of view than he acknowledged. Several critics have argued that Dewey's philosophy goes too far in separating the religious and religion.

More recently, Cornel West has developed his own brand of "prophetic pragmatism" that seeks to integrate Dewey's ethical and social thought with the work of W. E. B. DuBois, Reinhold Niebuhr, and Antonio Gramsci.[27] Robert Westbrook, who shares Dewey's democratic faith, has argued in his illuminating study of Dewey's life and thought that even though the ideal of participatory democracy is central to Dewey's vision of the democratic life, he was not very effective as a political theorist in identifying the means needed to realize this ideal.[28] In his appreciative study of Dewey's social and political philosophy, Alan Ryan recognizes the importance of the religious dimension of Dewey's thought, but describing himself as "an aggressive atheist" Ryan joins Sidney Hook in criticizing Dewey's use of God language. Ryan is skeptical as to whether "it is possible to have the *use* of religious vocabulary without the accretion of supernaturalist beliefs that Dewey wishes to slough off."[29] However, Richard Rorty, whose writings have been especially influential in generating a renewal of interest in Dewey and pragmatism, has reconstructed William James's argument in "The Will to Believe" and offered a pragmatist defense of the right of Dewey or any other "religious pragmatist" to use God language in their private religious life if they find it a source of personal "comfort and joy."[30] Some of Rorty's statements seem to involve a dualism of science and religious faith that Dewey worked to overcome, but Rorty's defense of a pragmatist's right to believe extends only to forms of faith that from the point of view of practical action are noncompetitive with science. There are important differences between Dewey's experimentalism and Rorty's linguistic pragmatism, but Rorty's attempt to conceive religious faith and scientific knowledge in such a way that they are understood to be noncompetitive is consistent with Dewey's general approach.[31]

To the end of his long life Dewey remained unwavering in his passionate faith in democracy, social intelligence, and the possibilities of human experience, which together with his larger vision of nature brought him the wholeness, unity with the world, and sense of meaning and value that he had set out to realize as a young man. In a postmodern world struggling to create democratic societies and a multicultural global community, Dewey's understanding of the democratic faith continues to be of critical importance. He knew, for example, that without a unifying social faith in moral democracy as a regulative ideal governing all human relations, free elections and free markets are not sufficient to create democratic societies. At a time when humanity faces severe environmental problems and must establish a mutually enhancing relationship with the larger earth community, Dewey's evolutionary naturalism, piety toward nature, and faith in a scientific approach to the moral evaluation of human behavior have acquired a new relevance. Dewey's distinctive combination of empirical naturalism and a democratic-ecological spirituality that pursues a middle way between an otherworldly supernaturalism and a despairing atheism constitutes an American religious vision of enduring significance.[32]

Notes

1. John Dewey, "From Absolutism to Experimentalism" [LW5:153].

2. John Dewey, as quoted by Herbert Schneider in Corliss Lamont, ed., *Dialogue on John Dewey* (New York: Horizon Press, 1959), p. 15.

3. Max Eastman, "John Dewey: My Teacher and Friend," in *Great Companions* (New York: Farrar, Strauss and Cudahy, 1959), pp. 255–57.

4. John Dewey, "From Absolutism to Experimentalism" [LW5:153].

5. John Dewey, as quoted in Robert M. Wenley, *The Life and Work of George Sylvester Morris* (New York: Macmillan, 1917), pp. 316–17.

6. John Dewey, *Psychology* [EW2:357–63].

7. John Dewey, "Christianity and Democracy" [EW4:7–8]; John Dewey, "Reconstruction" [EW4:99–101].

8. John Dewey, "Experience, Knowledge and Value: A Rejoinder" [LW14:79].

9. John Dewey, "The Historical Value of Christianity" [LW17:531–32].

10. John Dewey, *The Ethics of Democracy* [EW1:248].

11. John Dewey, "Creative Democracy—The Task Before Us" [LW14:226].

12. John Dewey, *Democracy and Education* [MW9:129].

13. John Dewey, *Reconstruction in Philosophy* [MW12:186].

14. John Dewey, "Creative Democracy—The Task Before Us" [LW14:229–30].

15. John Dewey, *The Quest for Certainty* [LW4:240–43].

16. John Dewey, *A Common Faith* [LW 9:8].

17. John Dewey, *Art as Experience* [LW10:23].

18. John Dewey, *A Common Faith* [LW9:13–14].

19. John Dewey, *Ethics* [LW7:198–99, 302].

20. John Dewey to Scudder Klyce, 29 May 1915, Scudder Klyce Papers, General Correspondence: John Dewey, Manuscript Division, Library of Congress, Washington, D.C.

21. John Dewey, *A Common Faith* [LW9:54].

22. John Dewey, *Experience and Nature* [LW1:144–45, 157–60].

23. John Dewey, "Religion in Our Schools" [MW4:176].

24. John Dewey, *Human Nature and Conduct* [MW14:180–81; 226–27]; John Dewey, "Intimations of Mortality" [LW11:425–27].

25. See, for example, Sallie McFague, "A Square in the Quilt: One Theologian's Contribution to the Planetary Agenda," in S. Rockefeller and J. Elder, eds., *Spirit and Nature* (Boston: Beacon Press, 1992), pp. 56–57; and J. Baird Callicott, *In Defense of the Land Ethic: Essays in Environmental Philosophy* (Albany: State University of New York Press, 1989), pp. 101–14. There are many elements of an ecological worldview in Dewey's naturalism. However, he died before the science of ecology became a major influence and before the emergence of the environmental movement, and one will not find in his writings the kind of ecocentric orientation that is characteristic of environmental thinkers like Callicott. Dewey remained basically an ethical humanist who had a deep sense of belonging to, interdependence with, and respect for nature.

26. The ongoing influence of Dewey on the American tradition of naturalism and empiricism in religious thought is well illustrated in the pages of the *American Journal of Theology and Philosophy* published by the Highlands Institute for American Religious Thought. See also, for example, Jerome Paul Soneson, *Pragmatism and Pluralism: John Dewey's Significance for Theology*, Harvard Dissertations in Religion, no. 30 (Minneapolis, Minn.: Fortress Press, 1993).

27. See Cornel West, *The American Evasion of Philosophy: A Genealogy of Pragmatism* (Madison: University of Wisconsin Press, 1989).

28. Robert B. Westbrook, *John Dewey and American Democracy* (Ithaca, N.Y.: Cornell University Press, 1991), pp. 317–18, 549. Robert B. Westbrook, "Democratic Faith: A Response to Michael Eldridge," *Transactions of the Charles S. Peirce Society* 32 (Winter 1996): 31–38.

29. Alan Ryan, *John Dewey and the High Tide of American Liberalism* (New York: Norton, 1995), p. 274.

30. Richard Rorty, "Religious Faith, Intellectual Responsibility, and Romance," *American Journal of Theology and Philosophy* 17, 2 (May 1996): 121–40. Richard Rorty, "Something to Steer By," a review of Alan Ryan, *John Dewey*

and the High Tide of American Liberalism (New York: Norton, 1995), in *London Review of Books*, 20 June 1996, p. 8.

31.   On the differences between Dewey and Rorty, see Robert Westbrook, *John Dewey and American Democracy*, pp. 539–42, and James Kloppenberg, "Pragmatism: An Old Name for Some New Ways of Thinking?" *Journal of American History* 83, 1 (June 1996): 101, 109–12, 116–18, 123–25, 131.

32.   The aspects of Dewey's thought considered in this essay are explored more fully in Steven C. Rockefeller, *John Dewey: Religious Faith and Democratic Humanism* (New York: Columbia University Press, 1991).

8 Dewey's Metaphysics: Ground-Map of the Prototypically Real

Raymond D. Boisvert

Maps

In 1984 a well-publicized challenge was raised against four hundred years of cartographic orthodoxy.[1] Arno Peters, a German historian, supported by the National Council of Churches, sought to discredit and replace the world map that had graced classroom walls since the sixteenth century, that of Gerhard Mercator (1512–94). The controversy woke many of us from dogmatic slumbers. Philosophy, we realized, was unavoidably contentious. But geography? Did this not involve, as its etymology suggests, graphing the earth, sketching an accurate portrait of the globe's land and water masses? Could a study be all that controversial whose task involved merely mirroring the globe's contours?

The term *merely* is a great soporific, inducing especially the dogmatic sort of slumbering.[2] Geographers, the Peters/Mercator controversy made abundantly clear, cannot "merely" sketch a representation of the earth, the way someone might take a snapshot of a scene. Producing a two-dimensional map of a spherical globe is a complex process. Mercator's aim had been to aid the navigators plying the Atlantic in ever increasing numbers. In order to maximize his map's effectiveness, he fastened upon a particular projection scheme.[3] This had the side-effect of distorting land masses in such a way that the northern hemisphere, with its 18.9 million square miles, appears much larger than the southern hemisphere with its 38.6 million square miles.[4]

Why begin a discussion of Dewey's metaphysics by referring to controversies within the mapmaking world? The reason is simple: mapping is the metaphor used by Dewey to describe the nature of metaphysics. He characterizes this study as the "ground-map of the province of criticism"

[LW1:309]. Any attempt to grasp what is involved in Dewey's metaphysics will have to come to terms with this central image.

The map metaphor is immediately useful in helping sort out Dewey's conception of metaphysics from that of other philosophers. Metaphysics is traditionally associated not with maps, but with "systems." Philosophical systems, since Descartes, have sought to discover a central, unassailable starting point (sense data, atoms, protocol sentences, innate ideas) upon which can be erected a logically consistent, rigorously developed system. The guiding image has been that of an edifice meticulously constructed upon the single foundation.

Charles Sanders Peirce, father of pragmatism, denied that this sort of foundationalism had anything to do with how human inquiries were actually carried out. He altered the edifice image completely. Truth was more like a cable, he argued. We do not begin from any apodictic foundation. Rather, we gather threads from many different areas and weave them together. The more threads that go together, the stronger is the cable. The stronger the cable, the more likely is it that the position is justifiable and approximates truth.[5]

Dewey, continuing in the antifoundationalist footsteps of Peirce, suggested the map metaphor as his own alternative. Why this particular choice? The map/philosophy parallel is instructive in three ways. (1) Neither should pretend to occupy a detached, disinterested standpoint that provides *the* snapshot of the world. Maps are constructed on the basis of certain interests, such as Mercator's wish to aid navigation. Metaphysics, too, seeks to satisfy a particular interest, examining the issue of "being qua being" (traditional formulation) or of "appearance versus reality" (modern formulation).

(2) Both involve selectivity and choice. Peters and Mercator each made different choices with regard to the projection scheme for adequately translating the three-dimensional globe onto a two-dimensional sheet of paper. For the pragmatists in general, and for Dewey in particular, choice goes all the way down. There is no foundational data that simply offers itself up to the inquirer as absolutely fundamental. We are surrounded by a profusion of data. They are, in that sense, "given": we do not invent them. However, as multifarious "givens" they represent a limitless concatenation that is unhelpful for intellectual advance. Different interests, different problems, will involve "takens," those data and perspectives selected as best able to satisfy the interest or resolve the problematic situation.

(3) Both maps and philosophical analyses are provisional, always open

to revision, improvement, and emendation. The dialogical interplay between data and interests means that no single charting of territory, whether physical or intellectual, should be considered fixed and final. The mapmaker's task of translating a three-dimensional sphere onto a two-dimensional flat surface brings with it inherent and ineluctable limitations. Each attempt, using different projection techniques, will result in some successes. Each will also be accompanied by side effects of distortion and limitation with regard to alternative interests. Such drawbacks, though, do not mean that the procedure of mapmaking is to be abandoned. Awareness of drawbacks means only that mapmakers must be sensitive to the unavoidable limitations that attach to their craft.

Such introductory comments about maps are necessary because Dewey has been criticized, most notably by Richard Rorty, for seeking a "magisterial neutrality" in his metaphysics.[6] The choices, for Rorty, are simple. If a metaphysics is "empirical," as Dewey wanted his to be, then it must, regardless of Dewey's claims to the contrary, aim at inhabiting a bias-free, spectatorial standpoint. If, on the other hand, metaphysics is not empirical, not "magisterially neutral," then it quickly dissolves into cultural criticism. Nothing called "metaphysics" need be recognized.

If we take seriously, however, both Dewey's map metaphor and the intricacies of cartography, another option emerges. Mapmakers combine elements that Rorty believes to be incompatible. Their methodology must be empirical, *and* they are guided by interests. The worst sorts of one-sided biases can be avoided by keeping in mind the twin ideals of fairness to the data and self-conscious awareness of one's interests.

Rorty also claims that Dewey, aping traditional metaphysics, sought to provide "a permanent neutral matrix" for inquiry.[7] Here again, the map metaphor is instructive. As new information is gathered, as the ground being charted alters, as improved cartographic methods are developed, the maps are changed. Maps are always provisional, never fixed, final, and "permanent."

Philosophically, the epoch covering Dewey's education and maturation, the late nineteenth and the early twentieth century, was divided into competing schools with sharply differing views on how to map the territory of appearance and reality. Materialists sought to explain everything in terms of a physical substrate. Some materialists pronounced atoms to be the "really real." The world of ordinary experience was explained away as a realm of appearance. The limitations of this view led opponents to posit a nonphysical force, like Bergson's élan vital, by whose presence alone could be explained the full complexity of the world. The ultimate ontological[8] category was here the "vital." Members of the idealist school still preferred the "mental" as the inclusive category. Scientifically minded philosophers like Whitehead tended toward the "organic."[9]

Dewey was not content with any of these choices. He sought a perspective that would do justice equally to ordinary experience and to science.[10] Articulating such a perspective, he came to realize, would mean formulating a metaphysics. He did not, it is true, embrace metaphysics as enthusiastically as did his contemporaries Whitehead and Heidegger. Nonetheless, he came to realize that philosophers worked with assumptions about answers to questions like "what sorts of things are there?" and "what is existence like?" Although philosophers could choose not to articulate their answers to such questions by developing a metaphysics, an honestly exhaustive presentation of one's position would have to include it.

Recapturing a Marginalized Sense of Metaphysics

Dewey's understanding of metaphysics differs sharply from the widely held view that this study aims at getting beyond the physical. Descartes voiced this clearly when he linked together the study of metaphysics with an ability of the mind to "withdraw itself from commerce with the senses."[11] Kant, a century later, accused metaphysics of seeking to "transcend the limit of possible experience."[12] G. E. Moore opened the twentieth century by complaining that metaphysicians overextend themselves by making claims about "supersensible reality."[13]

Not surprisingly, philosophers have recoiled from a discipline so understood. Nietzsche attacked "being," the central concept of metaphysics, as a "concept-mummy" that substitutes death and stagnation for the vibrancy of life itself.[14] A. J. Ayer, the greatest antimetaphysics polemicist in the first half of this century, was anything but subtle in his opposition. In 1934 he published an article with the unambiguous title "Demonstration of the Impossibility of Metaphysics."[15] His widely popular book *Language, Truth, and Logic*[16] demeaned metaphysics as not only wrong headed, but as utterly meaningless.

Today, metaphysics remains a discipline on the defensive. Derrida, associating it with intellectual imperialism, has derisively referred to metaphysics as "white mythology."[17] Within the camp of Dewey supporters, Richard Rorty has been most vocal in charging that Dewey's attempt at developing a naturalistic metaphysics was doomed as a "contradiction in terms." [18]

Given such a history of criticism, an interpreter must circumscribe carefully what is meant by metaphysics. If its meaning were exhausted by concern for the supersensible, then Dewey would join the Kant, Moore, Derrida, and Ayer chorus of rejection. The philosophical tradition, however, is not limited to this meaning.

Aristotle, who gave the study its first systematic formulation, never used the word *metaphysics*. The term, etymologically connoting "going beyond the physical," came into currency a full three centuries later. [19] The names used by Aristotle fell into two categories, "first" philosophy [20] and "theology." [21] Much of subsequent philosophy went the route of highlighting the "theology" side of metaphysics. But "first" philosophy need not be read simply as a synonym for "theology." It also identifies a study both more comprehensive, and more mundane, that of "being as being." [22]

Plato had already warned philosophers about taking too thin, too limited a view of what is real. His divided line simile had held together a continuum stretching from images and copies at one end, through living things, mathematical concepts, all the way to ideals (Forms) at the other. [23] Each of these was to be regarded as real, as "being" in some sort of way.

Indeed, for Plato, the Forms, like justice and beauty, actually possessed greater dynamism, and were thus more real, than the plants and animals that surround us. The sign of whether something is real or has "being," is not whether it is accessible to the senses, but whether it has "power" to affect "anything else or to be affected." [24] Thus articulated, Plato's metaphysics is both generous and hierarchical. He wishes to cast the metaphysical net as widely as possible, but, at the same time, to make some important distinctions about degrees of reality.

Aristotle continued this "thick" yet nuanced approach to metaphysics. He admits, Plato-like, that "there are many senses in which a thing may be said to 'be.' " [25] He also admits, Plato-like, that these senses are not all equivalent. The distinguishing principle for him, however, is not "power." Rather, he goes on to assert that the "many senses" all resonate around a central core. That central core is what Aristotle calls *ousia*. This is a term misleadingly translated as "substance." A more accurate translation, as one well-versed commentator has suggested, would be "entity." [26]

Aristotle is here attempting to preserve both the thick inclusivity of "being" while at the same time not allowing that inclusivity to slide into equivocation. This attempt is of utmost importance. It defines the central move in Aristotelian metaphysics. It is also, as I hope to indicate, what characterizes Dewey's metaphysics at its best. But how exactly can inclusivity be preserved and equivocation be avoided within a perspective which self-consciously resonates about central exemplars?

Fortunately, some guidance is provided by another field, lexicography. Josette Rey-Debove, who has worked on France's *Petit Robert,* explains the procedure well. Writing dictionary definitions, she claims, does not follow the model of providing necessary and sufficient conditions, "X is a bird if and only if C1, C2, C3, etc."[27] Rather, the lexicographer works with "prototypes."

A "prototype" is "developed on the basis of an individual who is considered to be the best example of a category." For "bird" the prototype might, for example, be a sparrow.[28] The sparrow best incorporates that cluster of traits associated with birds—hollow bones, feathers, flight, behavioral attributes, size. This makes it more suitable for exemplary status than, say, the penguin or the ostrich whose inability to fly, lack of feathers (penguin), or size (ostrich) situates them as peripheral members of the group being identified.

Aristotle, at his metaphysical best, is working in just this "prototype" manner. Many things are said to "be." Clouds, ideas, numbers, space, qualities are all, in some sense, real. In order to avoid complete equivocation, however, these are said to exist as a cluster around the term "entity." In the *Categories,* Aristotle provides, as examples of "entity," "the individual man or horse."[29] These are the prototypes, those things which, as described in the *Categories* at least, serve as exemplars of "what is." This Aristotelian insistence on identifying a prototype will provide important guidance in sorting out the lesser known but more fruitful aspects of Dewey's metaphysics from those better known but, in my view at least, more sterile ones.

Dewey on Metaphysics

The Unsatisfactory Map of Generic Traits

Dewey's own writings, which cover a span of seventy years, take various positions with regard to metaphysics. His earliest essays, situated within the stream of Idealism, assume the importance of metaphysics.[30] Later on, influenced by the natural sciences, Dewey, understanding metaphysics more in line with Nietzsche, Moore, and Descartes, was to reject it in favor of a carefully developed methodology. This philosophical shift occurred about the time of his move to the University of Chicago in 1894 and reflected the first inklings of a "pragmatist" dimension to his thinking.[31]

It was the influence of a new colleague, F. J. E. Woodbridge, after his move to Columbia in 1905, that occasioned a rethinking of metaphysics in the "descriptive," rather than supraphysical, sense.[32] Discussion with Woodbridge[33] was fertile for Dewey's development of a metaphysics because Dewey already possessed a sensibility that is the *sine qua non* for any metaphysician. Put negatively, this is the conviction that compartmentalization is artificial and barren. Put positively, the German term *zusammenhangen* best expresses this attitude. It is a sense that somehow things hang together. Reflections on the natural world, the social world, the cultural arena are presumed somehow to be interlinked and analogous. Dewey openly embraced such an attitude: "Before taking up the issue raised by Mr. Parodi, I want to thank him for his grasp of the main purpose of my philosophical writings: 'To re-integrate human knowledge and activity in the general framework of reality and natural processes' " [LW14:80].

We can now begin to understand more fully why the "map" metaphor is utilized by Dewey. The cartographer seeks a set of symbols and techniques that will most adequately deal with the aims and interests of particular map users. Just so, metaphysicians seek to come up with concepts (understood etymologically as those constructs "which seize things together") allowing as comprehensive a grasp of reality as is possible. Such concepts then become signposts which help guide our exploration of the territory.

One of the most astute commentators on Dewey, John E. Smith, has gotten the sense of this project exactly right. Merely noting that reality is a "miscellaneous collection" of things is not adequate. What is needed is a "differential standpoint or interpretative principle such as organism, matter, selfhood from which we attempt to understand reality in its wholeness. . . ."[34] Dewey had admitted as much in "Philosophy and Civilization" when he claimed that the "intellectual registrations which constitute a philosophy are generative just because they are selective and eliminative exaggerations" [LW3:7]. The alternative "spectator view" is not generative. It simply leads to "a transcript, more or less accurate but otiose, of real things" [MW10:41].

Based on these texts, we can identify a threefold challenge facing Dewey in his quest to develop a viable philosophy. To begin with, if philosophy is to be "generative," that is to say fruitful in guiding humans in their under-standing of the world as well as in their comportment, it will need to be careful about its "selective and eliminative exaggerations." The "differential standpoint" of which Smith spoke will have to be specified adequately enough to mark out Dewey's philosophy from competing ones. Second, the differential standpoint will have to provide a perspective from which to grasp the real. A good map is not simply a "transcript, more or less accurate but otiose, of real things." It affords a mode of access.

A third challenge must be added with specific regard to metaphysics. This branch of philosophy is to provide a "ground-map of the province of criticism" [LW1:309]. What Dewey is getting at here is that suggestions for improvement, evaluations, and prescriptions will somehow "hang to-gether" with one's metaphysical understanding of the world. "The more sure one is that the world which encompasses human life is of such and such a character (no matter what his definition), the more one is committed to try to direct the conduct of life, that of others as well as of himself, upon the basis of the character assigned to the world" [LW1:309].

Some of his formulations, it must be admitted, do not satisfy this three-fold test. This is especially true of the attempt most widely accepted as the canonical formulation of Deweyan metaphysics: that given in terms of "generic traits." In "The Subject-Matter of Metaphysical Inquiry" (1915) he specifies that metaphysics seeks to articulate "the most general traits of the matter of scientific inquiry." In the same essay, he also speaks of "ul-timate, or irreducible traits." It is these that "may be made the object of a kind of inquiry differing from that which deals with the genesis of a par-ticular group of existences, a kind of inquiry to which the name meta-physical may be given" [MW8:6].

This position is echoed in the book that John E. Smith called "the most fully elaborated naturalistic metaphysics in American thought," *Experi-ence and Nature.*[35] Reprising his earlier formulation, metaphysics is there described as that field which studies "the generic traits manifested by ex-istences of all kinds without regard to their differentiation into physical and mental" [LW1:308].

Commentators on Dewey's metaphysics tend to fasten on such formu-lations as providing *the* definitive articulation of what his metaphysics seeks to accomplish.[36] I would like to suggest that this attempt at describ-ing the work of metaphysics is less than successful. It does not fully meet the threefold challenge described above. There are Deweyan formulations that do meet the challenge. But they are found elsewhere.

What are the limitations inherent in the attempt to define metaphysics as the study of "generic traits"? A brief response takes us back to the three-fold challenge. (1) It does not distinguish Dewey's philosophy sharply enough from that of other thinkers. (2) What it does provide comes close to the "transcript, more or less accurate but otiose" that Dewey criticized as belonging to "spectator" attitudes in philosophy. (3) Because of these limitations, it is not very helpful in laying out a "ground-map for the province of criticism."

By themselves, traits like contingency, change, stability, interaction, precariousness, only begin to help provide a "ground-map of the province of criticism." As a decontextualized listing, they fall short of providing the perspectival access that any metaphysics as mapping should offer. Here we need to go back to John E. Smith's claim that what is needed is a "differential standpoint or interpretative principle such as organism, matter, selfhood." Such a "differential standpoint" is precisely what is lacking in the approach via generic traits.

The main weakness of the "generic traits" approach has been well stated by Richard Rorty. Recognition of generic traits can too readily be understood as a neutral ticking off of attributes.[37] Dewey, it is true, goes to great lengths to indicate how this identifying of traits is inseparable from "criticism" or evaluation. Still, there is a kind of static, almost non-Deweyan, quality about identifying generic traits as the extent of metaphysical discourse.

Generic traits may be somewhat helpful as ways of emphasizing certain conditions, for example, contingency, interaction, and precariousness, that were minimized in earlier philosophies. Dewey was overly hasty, however, in thinking that articulating generic traits was the same as production of a ground-map that would guide cultural criticism. Such a conflation both impoverishes metaphysics and limits its ability to suggest directions for cultural criticism.

This is especially true as the traits begin to multiply.[38] To be helpful, a philosophical map has to be distinctive. Only then can it orient us in a specific way. As generic traits are multiplied, the unique character of Dewey's position comes to be more and more diluted. Its specific perspective is eroded because, as it grows, the list of traits is one that can be embraced by philosophers of quite different philosophical dispositions. It is hard to imagine, for example, Mill, Russell, and Hume not agreeing that the world of experience is a combination of the precarious and the stable, of possibility and interaction, of temporality and contingency.

The More Satisfactory Map of Paradigmatic Instances

This is not, however, the whole story of Dewey's metaphysics. The "prototype" approach is present as well. It can be found, along with the generic traits approach, in *Experience and Nature* (1925). There are also important formulations of it in three articles: "The Need for a Recovery of Philosophy" (1917), "The Inclusive Philosophic Idea" (1928), and "Philosophy" (1928). In these texts, as I have argued elsewhere,[39] Dewey goes beyond merely listing generic traits. He provides instead the sort of "differential standpoint" mentioned by Smith. By so doing, he charts a genuinely distinctive metaphysics, one that can serve as a vibrant, definitive, ground-map for criticism.

Pragmatism, Dewey points out, differs from other philosophical positions by occupying "the position of an emancipated empiricism or a thoroughgoing naive realism" [MW10:39]. "Naive" here should be taken as signaling a generous, inclusive attitude that results in a Plato- and Aristotle-like, "thick" metaphysics. Traditional empiricism was too "thin." It privileged sense data (which Dewey regarded as the results of abstractive mental processes) and made them foundational. In this way empiricism fell into what Dewey called, variously, "the standing temptation" of philosophy [LW1:26], "the commonest of all philosophical fallacies" [LW1:352], and, most straightforwardly, "*the* philosophic fallacy," namely "conversion of eventual functions into antecedent existence" [LW1:34].

The importance of identifying what is prototypically real becomes more evident when we reflect on this "metaphysical" difference between Dewey and other empiricists. Sense data result from an abstractive process undertaken within a particular inquiry. They are not antecedent, isolated building blocks of existence. They should not be confused with what is prototypically real.

Dewey's "naive" approach begins not with the results of abstractive, eliminative mental processes, but with the world that is given in ordinary experience. "Reality," as he points out, "is a *denotative* term." It designates "indifferently everything that happens. Lies, dreams, insanities, deceptions, myths, theories are all of them just the events which they specifically are" [MW10:39].

Philosophy has erred in the past by looking for a single Reality that was either beyond, or hidden beneath the world as it is given in ordinary experience. One antidote for this eliminative attitude is to accept the rich, complex diversity of ordinary experience as "real." "The only way in which the term reality can ever become more than a blanket denotative term is through recourse to specific events in all their diversity and thatness" [MW10:39].

In this regard Dewey can be seen as incorporating the components of the "prototype" perspective rooted in certain of Aristotle's texts. First of all, there is the desire for an inclusive, "thick" metaphysics. Second, there is the recognition that such a "thick" metaphysics cannot be strictly egalitarian, that is, one in which everything is real in the same sense and to the same degree. Third, although one way to avoid the egalitarian attitude would be to go the path of reductionism and seek to identify a "really Real" either beyond or beneath the "appearances" of lived experience, Dewey avoids this temptation. Fourth, what we find in his texts is something similar to Aristotle's selection of a paradigmatic instance of the real.

Dewey's steps in this "prototype" direction are not as well formulated as we might like. He was, after all, a reluctant metaphysician, mindful of the misguided paths too often followed in the name of such undertakings. Nonetheless, Dewey does offer some constructive analyses that stake out a distinctive position more successfully than his approach via generic traits.

His writings identify two versions of what will serve as prototype: "event" and "the social." "Event" is the ontological category that is present as a leitmotif in *Experience and Nature*. An explicit elaboration of the need to select a paradigmatic instance occurs in a later article originally entitled "Social as a Category," then reprinted under two different titles, "The Inclusive Philosophic Idea" and "The Social."[40]

As we have seen, the early twentieth century was not lacking in candidates for the "inclusive philosophic idea." Matter, mind, the vital, and the organic all had their adherents [LW3:44]. Metaphysical maps have traditionally selected one of these as the central concept for allowing the most adequate orientation toward existence. Dewey opts for a new symbol. He calls it "event" and "the social."

This is where we can locate the characteristic mark of what distinguishes Dewey's orientation. His choices, "event" and "the social," help provide a perspective for grasping certain dimensions of the real not emphasized enough in other philosophies. A map dominated by "event" and "the social" is one armed with the "interpretive principle" or "differential standpoint" mentioned by Smith. Together, "event" and "the social" provide the core concepts around which cluster those elements that make Dewey's position unique.

The first of these is interaction. Whatever is real in the fullest sense is not static and isolated. An "event" has no existence outside of or prior to its varied transactions with other events. The second is complexity. Dewey rejects definitively the lengthy philosophical tradition, extending from Democritus through Locke, Dalton, Russell, and the early Wittgenstein, which sought to identify those ultimate simples (atoms, sense data, atomic facts) that were to provide the most secure guideposts on the metaphysical map. There are for Dewey no ultimate simples. "The social" goes all the way down. In this sense, we might say that he develops a "cellular," as opposed to an "atomic," metaphysics. Like a cell, whatever we carve out as elemental will be heterogeneous, complex, and open to its surroundings. Third, temporality is an inherent component of the most fully real. Time must be factored in as a component of all understanding. Finally, the event is a unique composite, with a definitional persistence and irreducibility. Each event has a certain stability of characteristic pattern that delimits it as this particular event.

The texts in which Dewey describes "events" and "the social" highlight the importance of these dimensions. Detailing the "indispensable character of anything which may be termed an event," Dewey lists the following: "a qualitative variation of parts with respect to the whole which requires duration in which to display itself" [LW2:62]. Events, in other words, are heterogeneous and temporal. At the same time, as enduring patterns, they are definable. They have a phase of "brute and unconditioned isness, of being just what they irreducibly are" [LW1:75]. "Only if elements are more than just elements in a whole, only if they have something qualitatively their own, can a relational system be prevented from complete collapse" [LW1:75]. An event, say fermentation, is (1) "cellular," composed of many elements, (2) temporal, involving a duration in time that is inseparable from its definition, and (3) marked by a qualitative tone that characterizes it, sets it off from other events with which it overlaps.

The most fundamental dilemma that has faced metaphysicians is whether to privilege ultimate units as the realities that underlie the world of appearances or to privilege the complex wholes that incorporate these component units. Whereas this choice is often made unself-consciously by philosophers, Dewey consciously confronts it. "The question of whether we should begin with the simple or the complex appears to me the most important problem in philosophic method at the present time" [LW3:42].

Do we, in other words, draw a conceptual map that grasps the world around us by directing us toward that to which everything, theoretically, can be reduced, or do we draw a conceptual map that turns our attention toward that which, theoretically, incorporates and embodies the elements and energies of the natural world? Dewey's choice is clear. He opts for the "inclusive philosophic idea." The most inclusive, which specifically includes even human life, is "the social."[41]

The Atlas

Dewey's metaphysical alignment, as presented thus far, can be summarized as follows: (1) When we examine Dewey's texts for his metaphysics, we are better served by passing over the incipient and minimally helpful comments about generic traits. The metaphysical perspective that is fruitful is found in those texts where Dewey, like Aristotle before him, articulates paradigmatic instances of the real. For Dewey, these are "events" and "the social."

This, in turn, is (2) consistent with Dewey's overall philosophical orientation. What he says in logic, in political philosophy, in his philosophical anthropology, all blend together, "hang together" in a way that makes for a harmonious overall philosophy. Articulations in one area find their analogues in others.

His criticisms of Montessori schools provide an instructive example. Madame Maria Montessori erroneously taught "that there must be isolation or separation in order to get individuality" [MW15:176]. Since, for Dewey, the social is primordial, what counts is not isolation for self-development, but the distinctive way an individual contributes to a communal project. "Only in social groups does a person have a chance to develop individuality" [MW15:176]. Montessori, assuming a metaphysical map inscribed with ultimate simples, quite naturally identified "individuals" as primordially real. Such a map then led consistently to a certain program for pedagogy. Dewey's alternative map, in turn, provides signposts for a different approach to pedagogy.

(3) Though Aristotelian in spirit, Dewey's metaphysics does not accept the full range of Aristotelian positions. His notion of metaphysics seeks to fall within a fully naturalistic perspective. There is no transcendent principle that supplies an absolute foundation on the basis of which a rigid superstructure of philosophy can be built. Instead, Dewey's positions, as he admitted late in life, "hang together"[42] as a series of specific analyses in which mutually supportive orientations are articulated.

(4) Had Dewey expanded his ground-map metaphor, he could have argued that his philosophical work comprised an "atlas." Such an atlas would

provide a series of maps serving as guides for navigating the territory opened up by ordinary experience. As the atlas got thicker, it, like Peirce's cable, would gain in plausibility. Within such an atlas the metaphysical map would have an important place. It would be that chart which guides us into the world by asking what, in the end, we are willing to fasten upon as exemplary cases of the "real." For Dewey, the answer is given in terms of "events" or "the social." These, not ultimate simples, are the most fully and so most prototypically real.

Some philosophers have produced atlases with different metaphysical maps. Others have come up with an atlas that has no metaphysical map at all. The use of "events" and "the social" distinguishes Dewey from the former. With the latter, Dewey realizes that other maps in the atlas could be prepared without an explicit metaphysical map. Its presence, though, is important if a philosopher is to provide a perspective that is honest, self-conscious, and complete. Dewey was consistent, rigorous, and thorough enough to do just that. He was somewhat muddled in his attempts to provide formulations. But that is no reason to overlook the importance of his contribution.

Notes

1. The original draft of this chapter included a bibliography that was subsequently incorporated into these endnotes as the references arose throughout the document. The following books appeared in that bibliography without corresponding reference in the text. Mary Midgley, *Wisdom, Information, and Wonder: What is Knowledge For?* (London: Routledge, 1989); idem, *Can't We Make Moral Judgements?* (New York: St. Martin's Press, 1991); and Michel Serres, *Atlas* (Paris: Editions Julliard, 1994).

2. As Dewey puts it, "The word *mere* plays a large role in anti-naturalistic writings" [LW15:47].

3. "The earth's surface is shown [on Mercator's map] in the form of a flattened-out cylinder, with the meridians and parallels represented by perpendicular straight lines intersecting at right angles, and the spacing between the parallels progressively increasing from the equator to the poles. This arrangement gives rise to some distortion in the representation of distances, but it enables navigators to set their course and ensure that the route they take tallies with the map." Jean Portante, "Mercator, Cartographer of Genius," *Unesco Courier* 47 (1994): 39.

4. "The Real World," *Harpers* 268 (April 1984): 15. The details of Mercator's scheme are clearly explained by the mathematician Robert Osserman in a

delightful book on the wonders of mathematics. See Robert Osserman, *Poetry of the Universe* (New York: Anchor Books, 1995), pp. 30–40.

5. Charles Sanders Peirce, "Some Consequences of Four Incapacities" (1868), in *Classical American Philosophy,* ed. John Stuhr (New York: Oxford University Press, 1987).

6. Richard Rorty, *Consequences of Pragmatism* (Minneapolis: University of Minnesota Press, 1982), p. 74.

7. Ibid., p. 80.

8. "Ontology," "speech about being," is an etymologically more correct way of referring to the study that Aristotle said concerned itself with "being qua being." My own usage employs the terms "metaphysics" and "ontology" interchangeably.

9. Speaking of the various modes of association "to be used in an enterprise of philosophic description and understanding," Dewey says the following: "Aside from social, whose thoroughgoing admission still awaits adequate acknowledgment, they are the physical, the vital or organic, and the mental" [LW3:44].

10. "Pragmatism is content to take its stand with science; for science finds all such events to be subject-matter of description and inquiry—just like stars and fossils, mosquitoes and malaria, circulation and vision. It also takes its stand with daily life, which finds that such things really have to be reckoned with as they occur interwoven in the texture of events" [MW10:39].

11. René Descartes, *Meditations on Philosophy* (1641), trans. Donald A. Cress (Indianapolis: Hackett Publishing, 1980), p. 47.

12. Immanuel Kant, *Critique of Pure Reason* (1787), trans. Norman Kemp Smith (New York: St. Martin's Press, 1965), p. B, xix.

13. G. E. Moore, *Principia Ethica* (London: Oxford University Press, 1962), p. 111.

14. Friedrich Nietzsche, *Twilight of the Idols* (1888), in *The Portable Nietzsche,* ed. Walter Kaufmann (New York: Viking Press, 1954), p. 479.

15. A. J. Ayer, "Demonstration of the Impossibility of Metaphysics," *Mind* 43 (1934): 335–45.

16. A. J. Ayer, *Language, Truth, and Logic,* 2d ed. (1946; reprint, New York: Dover Publications, 1952).

17. Jacques Derrida, *Margins of Philosophy,* trans. Alan Bass (Chicago: University of Chicago Press, 1982), p. 213.

18. Rorty, *Consequences of Pragmatism,* p. 81.

19. The name "metaphysics" was provided by a later editor of Aristotle's writings who, for the sake of convenience, labeled a collection as "those which come after the physics," *ta meta ta physica.*

20. Aristotle, *The Basic Works of Aristotle,* ed. Richard McKeon (New York: Random House, 1941), Met. IV, 2 1004a 3,4.

21. Ibid., Met. VI, 1 1026a 19.

22. Ibid., Met. IV, 1 1003a 21.

23. Plato, *Republic,* VII, 509D–511E, in *The Collected Dialogues,* ed. Edith Hamilton and Huntington Cairns (New York: Bollingen Foundation, 1963).

24. Plato, *Sophist,* 247e, in *Collected Dialogues,* ed. Hamilton and Cairns.

25. Aristotle, *The Basic Works of Aristotle,* Met. IV, 1 1003a 33.

26. Joseph Owens, *The Doctrine of Being in the Aristotelian Metaphysics* (Toronto: Pontifical Institute of Medieval Studies Press, 1951), p. 72.

27. Josette Rey-Debove, "Prototypes et Définitions," in *L'Objet: Colloque en Homage à Gérard Deledalle* (Perpignan, France: Unpublished Conference Proceedings, 1991), p. 47.

28. Ibid., p. 43.

29. Aristotle, *Categories,* 4. 2a 11–14, in *The Basic Works of Aristotle.*

30. See, for example, "The Metaphysical Assumptions of Materialism" [EW1].

31. The shift away from metaphysics is evident in an 1896 commentary on a critic who would place a more secure metaphysical foundation under Dewey's ethical theory. Dewey's conclusion: "For my own part, I believe that an ethical doctrine with less 'foundations' under it is likely to go farther and last longer" [EW 5:33]. Later on, he would argue that if the "scientific method" were properly understood and implemented, the need for metaphysical (read supersensible) entities to explain phenomena would be eliminated. There would be no need to indulge in a "metaphysic of a purely hypothetical experience" [MW2:334].

32. In the autobiography edited by his daughter Jane, the importance of Dewey's new colleague at Columbia is made evident. He is the first philosopher mentioned in connection with the Columbia years. The impact of Dewey's relationship with him is immediately described in terms of metaphysics. "Contact with him [Woodbridge] made Dewey aware of the possibility and value of a type of metaphysical theory which did not profess to rest upon principles not empirically verifiable." Paul Arthur Schilpp, ed., *The Philosophy of John Dewey: The Library of Living Philosophers,* vol. 1 (Evanston: Northwestern University Press, 1939), p. 36.

33. See F. J. E. Woodbridge, "Confessions" (1930), in *Nature and Mind: Selected Essays of Frederick J. E. Woodbridge* (New York: Russell and Russell, 1965).

34. John E. Smith, "John Dewey: Philosopher of Experience," *Review of Metaphysics* 13 (1959): 77.

35. John E. Smith, *The Spirit of American Philosophy* (New York: Oxford University Press, 1963), p. 212.

36. This is true, for example, of two thinkers who have reservations about Dewey's metaphysical project, Sidney Hook (who authored the 1981 "Introduction" to *Experience and Nature* in *Later Works* 1) and Richard Rorty. It is also true of someone like Craig Cunningham who supports Dewey's attempt to formulate a metaphysics (see note 38 below). My own earlier study, *Dewey's Metaphysics* (New York: Fordham University Press, 1988), also tended to embrace this position too uncritically.

37. Rorty, *Consequences of Pragmatism,* pp. 73–74.

38. In a recent study of Dewey's metaphysics, Craig Cunningham has identified forty such traits, which he lists in a helpful table. See Craig Cunningham, "Dewey's Metaphysics and the Self," in *The New Scholarship on Dewey,* ed. Jim Garrison (Dordrecht: Kluwer, 1995), p. 348.

39. Raymond Boisvert, "Metaphysics as the Search for Paradigmatic Instances," *Transactions of the Charles S. Peirce Society* 28 (1992): 189–202.

40. The essay first appeared in the *Monist* 38 (1928): 161–77. It subsequently was reprinted in *Philosophy and Civilization* and in *Intelligence in the Modern World.*

41. "Denial of opposition between the social and natural is, however, an important element of the *meaning* of 'social' as a category" [LW3:44].

42. "I find that with respect to the hanging together of various problems and various hypotheses in a perspective determined by a definite point of view, I have a system. In so far I have to retract disparaging remarks I have made in the past about the need for system in philosophy" [LW14:141–42].

9   Dewey's Theory of Inquiry

Larry A. Hickman

John Dewey did not develop a theory of knowledge in the usual sense of "epistemology," but he did have a well-developed theory of inquiry. He was in fact highly critical of what he called "the epistemology industry" because of its tendency to treat knowledge as something separated from the contexts in which actual inquiry takes place.

He thought that when epistemologists start out by positing cases of "certain" knowledge, or "justified true belief," as they sometimes do, and then attempt to find out *how* it is justified, they tend to get matters backward. It is more productive, he suggested, to examine how actual cases of inquiry are related to one another and how they increase our stock of guides for future action. In other words, analysis should be a tool for the production of satisfactory outcomes, and not an end in itself. Epistemology as usually practiced was in Dewey's view a conflicted mixture of proven and relevant logical tools, on the one hand, and irrelevant psychological and metaphysical preconceptions, on the other. If such preconceptions could be jettisoned, he thought, then epistemology would be freed to do its real work as a theory of inquiry. The terms "epistemology" and "logic" would then become synonymous.

Although he did in fact use the term "knowledge" quite frequently, Dewey thought that it had so many infelicitous connotations that it needed to be replaced. He tried to do this in two ways. First, for the reasons I just indicated, he often used the gerund "knowing" in place of the substantive term "knowledge" in order to emphasize the fact that knowing is always a part of a larger process of inquiry.

But even this did not entirely convey what he had in mind, so he invented the phrase "warranted assertibility." The two parts of this somewhat cumbersome but descriptive phrase point in different directions. "Warranted" denotes an individual outcome, and thus points backward in time toward something that has been accomplished. What is warranted is the result of reflection that has been effective in the sense that some specific doubt or difficulty has been resolved. "Assertibility" points forward in time toward something yet to be done. What is assertible is something general, and therefore something potentially applicable to future cases that are relevantly similar to the one by means of which it was produced. Unlike the alleged knowledge (or justified true belief) studied by most epistemologists, however, warranted assertibility is claimed to be neither certain nor permanent. The best it can offer is a measure of stability in an otherwise precarious world.

Inquiry as Organic Behavior

The work of Charles Darwin exerted a profound influence on Dewey's thought from the time Dewey was an undergraduate during the 1870s until his death in 1952. In 1909, on the occasion of the fiftieth anniversary of the publication of *The Origin of Species,* Dewey wrote an essay in which he characterized his own work as doing for philosophy what Darwin had done for biology. Just as Darwin had proved the notion of fixed biological species untenable, he, Dewey, would seek to demonstrate that there are no fixed or certain truths. Contrary to the claims of some of his critics, however, this project was motivated by neither skepticism nor nihilism. It was based on a candid recognition of the observable fact that living beings must constantly adapt to changing environmental circumstances. Even though they require overlapping and interpenetrating patterns of stability for their continued existence, their lives are at bottom and in the long run highly precarious.

Dewey identified inquiry as the primary means by which reflective organisms seek to achieve stability through adaptation. It is by means of inquiry that humans are able to exert control over their own habit formation, thereby creating new instruments. In the short run, these instruments enable us to improve conditions that we deem unsatisfactory. In the long run, they enable us to influence the course of our own evolution.

Because inquiry is an organic activity, and because organisms encounter constraints as well as facilities, assertions must continually be tested and new warrants must continually be issued. Successful living requires an active and ongoing reconstruction of experienced situations. Dewey's notion of warranted assertibility, therefore, unlike the concept of knowledge as it has functioned in systems such as those of Plato, Descartes, and many contemporary philosophers, is not a matter of a spectator getting a better view of a fixed state of affairs that is already "out there."

Dewey constantly reminded his readers that if contemporary science has taught us anything, it is that there is nothing "out there," in any permanent sense of "out there," of which we can get a better view. At the level of immediate or unreflective experience, what is "out there" is always changing. And at the level of reflective or organized experience, what we count as being "out there" at any given time is a result of the activity of human intelligence as it takes into account the materials it finds in immediate experience and the tools currently at its disposal. The aim of inquiry is therefore to reconstruct both found materials and available tools in ways that render them more richly meaningful.

Inquiry as Instrumental

Dewey rejected versions of naive realism which claim that things already are as they will eventually be for us, even prior to our taking them into account. He also rejected the version of scientific realism just described, which claims that there is a fixed reality that is simply discovered by scientists and to which scientific "laws" therefore correspond. As a result, some of his earlier critics read him as advancing one or another variety of idealism, such as the view that the laws of science—or logic—are wholly a matter of coherence within a human or divine mind.

More recently, some of Dewey's interpreters have argued that he held a type of relativism similar to that of some of the French postmodernists, according to which human beings as language-users are caught in an infinite web of metaphors or tropes, none of which are any more privileged or warranted than any other. Richard Rorty, for example, has claimed Dewey's authority in advancing the view that there is no real distinction between the sciences and the arts, but that both are just types of literature. Dewey regarded both of these views—scientific realism and extreme relativism—as flawed and he vigorously opposed them.

His name for his own view was "instrumentalism." In 1903 he and his students and colleagues at the University of Chicago published a collection called *Studies in Logical Theory* which announced instrumentalism as a school of thought and attempted to work out its implications.

Seen in the context of his instrumentalism, warranted assertibility results from the experimental manipulation of tools, materials, and conditions as they are experienced. And the whole point of experimentation is to see whether we can make things better by finding out how experienced situations (which of course include ourselves as components) can be reconstructed.

Contrary to the position advanced by much of traditional philosophy, Dewey was convinced that the tools that we use in inquiry are not given to us a priori. They are instead instruments that have been developed in the course of inquiry that have proven successful. Inquiry is thus a reflective activity in which existing tools and materials (both of which may be either tangible or conceptual) are brought together in novel and creative arrangements in order to produce something new. The byproducts of this process often include improved tools and materials that can then be applied to the next occasion on which inquiry is required.

To miss this point is to misunderstand the radical nature of Dewey's theory of inquiry. His view was that logical forms *accrue* to inquiry as a result of the subject matter it takes up and the conclusions it finds warranted. He put this matter very precisely in 1938, in *Logic: The Theory of Inquiry:* "logical forms accrue to subject-matter in virtue of subjection of the latter in inquiry to the conditions determined by its end—institution of a warranted conclusion" [LW12:370].

One of the things that makes this claim so controversial is that traditional logic had claimed just the opposite—that logical forms are *imposed* upon the subject matter of inquiry. Dewey thus turned traditional logic on its head. This is an extremely important point, so I shall return to it later in this essay.

The Role of the A Priori in Inquiry

Especially since Kant, the concept of the a priori has played an important role in philosophical discourse. It is therefore important to understand the two senses in which Dewey employed the term. What he called the "external" a priori corresponds to the way the term was used by Kant and subsequently in much of Anglo-American analytic logic and epistemology. What is a priori in this sense is strictly speaking prior to *any* experience. In Kant, for example, what is a priori provides the very conditions under which any experience is possible. Kant thus treats space and time as a priori forms that must be imposed on what is perceived in order for there to be any experience at all. Dewey denied that there is any such thing as an a priori in this sense. In his view, for example, space and time are not forms that are brought *to* experience, but conceptions that are constructed *on the basis* of experience.

What Dewey did allow, however, was something that he called the "operational" a priori. In inquiry, he observed, we develop habits of action that are known as "laws of inference." Because these are habits, rather than specific actions, they are general. Like other sorts of habits, they have been adopted (and they continue to be adapted) over time because they have been found to produce successful consequences. Dewey used the term *successful* in its precise instrumental or pragmatic sense. The laws of inference, he wrote, are successful when they are "operative in a manner that tends in the long run, or in continuity of inquiry, to yield results that are either confirmed in further inquiry or that are corrected by use of the same procedures" [LW12:21].

He provided several excellent examples of what he meant by this. Take a logical postulate, he suggested, such as the "law" of the excluded middle (which states that a thing is either A or not A but not both, say, either a liquid or a nonliquid but not both). This is a logical "law" in the sense that if we are going to reason at all, then we must take it (as well as other logical laws) into account. But there is nothing a priori in the external, or Kantian sense, about these laws. Dewey called such "laws" stipulations, or "formulations of formal conditions . . . to be satisfied." As such, he said, they are "valid as directive principles, as regulative limiting ideals of inquiry" [LW12:345]. Dewey called our attention to the obvious fact, for example, that at a certain temperature near the freezing point, water is neither precisely a liquid nor precisely a nonliquid.

Dewey argued that these "laws" are stipulations in much the same sense that the laws of contracts are stipulations that regulate business arrangements. If we are going to do business at all, then we must take into account as "directive principles" certain forms that have *proven* to be successful, that is, that have been *proven* to regulate a wide range of particular transactions in ways that keep the business community functioning. And if we are going to engage in inquiry at all, then we must take into account, again as "directive principles," certain logical forms that have been *proven* to be successful in precisely the same sense.

But these "laws" are not a priori in the sense that they are applicable regardless of subject matter. They accrue to inquiry *in virtue of* its subject matter. They arise out of subject matter, and they are returned to subject matter as tools for testing our conceptions of it: as such, they are conditions to be satisfied. In his treatment of the law of excluded middle, for example, Dewey pointed out that the "fact that disjunctions which were at one time taken to be both exhaustive and necessary have later been found to be incomplete (and sometimes even totally irrelevant) should long ago have been a warning that the principle of excluded middle sets forth a logical condition *to be* satisfied in the course of continuity of inquiry. It formulates the ultimate goal of inquiry in complete satisfaction of logical conditions. To determine subject-matters so that no alternative is possible is the most difficult task of inquiry" [LW12: 344].

What is operationally a priori, then (and this is the only kind of *a priori* that Dewey admitted), is what has been brought to current inquiry as a byproduct of prior inquiry. There is nothing that is a priori in the Kantian sense. There is no a priori that is absolutely prior or external to experience.

Common Sense and Science

Dewey thought that the splits within experience posited by most philosophers, especially since Descartes, were not only unwarranted but debilitating. He thought that the split between scientific inquiry and common sense which resulted from these philosophers' penchant for skepticism was no exception. Dewey characterized common sense as the part of experience in which humans make required behavioral adjustments as a response to "direct" involvement with the circumstances of their environing conditions. In other words, common sense involves ordinary use and enjoyment, and it is concerned with what is *practical.*

Dewey rejected the common notion that there are metaphysical or ontological differences between common sense and science. He did think, however, that there was a *logical* difference between these two types of inquiry: they utilize different logical *forms.* Science grows out of common sense as its tools of inquiry become more refined. But science is not "final" in the sense of being the end or point of inquiry. It does not tell us how the world "really" is in any final sense, and it is not the paradigm for all other forms of inquiry. It is not, to use a phrase recently made popular by Jean-François Lyotard, a "master narrative." Scientific inquiry is in Dewey's view inquiry *for.* It is a theoretical enterprise that must ultimately return to the world of use and enjoyment in order to check its results.

Historically, one of the great philosophical errors has been the treatment of objects produced by abstraction from common sense experience as if they were prior to and independent of the experience from which they were abstracted. They are then said to exist in a realm that is separate and superior to common sense. Having then created this fracture within experience, some philosophers have spent inordinate amounts of time attempting to show how the two realms might be related.

Dewey thought this utter nonsense, and referred to it as "the philosopher's fallacy." His suggestion was that once it is recognized that there is a continuity between common sense and science, the purported fracture between these areas of inquiry will be recognized for what it is—nothing more than a difference of logical form. Metaphysical or ontological fractures will never open up in the first place.

Logical Objects

In 1916 Dewey gave a talk to the philosophy club at Columbia University in which he shed a good deal of light on these matters. The subject of his remarks was what he called "logical objects" or "logical entities." These were said to include such items as "between," "if," numbers, and essences. Historically, Dewey observed, these entities have been treated as (a) physical properties of objects, (b) mental or psychical properties, or (c) some sort of "tertium quid" which is neither physical nor mental but "metaphysical."

Dewey rejected all three of these views. He argued instead that logical objects are just that—logical. By this he meant that they are the byproducts of inference. They are thus "things (or traits of things) which are found when inference is found and which are only found then" [MW10:90].

The key to understanding Dewey's radical innovation on these matters lies in his argument that what is logical must be separated from what is purely mental, or psychical. Of course Dewey did not wish to deny that inquiry involves mental processes, or that there are psychological factors that are present in inquiry. His point was rather to insist that inquiry is always a behavioral response of a reflective organism to its environing conditions. As such, he wrote, it belongs to "action, or behavior, which takes place in the world, not just within the mind or within consciousness" [LW10:90]. This means that whatever mental processes may accompany a particular inquiry, it is its behavioral results, and not some accompanying psychic or mental process, that identifies it as inquiry. Inquiry, just as much as walking or eating, is what Dewey termed an "outdoor fact."

Dewey's treatment of this subject was typical of his broader philosophical outlook. He undermined the customary ontological approach to the problem of logical objects (which relied on sorting them into pre-existing categories) and then he argued that they should be treated in functional terms. He thus identified inquiry as an art, and its products and byproducts (including logical connectives such as "and," and "or," and numbers) as manufactured articles. Such artifacts, he reminded us, are manufactured for some purpose; or at least they are connected to some process. To treat them as having existence apart from such purposes and processes is to fall back into the older practice of giving them a spurious ontological status.

Geometrical points, temporal instants, and even logical classes provide excellent examples of what Dewey had in mind. They refer to a kind of reality that is neither physical, psychical, nor metaphysical. The reality to which they do refer is no more or less than the behavioral reality of controlled inquiry. To treat them as something apart from inquiry, as has traditionally been the case, would be to make the same type of mistake that a biologist would commit if he or she were to infer from the conditions of a fish in water the conditions of a fish out of water [MW10:95].

Abstraction

That Dewey used this particular figure of speech as a part of his discussion of abstract objects was perhaps occasioned by his reading of William James. James had observed that anyone who looks up through the side of an aquarium can see an object across the room, such as a candle, reflected from the bottom of the water's surface back down into the water. The water, he suggested, is like the world of sensible facts. And the air above it is like the world of abstract ideas.

> Both worlds are real, of course, and interact; but they interact only at their boundary, and the *locus* of everything that lives, and happens to us, so far as full experience goes, is the water. We are like fishes swimming in the sea of sense, bounded above by the superior element, but unable to breathe it pure or penetrate it. We get our oxygen from it, however, we touch it incessantly, now in this part, now in that, and every time we touch it, we are reflected back into the water with our course re-determined and re-energized. The abstract ideas of which the air consists are indispensable for life, but irrespirable by themselves, as it were, and only active in their re-directing function. All similes are halting, but this one rather takes my fancy. It shows how something, not sufficient for life in itself, may nevertheless be an effective determinant of life elsewhere.[1]

In his own treatment of abstraction, Dewey elaborates on James's simile. First, there is a living relation of transaction between the abstract and the concrete. Just as the fish draw their oxygen from the air above their everyday environment, human experience draws nourishment from abstract entities and relations. When this living relation is ignored, abstraction tends to become something negative and even the subject of parody. It becomes something arbitrary and aloof from everyday experience.

Second, the living relation between abstract and concrete is maintained by means of experimentation. Abstraction is not an end in itself, but instead a tool for developing new meanings that can be brought back down into the realm of concrete, existential experience. Inquiry always involves abstraction, since it always involves hypotheses that articulate alternative courses of action. It also relies upon relations (and relations of relations), which are the byproducts of previous inquiries. Ultimately, however, inquiry is undertaken for the sake of effecting change in a concrete, existential world; it is there and only there that abstractions are determined to have succeeded or failed, that is, to have been useful or not.

Third, and contrary to the long tradition of western philosophy, abstractions do not belong to a metaphysical or ontological order that is higher or more noble than that of concrete experience. James uses the term *superior* in his analogy to designate spatial location, not metaphysical preeminence, and Dewey's account makes it clear that abstract and concrete are coequal phases or moments within inquiry. In his account of the history of abstraction, Dewey reminds us that Socrates rendered a great service to his fellow Athenians by urging them to avoid excessive reliance on the concrete, that is, to avoid reasoning by simple enumeration of examples. Socrates' attempts to get his fellow Athenians to engage in hypothetical reasoning constituted a great step forward in the history of inquiry. But Plato made the opposite mistake: when he began to treat abstractions as metaphysical entities, he set an unfortunate course for twenty-five hundred years of western philosophy.

One of the reasons why philosophers since Plato have tended to think of abstractions as higher and more perfect than concrete experience is that they are said to afford a level of "certainty" that ordinary experience does not. The mathematical proposition "2+3=5" has, for example, been treated as a timeless truth, metaphysically superior because applicable everywhere and at all times. But Dewey saw matters differently. The reason why mathematical propositions are often taken as timeless truths is that

> *qua* mathematical, [they] are free from the conditions that require any limiting interpretation. They have no meaning or interpretation save that which is formally imposed by the need of satisfying the condition

174 *Larry A. Hickman*

of transformability within the system, with no extra-systemic reference whatever. In the sense which "meaning" bears in any conception having even indirect existential reference, the terms have no meaning—a fact which accounts, probably, for the view that mathematical subject-matter is simply a string of arbitrary marks. But in the wider logical sense, they have a meaning constituted exclusively and wholly by their relations to one another as determined by satisfaction of the condition of transformability. [LW12:395–96]

In other words, mathematical propositions may be meaningful in either of two senses. In terms of their relation to other elements of a formal system, they are meaningful in virtue of satisfying certain conditions of transformability within a system. It is in this sense that they *appear* to be true everywhere and at all times. Their place in the formal system is secure, and results of transformation within the system that depend on them are uniform and dependable within that limited scope. In this sense, mathematical propositions refer to *no* existential individuals.

In a second sense, however, the sense in which mathematical propositions refer to *some* existential individual or another, they are not dependably applicable. Experimental science, as well as everyday experience, is replete with cases in which abstract mathematical propositions are too "thin" to apply to experience in all its robustness. It is important to note that Dewey does not think that mathematical propositions, or any other type of propositions, for that matter, are true or false. I shall discuss this matter in more detail later, in the section on propositions.

Matter and Form in Inquiry

It is now time to return to the matter of the relation of form and matter within inquiry. According to his critics, one of the scandals of Dewey's *Logic: The Theory of Inquiry* was its paucity of symbols. How, they asked, in a time when logic was increasingly symbolic, could they be expected to take seriously a book about logic that contained so few symbols?

Dewey addressed this question in the introduction to his book. Many of the problems of logic, he argued, have been the result of the separation of form and matter. This has in turn been the result of a rush to symbolize in the absence of a "general theory of language in which form and matter are not separated" [LW12:4].

Dewey thought that logical forms are *disclosed* as inquiry is undertaken, but even more importantly, he thought that they *originate* as the byproducts of inquiry. In order to understand this point it is necessary to differentiate inquiry, which Dewey sometimes calls "primary" inquiry, from logic, which he terms the "theory" of inquiry. "Primary inquiry," he writes, "is itself *causa essendi* of the forms which inquiry into inquiry [or logic] discloses" [LW12:12]. It is the function of (primary) inquiry to arrange its subject matter into settled forms. It is the function of inquiry into inquiry (logic) to take account of those forms, disclosing their relations to other forms and arranging them in ways that facilitate their use in further inquiries. When these things (settled forms) are used in further inquiries, they become the *means* to further results. But viewed retrospectively, they become *objects*. Dewey thus makes a radical move: he functionalizes objects by characterizing them in terms of their roles in continuing inquiry. "Objects," he writes, "are the *objectives* of inquiry" [LW12:12].

Once established, objects (or settled forms) tend to persist long after their originating subject matter has been altered. Old forms are imposed on new subject matter. In some cases this works well enough, but in other cases the old forms are not really relevant to the new subject matter. Their use results in error and confusion. Dewey thought that this is precisely what had happened in the case of the Aristotelian syllogism. "The perpetuation of the forms of the Aristotelian tradition," he argued, "with elimination of the subject-matter of which they were the forms, also ruled out inquiry (which is effective reflection) from the proper scope of logic. The syllogism in the original logic was in no way a form of inferring or reasoning. It was immediate apprehension or vision of the relations of inclusion and exclusion that belong to real wholes in Nature" [LW12:93].

Dewey freely admitted that logic has to do with formal relationships, and he accepted the widely held notion that this is what sets logic off from other sciences. But he also noted that logicians have tended to disagree about what this means. Their debates have been particularly sharp regarding the question of how logical form is related to subject matter. Logical formalists, for example, tend to hold that there is no relation between logical form and subject matter. But they disagree among themselves about how this tenet is to be interpreted. Some of them argue, for example, that forms constitute a separate realm of metaphysical possibilities (possible worlds). Others, exhibiting a less mystical temper, hold that logic is the study of the formal syntactical properties of sentences or propositions. Still other logicians, of a more realistic bent, oppose both types of formalism. They argue that logical forms are abstracted, rather like Aristotle's "intelligible species," from pre-existing materials.

Dewey rejected each of these views. As I have already indicated, he argued that "logical forms accrue to subject-matter in virtue of subjection of the latter in inquiry to the conditions determined by its end—institution of a warranted conclusion" [LW12:370]. In other words, logical forms accrue to subject matter in the process of inquiry. The subject matter does not have the logical forms prior to inquiry.

Dewey illustrates these points by drawing our attention to the history of jurisprudence. He observes that there have been numerous occasions on which

> forms of procedure had become the controlling factor at the expense of substance. In such cases, they ceased to be forms-of-matter and were so isolated that they became purely formalistic—a fact which perhaps contains an instructive lesson for logic, since it is clear that legal forms should be such as to serve the substantial end of providing means for settling controversies. . . . These rules of law provide multifarious examples of the ways in which "natural" modes of action take on new forms because of subjection to conditions formulated in the rules. As new modes of social interaction and transactions give rise to new conditions, and as new social conditions install new kinds of transactions, new forms arise to meet the social need. When, for example, a new type of industrial and commercial enterprise required large capital, the form known as limited liability supervened upon the forms constituting the legal rules of partnership. [LW12:370–71]

It is the business of controlled inquiry, then, to manipulate its subject matter in ways that allow new forms to accrue to it. After these new forms originate, it is the business of logic (as the theory of inquiry) to disclose the ways in which they are related to one another and to determine their potential use in further inquiry.

Judgments

Books about logic often begin with a discussion of terms. They then take up the various ways in which terms are joined to make propositions or judgments, and the various ways in which propositions or judgments are combined to make arguments. Aristotle, for example, combined terms into four forms of judgment: All S is P, Some S is P, No S is P, and

Some S is not P. He demonstrated that when these judgments are combined into forms consisting of two premises and a conclusion (a syllogism), some of the arguments thereby constructed are valid, while others are invalid.

Dewey begins differently. In his view, terms and propositions can only be understood as *correlative* with judgment, which he terms the "settled outcome of inquiry" [LW12:123]. As already indicated, inquiry begins when a situation is doubtful or problematic. Tools and materials are then brought to bear on the situation in question. Hypotheses are formed and then tried out in what he calls "dramatic rehearsals" with a view to alleviating the undesirable circumstances of the situation. Along the way appraisals are made. Finally, where inquiry is successful, the situation is reordered in a way that renders it stable and unproblematic.

In Dewey's usage, therefore, a judgment is not the same as a proposition. A proposition is just that—a proposal which is only intermediate within inquiry. A judgment, on the other hand, carries what he calls "existential import." Whereas propositions *assert*, judgments *affirm*. Dewey uses a baseball metaphor to clarify this point. Drawing on the slang of his day, he writes that "a pitched baseball is to the batter a 'proposition'; it states, or makes explicit, what he has to deal with next amid all the surrounding and momentarily irrelevant circumstance" [MW10:356]. Continuing this analogy, we could say that a judgment is what is made by the batter as a result of (rapid) deliberation about whether he or she will swing the bat at the ball. The pitched ball is thus the proposition and the swing of the bat is the judgment. In this case, as others, deliberation takes into account observed conditions as well as established rules, such as those established to determine strike zones.

Switching to a different analogy, we might say that a proposition in a court of law is what is asserted by one of the parties to a dispute, whereas a judgment is the affirmation that is handed down by the court as a result of deliberation with respect to the evidence and its relation to established legal precedent. Of course intermediate judgments, or what Dewey calls "*appraisals*," such as those that determine the admissibility of evidence, are also a part of the overall process of inquiry that eventuates in a final judgment or settlement of the affair before the court. But whereas both propositions and intermediate judgments (appraisals) are intermediate, propositions are less determinate than are intermediate judgments (appraisals).

Many logic texts treat the subject of a proposition as something given in a determinate fashion to the senses, and the predicate of a proposition as something conceptual that is attributed to the already determinate subject by means of an act of judgment. Dewey rejected this view. He argued that the subjects and predicates of judgments are determined correlatively to one another as a part of the process of inquiry [LW12:128]. The subject of a proposition is not given as already determined, he argued, since if it were there would be no occasion for inquiry in the first place. Since the point of inquiry is to *find out*, it follows that the subject of a proposition is something vague that requires further definition.

It may well be that what is taken as the subject of a proposition will have received determinate form in a *prior* instance of inquiry; but that does not insure that it will be relevant *as such* to the inquiry at hand. Progress in the sciences, as well as in common sense inquiries, requires that the results of prior inquiries be treated as raw materials for further inquiries, and not as determinate results, established once and for all.

It is sometimes argued that pure reference can be established for the subject of a proposition merely by pointing to something and by referring to it as "this." But Dewey argues that there is no such thing as pure referentiality. He makes the point (later taken up and capitalized upon by Quine in his famous remarks on "rabbit stages") that even the act of pointing does not establish pure reference, since any of several sensory traits of an object (including its temporal stages) may be the object of the pointing. The fact is that subjects and predicates of propositions are determined correlatively to one another. Their definitions are refined as they are checked against one another. To establish a "this" in the first place is to establish it in terms of a predicate, that is, as *provisionally* one instance of a particular kind. A proposition, which associates a subject and a predicate, is therefore indefinite. It is an indication of tests to be made—of operations to be performed.

Dewey's view also differs from mainstream theories of logic in terms of what it is that judgment accomplishes. It is a commonly held view that the point of judgment is to make a difference in the mental states or attitudes of the judging subject. But Dewey thought that this view yields too much to subjectivism. According to his own view, the point of a judgment is to make a difference in the existential conditions which gave rise to the inquiry of which the final judgment is the termination. Changes in wider existential situations may involve alterations of mental states and attitudes, to be sure, since mental states and attitudes are also existential. But to ignore the wider existential situation and to focus exclusively on mental states and attitudes is to open the door to the prospect of pure fantasy [LW12:162].

This is particularly apparent in the case of what Dewey calls "judgments of practice," or judgments which involve considerations of value. The point of a moral decision is not to choose from among certain pre-established ends and thereby to change one's mental state. The point of a moral decision is to assess an existential situation, to bring the best instruments currently at one's disposal to bear upon it, and to arrive at a judgment that changes the "*indeterminate situation into one that is so determinate in its constituent distinctions and relations as to convert the elements of the original situation into a unified whole*" [LW12:108].

Propositions and Their Relations

As I have already indicated, Dewey characterized propositions as different from judgments in the sense that propositions are intermediate, that is, instrumentalities for the final settlement (judgment) of a particular case. Beyond that, however, Dewey divides propositions into two distinct but correlative types. What he calls *existential* propositions have to do with "actual conditions as determined by experimental observation," whereas what he calls *ideational or conceptual* propositions have to do with "interrelated meanings, which are non-existential in content in direct reference but which are applicable to existence through the operations they represent as possibilities" [LW12:284]. As we would expect, given the foregoing discussion of his treatment of abstraction, Dewey indicates that these two types of propositions are related not as inferior and superior, but as equal partners. He suggests that they represent a "division of labor" within inquiry.

From the viewpoint of some logic textbooks, Dewey's contention that propositions are neither true nor false is nothing short of scandalous.[2] But his point becomes clear enough when it is remembered that he views propositions as means rather than ends. As such, they may be said to be effective or ineffective, strong or weak, or even relevant or irrelevant; they are not, however, said to be true or false. Propositions that are effective, strong, and relevant with respect to the advancement of inquiry are said to be "valid." Propositions that are ineffective, weak, or irrelevant are said to be "invalid." Judgments are said to be true or false to the extent that they involve warranted assertibility. And arguments are said to be formally correct or incorrect. This usage has been the occasion for great offense to some mainstream logicians who are accustomed to characterizing propositions as either true or false and arguments as either valid or invalid.

In an attempt to clarify these matters, Dewey provides the following example. "The syllogism 'All satellites are made of green cheese; the moon is a satellite; therefore, it is made of green cheese' is formally correct. The propositions involved are, however, *invalid,* not just because they are 'materially false,' but because instead of promoting inquiry they would, if taken and used, retard and mislead it" [LW12:288]. In a sequence of inquiry in which the judgment that "the moon is made of green cheese" was accepted as settling the matter, then, such a judgment would be false in the sense that it would lack warranted assertibility.

Dewey's full treatment of propositions is quite complex, so a complete discussion of it is well beyond the scope of this essay. Nevertheless, before concluding I want to call attention to several additional points of interest.

First, Dewey distinguishes "particular" propositions from "singular" propositions. Since they sometimes have the same grammatical form, he points out, these two types of propositions are sometimes confused. A *particular* proposition (such as "this is hard"), draws attention to some change, that is, to something taking place as a consequence of the operation of some sense organ [LW12:289]. Such propositions are particular in the sense that they have reference to a particular time and place; they do not in themselves allow further inference. Dewey tells us that particular propositions "represent the first stage in *determination of a problem;* they supply a datum which, when combined with other data, *may* indicate what sort of a problem the situation presents and thereby provide an item of evidence pointing to and testing a proposed solution" [LW12:290].

Although a *singular* proposition may be of the same grammatical form as a particular proposition (as in the case of "this is hard," for example), the two types of propositions function differently within inquiry. Whereas a *particular* proposition merely indicates the presence of a change, thus possibly instituting a problem, a *singular* proposition determines the "this" to be one instance of a certain kind. The logical structure of singular propositions is more obvious in the case of "this is a diamond," which asserts that "what occurs at the time is being taken as evidence of the permanent traits which describe a kind" [LW12:291]. Since they assert inference beyond the here and now to "permanent" or "general" traits not immediately experienced at the moment they are asserted, singular propositions are thus said to have a certain representative quality.

Dewey's Theory of Inquiry 181

Dewey introduces several technical terms to help clarify his treatment of these matters. When I merely notice at some moment that something is hard, he suggests, then I am aware of some *quality*. But since our experiences are complex and overlapping, many different qualities may be experienced in a given span of time. Some of these qualities are existentially *involved* with others. Mere recognition of existential involvement, however, does not do much to advance inquiry. There is still the need to discover *which* qualities are relevantly involved with one another (in terms of the problem at hand), and *how* they are so involved. As Dewey puts it, "reasoning and calculation are necessary *instruments* for determining definite involvements" [LW12:277].

In other words, *inference* is required: inquiry intervenes with a view to determining which involvement-relationships are relevant to the solution of a particular problem. The proposition "this is a diamond," for example, enables reasonably safe inference to still other qualities, such as that the "this" in question is not metallic. Under such conditions, a quality becomes a permanently distinguishing *trait* or *character*. Inference thus allows translation of existentially involved qualities into a form in which they can become useful in inference. They are taken as signs of something not present.

Generic propositions, such as "things that are diamonds are among the things that glass cannot scratch" are expressions of relations among kinds. Rather than proposing that something is one instance of a certain kind, as do singular propositions, generic propositions propose membership of one kind in another, more inclusive kind. Dewey's point here is not simply to construct a taxonomy of types of propositions. His point is rather to demonstrate how different types of propositions function differently within inquiry in ways that render judgment possible.

Generic propositions widen the scope of inference. They enable inference from traits of one kind to traits of another. And even more importantly, they provide the logical grounds for singular propositions. To say that something is one of a certain kind is unintelligible in the absence of a further condition, namely that "there are other kinds related to the one specified" [LW12:294].

Unlike generic propositions, which are existential, *universal* propositions are conceptual. They formulate possible actions which may or may not be executed. As such, they do not even pretend to have direct existential import; they are instead relevant to inquiry *into* existence [LW12:303]. Here, as elsewhere, grammatical form may be misleading. The term "all" (and its correlate "anything") may indicate an existential relationship between the terms of an existential proposition that expresses a high level of probability, such as is the case with "All diamonds are crystals." On the other hand, it may express "a necessary relation which follows, by definition, from analysis of a conception" [LW12:296], such as is grammatically more evident in the form "if anything is a diamond then it is a crystal." In the first case, the proposal is generic because it concerns existential singulars of a certain kind (this diamond, that diamond, and so forth) as belonging to a more inclusive kind. In the second case, the proposal concerns relations between meanings which may or may not have to do with existential affairs. If all diamonds were to disappear, and all crystals too, we might still (theoretically) make such a judgment. Universal propositions express meanings in terms of a system of related meanings. Rather than asserting existential relations, they advance procedures for finding out certain things about existential affairs. Generic and universal propositions are thus what Dewey calls "conjugate." They interact as partners within a sequence of inquiry, as inquiry moves back and forth between them.

Universal propositions exhibit *implication*. After qualities experienced as existentially involved with one another have been taken as traits and characters (by means of the formulation of singular and generic propositions and in ways relevant to the inquiry at hand), such traits and characters may be further abstracted. "This is a diamond" becomes a dependable sign of other, conjoined characteristics, such as "this is a crystal." Alternatively, "if anything is a diamond then it is a crystal." Once abstracted in this manner, what formerly functioned as a trait or character, allowing reasonably secure inference, is then termed a *property*.

Whereas existential things or qualities are *involved*, and whereas the determination of a thing as one of a certain kind is a matter of *inference*, fully abstracted (non-existential) properties are related as signs within a given conceptual system by means of *implication*. As Dewey notes, however, such systems do not come to us "from the blue." They are "evolved and explicitly formulated in terms of conditions set by the need of dealing with actual cases of human action" [LW12:278].

Dewey recognizes two logical types of universal propositions: those that may have quasi or limited existential import, and those that have no existential import. An example of a universal proposition of the first type is Newton's law of gravitation. Even though it relates abstract characters such as mass and distance, Dewey tells us, it is "framed with reference to the possibility of ultimate existential application [and so] the contents are affected by that intent. Such hypothetical universals do not exhaust the possible existential affairs to which they may be applied, and as a consequence *may* have to be abandoned in favor of other hypothetical universals which are more adequate or appropriate to the subject at hand. This is illustrated by the change from the Newtonian law of gravitation to the Einsteinian formulation" [LW12:395].

A second type of universal proposition is illustrated by a mathematical formulation. The proposition "2+2=4" is purely a relation of meanings within a constructed system of meanings, and is therefore free of any "privileged interpretation" [LW12:395]. Technically speaking, it has no extrasystemic reference whatsoever.

One final logical relation needs to be discussed. In addition to involvement, inference, and implication, ordered logical discourse includes what Dewey calls "*reference.*" As opposed to the logical formalists, Dewey thought that the point of inquiry is to settle existential difficulties. He therefore thought that the "excursus" into deliberation that involves the manipulation of conceptual material, that is, the determination of implicatory relations between signs within universal propositions, needs to be completed and complemented by a "recursus" that brings the results of such abstract thinking back down to the existentially doubtful situation that originated the particular sequence of inquiry in question. This is possible because of the conjugate relation between universal and generic propositions. In other words, symbol relations utilized in inquiry may have *reference* to existential affairs. The point of inquiry, it should be recalled, is to reorder involvement relations in such a way that a problematic situation is brought to a final resolution in terms of a judgment that carries warranted assertibility. It is also interesting to note that whereas standard treatments of logic tend to *start out* with reference, claiming that the subject term of a proposition has determinate reference, Dewey's theory of inquiry *ends up* with determinate reference, namely as a name for how the results of inquiry are applied to and checked against existential affairs. Reference is thus for Dewey a relation within inquiry as it comes to a close, and not something separate from inquiry that initiates it.

Inquiry as Social

Given that he characterized propositions as being of two types, namely those that are existential and those that are conceptual, Dewey recognized that his readers might wonder which comes first: the constitution of abstract meaning relations in discourse, or the constitution of existential significance relations. His answer to this question has two parts. First, because the existential and conceptual propositions work together as conjugate aspects of inquiry, he suggests that the question remains "rhetorical." He thus emphasizes what I have called the "excursus" and "recursus" movements within inquiry. As he puts it, the

> ability to treat things as signs would not go far did not symbols enable us to mark and retain just the qualities of things which are the ground of inference. Without, for example, words or symbols that discriminate and hold on to the experienced qualities of sight and smell that constitute a thing "smoke," thereby enabling it to serve as a sign of fire, we might react to the qualities in question in animal-like fashion and perform activities appropriate to them. But no inference could be made that was not blind and blundering. Moreover, since *what* is inferred, namely fire, is not present in observation, any anticipation that could be formed of it would be vague and indefinite, even supposing an anticipation could occur at all." [LW12:61-62]

Even if the question of priority is "rhetorical," however, it leads to a consideration that is itself quite fruitful. The context in which these conjugate aspects of inquiry work together is profoundly social both in origin and in import. The fact that existential things have signifying power is not a fact of nature per se, but a fact of a culture which supervenes upon it. Communication, which includes all the aspects of inquiry so far described in this essay, is the result of conjoint activities—both cooperative and competitive—among reflective beings. Culture is thus both a condition and a product of language [LW12:62].

Inquiry promotes cooperation among reflective organisms because it allows them to "rehearse" or try out activities before making a final irretrievable commitment to some overt action. At a very primitive level, the threatening gesture supplants and obviates the attack. At a higher level of organization, two friends "talk over" some disagreement rather than risking a rupture of their relationship. At a still more sophisticated level, complex political and economic plans of action are deliberated by a democratic electorate and orderly change ensues. These are among the developmental stages of inquiry. As Dewey puts it, "the habit of reasoning once instituted is capable of indefinite development on its own account. The ordered development of meanings in their relations to one another may become an engrossing interest. When this happens, implicit logical conditions are made explicit and then logical theory of some sort is born" [LW12:63].

It should by now be clear that Dewey rejected the notion of inquiry as an end in itself, and he also rejected the notion of the theory of inquiry (logic) as a strictly formal discipline complete in itself and devoid of relevance to the affairs of daily life. It was for these reasons that he thought that the next great scientific-technological revolution, if it should occur, will involve advances in the social sciences. Inquiry, and the theory of inquiry, were in Dewey's view among the most important tools at our disposal for learning to live together in ways that take into account the constraints of our environing conditions, as well as the full range of human needs and aspirations.

Notes

1.   William James, *Pragmatism* (Cambridge, Mass.: Harvard University Press, 1975), pp. 63–64.

2.   See, for example, Alonzo Church, *Introduction to Mathematical Logic*, vol. 1 (Princeton, N.J.: Princeton University Press, 1956), pp. 26–27.

10 John Dewey's Pragmatist Feminism
Charlene Haddock Seigfried

Making a Case for Pragmatist Feminist Philosophy

There can be little doubt that pragmatist philosophy in general and Dewey's philosophy in particular are not part of the impoverished tradition of discourse that feminists criticize. It is not among those philosophies that can "talk about the power of reason but not about the power of empathy," that can talk about rational knowledge but not the understanding brought about by a sense of compassion, one that robs feeling of any rationality. It fulfills Phyllis Rooney's call for a way to speak "about experience as embodied humans," and it answers the feminist need for "an empowering reason, one that doesn't require an opposing force over which it needs to gain transcendence."[1]

Dewey's political activism included support for the many women's issues for which feminists were campaigning at the time, including women's suffrage, women's right to higher education and coeducation, unimpeded access to and legalization of birth control, and just wages and worker control of the conditions of work for women as well as men. Explicit references in his philosophical writings to issues as they differentially affect women or to feminist theory are sporadic but insightful and consistently supportive even when critical of some feminist approaches in favor of others. His feminist perspective is surprisingly consistent with his pragmatism. It is surprising given the widespread lack of congruence of most philosophers' theories of rationality and human nature with their claims about race, ethnicity, class, and women that has been explored and documented in decades of feminist research.

Pragmatist theory itself provides strong resources for feminist thinking since many of its positions address current feminist interests and debates. Among these are a pluralism and perspectivism that go beyond theory to advocate the actual inclusiveness of appropriately diverse viewpoints, in-

cluding those of class, color, ethnicity, and gender, as a precondition for resolving problematic situations, whether these involve political, economic,
epistemological, or ethical issues. This position unites earlier feminist interests in nonhierarchical leadership styles and belief in "a woman's voice"
with more recent recognitions of the diversity of women and the complexity of multiple identities besides gender, as well as commitments to "let-
ting the subaltern speak." The pragmatist understanding of the developmental processes that characterize persons who dynamically interact
with their physical and social environments dissolves a knot of problems
evident in controversies over feminist standpoint theories as well as over
the oscillation between affirming the individual subject as a unique
Promethean entity or as a passive social construct.

The complex and nuanced understanding of experience and its role in
questions of understanding and inquiry that informs Dewey's rejection
of the epistemological turn opens a whole new approach to questions of
knowledge and reality. His explanation of the interactive character of experience, as both passive and active, subjective and objective, provides a
way for feminists to escape from false dualisms generated by the contemporary tendency to reduce philosophy to epistemology and sharply demar-
cate a privileged realm of theory from its applications in the real world.
The unproductive debate between realism and interpretivism can be ignored. We do not have to defend either a version of empiricist epistemology in order to objectively ground claims about women in reality or a version of postmodernist deconstruction of truth and assumption of the
self-referentiality of texts in order to recognize the subjective character of
understanding, the denial of which has contributed to rejecting the validity of women's experiences and perspectives.

On the other hand, the wealth of feminist scholarship about the explicit and implicit role of gender at every level of social, cultural, economic, political, religious, and intellectual organization enriches, critiques,
and transforms pragmatist theories. Dewey's conversion of a commitment
to social democracy into an emancipatory agenda that affects all aspects
of human individual and social development becomes more robust and effective insofar as it takes into account the barriers to inclusiveness exposed
in feminist research on racism, classism, sexism, and homophobia. He recognized that democracy can only work where there is faith in individuals
as unique resources and not in the superior insights of elites who claim
privileged access to reality. Individuals develop and flourish as persons
only in interaction with others in society. He showed how these insights, in

turn, require a changed conception of intelligence that is really a changed psychology, one which demonstrates that autonomy cannot develop except in situations of interdependence and that learning requires attention to the ways that those around us use things that lead to anticipated outcomes. It also signals a rejection of the model of truth as correspondence and as a function of a priori deduction and the development instead of a model of sympathetic inquiry into actually problematic conditions leading to desired outcomes. The democratic ideal Dewey seeks, which is the recognition that the achievement by individuals of their own freedom and prosperity requires the achievement of these goals by all, "in a fraternally organized society," cannot be obtained without the conscious articulation of the genuinely modern tendencies that inform the situation in which we find ourselves [MW4:39–40].

Although he analyzed many of these tendencies in his later writings, in 1908 Dewey said that such insight into the current conditions of life had not yet been satisfactorily achieved and that until it had been the ethics that characterizes our lives also remained undescribed [MW4:40]. Feminist philosophers have made great strides in the exploration of the concrete contexts influencing philosophical reflection. They have shown how unexamined assumptions of sexual, racial, and class superiority have distorted claims about reality and adversely affected the lives and opportunities of exploited members of society. They have consequently not escaped criticism from those who imagine that they themselves express a view from nowhere and who therefore severely criticize feminist theory for developing just such analyses of current cultural, economic, and political situations and for showing how the unanalyzed assumptions informing these various ways of life bias philosophical thinking.[2]

Because Dewey's philosophy was also concerned with concrete human experience in both its specificity and generality, he also had to defend himself against those who "seem to accept a dogma of immaculate conception of philosophical systems" and think it "derogatory to link a body of philosophic ideas to the social life and culture of their epoch" [LW6:17]. Pragmatist philosophy as envisioned and practiced by Dewey is therefore continued, deepened, and expanded by those feminist theorists who link knowledge with action, who take the goal of thinking to be emancipation, who recognize the multiple conditions that affect understanding, who demonstrate how a disembodied rationality distorts rather than reveals the world in which we find ourselves, who recognize the interpretive character of experience and who therefore deflate claims about the nature of reality as such and develop instead morally responsible intellectual criteria for adjudicating specific claims about particular realities.

The First Generations of Feminist Pragmatists

In 1949 in *The Second Sex* Simone de Beauvoir argued that one reason women did not organize themselves to dispute male sovereignty was that they had no past, no history, no solidarity of work and interest comparable to that of the proletariat. But in the same book she began to recover just such a past, as had Jane Addams in *The Long Road of Women's Memory*, written more than thirty years earlier.[3] There is now evidence that earlier generations of women studying pragmatist philosophy found resources in it for their own emancipation and that women contributed to pragmatist theory and practice. Even before Dewey moved to Chicago and inaugurated a pragmatist school of thought, Addams had invited him to be on the board of directors of the Hull House Settlement that she and Ellen Gates Starr founded, and they worked together to counter the civic and industrial exploitation of immigrants flooding into Chicago at the turn of the century. They collaborated in settlement work, in discussion, and they read each other's books.

The first generations of women to study pragmatist philosophy found two aspects of it particularly empowering. One was the pragmatist principle that theory arises from experience and is accountable to it. This changed the subject matter of philosophy from continued rehearsals of the works of generations long dead and the formalism of problem solving based on purely logical considerations to concern with "the perplexities, the troubles, and the issues of the period in which a philosophy arises" [LW6:17]. The changed focus also allowed them to trust their own experiences as a starting point for reflection even when they contradicted the received views of the time. The other principle was that the purpose of inquiry into experience was not to replicate it, but to interrogate problematic situations in order to satisfactorily resolve them. Not all resolutions are satisfactory because not all fulfill Dewey's criterion of a consummatory experience, that is, one which is the fulfillment of our being in interaction with the conditions of existence, a temporary state of harmony which is at the same time the beginning of further enriching interactions.[4] Because experience is a transaction between organisms and their physical and social environment, such resolutions are a means of growth for the self as well as a means of transforming oppressive situations into liberating ones.

Pragmatism's experimental method undermines the conservatism that seeks to preserve old standards despite changing conditions. According to Dewey: "What is needed is intelligent examination of the consequences that are actually effected by inherited institutions and customs, in order that there may be intelligent consideration of the ways in which they are to be intentionally modified in behalf of generation of different consequences" [LW4:218]. Women of many different ethnic groups and classes, and other minorities whose lives were severely circumscribed by convention and who bore the brunt of sexist, ethnic and racial prejudices, found a powerful resource in a philosophical position that questioned rather than justified convention and whose goal was transformation of given conditions to better meet the just needs of individuals and communities. Through reflections on the consequences for thinking of the Darwinian evolutionary model, pragmatists understood that a metaphysics of being could no longer be defended once the pervasiveness of temporality was acknowledged. To succeed in understanding things as they are, for example, requires a prior examination of how they came to be and is continuous with interest in how they will turn out. Accurate anticipation of outcomes that we have helped to bring about, not accuracy of representation, is the goal of knowledge.

But what did women bring to their reflections that derived from and challenged their particular situation? Lucy Sprague Mitchell is one example of a female undergraduate who has left evidence that her experiences were at odds with what she was hearing in the philosophy classroom. I first came across her name in my efforts to discover whether I, as a woman for whom pragmatism was an invaluable resource for developing feminist theory and practice, had any predecessors. Higher education for women was still the exception rather than the rule when Mitchell entered the class of 1900 at the Harvard Annex, the forerunner of Radcliffe College. She studied with William James, Josiah Royce, George Santayana, Hugo Munsterberg, and George Palmer and was the only one in her class to receive Honors in Philosophy. I was not surprised to learn that in an essay written for Royce she had rejected the knower as isolated subject because it was solipsistic and argued instead for a relational self. But I was intrigued by her rejection of free will in another paper. Recognizing that her belief in determinism was in fundamental disagreement with both Royce's and Palmer's beliefs, she also denied that reality was ultimately benevolent and rational, and asserted instead that "the reality of evil and disappointment" was one of her "strongest beliefs."[5]

Mitchell, who became a lifelong friend of John Dewey, had already met him, his wife, Alice, and Jane Addams in Chicago, read all of John Dewey's writings on education, avidly followed Addams's work, and later attended Dewey's lectures at Teachers College, Columbia University. I do not know whether the positions expressed in her undergraduate essays continued into her pioneering work in higher education for women and in progressive education, but her youthful sense of being determined by conditions over which she exercised little control and her recognition of the pervasiveness of evil and disappointment do not reflect the optimistic meliorism associated with pragmatist philosophy. They are more characteristic of the experiences of marginalized members of society whose choices are severely circumscribed and who bear the brunt of adverse social, economic, and physical conditions. Mitchell was privileged by her upper-class status and wealth but was still subject to the limitations imposed by patriarchal traditions of family life. She suffered from tuberculosis throughout her college years and after graduation, although chronically ill herself, assumed her role as dutiful daughter and cared for her mother until she died of tuberculosis and then continued to care for her ill and despotic father.

The sense of frustration she experienced growing up under continuous constraint in an authoritarian household and in deferring her own goals to meet the needs of others jars with the meliorism, creative possibility, and openness to the future characteristic of pragmatist philosophy. Her situation, like that of W. E. B. Du Bois, who studied philosophy at Harvard a decade earlier than Mitchell, illustrates the disruptive changes of attitude, tone, and subject-matter evident when pragmatism is approached from the perspectives of those differently positioned by gender, race, and/ or class from the norm. In Du Bois's 1890 commencement speech, for example, he says that "to say that a nation is in the way of civilization is a contradiction in terms and a system of human culture whose principle is the rise of one race on the ruins of another is a farce and a lie."[6] White commentators were predisposed to label such viewpoints "bitter" and to resent their militancy.[7] But such sentiments expose the limitations of their awareness of the unjust relations endemic in American society. Their lack of understanding of the suffering caused by racism unwittingly reveals their privileged positions as whites. Such marginalized perspectives as

Mitchell and Du Bois express, though, are not necessarily opposed to the hopeful tone of the pragmatist faith in reconstruction. If anything, such an emancipatory agenda can resonate with particular force for those traditionally excluded or oppressed, as Mitchell acknowledged when she said that Dewey freed her from her father's patriarchal attitudes and as is evident in Du Bois's calls for a social democracy.[8]

Prejudice, Alienation, and Oppression

Of central importance for a feminist interpretation of Dewey is the determination of whether he recognized and censured sexual, class, and racial discrimination and of whether his pragmatist philosophy can accommodate marginalized persons and alienated perspectives. What resources has it to offer in overcoming such alienation and discrimination and changing the social, economic, and political conditions that have brought them about? Over the years Dewey's political writings became increasingly radicalized in response to continued warfare, the Great Depression, the intransigence of entrenched economic and political forces, and the growing virulence of public discourse. But all his writings show an awareness of the negative effects of past unjust beliefs and practices and a desire to develop the resources needed for everyone, but especially those presently excluded, to overcome these obstacles and to be enabled to contribute to a better future for themselves and others.

Dewey argues that reflective thinking begins with the existential situation of everyday experience. He deliberately seeks to undermine the prevailing practice of philosophizing in a vacuum, as though rationality was a characteristic of disembodied minds unaffiliated with others and unaffected by society. He coins the term *body-minds* to emphasize that feeling plays an essential role in human understanding. Because we have the capacity of feeling, our responses to natural and social environments are selective. Our susceptibility to the useful and harmful in our surroundings eventuates in anticipation of consequences and intelligent foresight. Feelings, therefore, reveal and direct us toward objective features of experience. They are also affected by past experiences and beliefs: "Comfort or discomfort, fatigue or exhilaration, implicitly sum up a history . . . whereby . . . the past can be unravelled and made explicit" [LW1:197]. Such feelings reveal more than a particular individual's personal history because "experience is already overlaid and saturated with the products of the reflection of past generations and by-gone ages" [LW1:40]. Even experiences which seem uniquely one's own are filled with inherited interpretations.

Selective bias in interactions with social and physical environments is inevitable, which is why "philosophy is a critique of prejudices" [LW1:40]. None of us escapes bias because "interest, as the subjective, is after all equivalent to individuality or uniqueness" [LW6:15]. To be a person, an individual center of action, is to uniquely undergo and actively apprehend the world of which one is a part. These undergoings and doings are expressions of a history, habits, and perspectives.[9] Critical reflection is needed in order to determine whether these inherited interpretations, welded onto the genuine materials of firsthand experience, will eventuate in a fuller and richer grasp of our situation or will impoverish it through distortion. One great task of philosophy, therefore, is to emancipate us from prejudice [LW1:40]. Dewey's pragmatist philosophy is thus allied with other emancipatory theories such as feminism that aim at exposing prejudices and that work to empower the oppressed.

But although his analyses reveal the ubiquity of unconscious biases, some of which are helpful and some of which are harmful, Dewey nevertheless thinks that "deliberate insincerity and hypocrisy are rare" [LW4:224]. What seems to be hypocrisy is more often a reflection of the difficulty we have in consistently integrating theory and practice, attitudes and responses [LW4:224]. His lack of suspicion of the motives of others leads him to underestimate the extent and depth of misogyny, racism, homophobia, and classism in personal habits and societal institutions and to neglect the development of an account of the more irrational sides of human understanding and use of power. This has paradoxical results for his analysis of feminist issues. On the one hand, Dewey's realization that selective interest plays a necessary role in our ability to organize our experiences satisfactorily, even when the organization is intellectual, motivates him to develop a methodology of inquiry that takes such bias into account. Recognizing that we cannot achieve impartiality merely by wanting to do so, he makes inclusiveness of others in decision-making processes a condition of objectivity. It is not just morally wrong to refuse to include in deliberations that affect their lives those members of society that are believed to be inferior. It is also an intellectual fallacy to suppose that limiting points of view to those of an intellectual elite would more adequately achieve the objectivity expressed in the resolution of problematic situations than a more inclusive approach would. Dewey also makes emancipation from prejudice a central concern of pragmatist philosophy and a necessary part of the steps needed to accomplish its goal of reconstructing society.

On the other hand, once having recognized the sources of oppression in the intention of ruling elites to preserve their power and after demonstrating the negative effects this has had both in theory and practice, he fails to follow through with an account of the role that power plays in human affairs. He seems curiously uninterested in accounting for the virulence of prejudice and its persistence or in exploring in detail how it alters the lives of those affected by it. By locating conflicts in different approaches to life and not in struggles for power, he frequently underestimates what is required to overcome them. He seems to think that once someone has participated in a rational process of inquiry, she or he would not persist in holding onto prejudices or unilateral power. I am not claiming that he ignores the forces opposing personal and societal liberation—quite the contrary—but only that his analyses often do not go far enough. He sometimes attributes stubborn intransigence to the force of habit which tends to conserve and reinforce traditional models of behavior long after they have ceased to be intellectually justified. He consistently links the traditional dualisms which still distort contemporary philosophical reflections to the origins of philosophy in an ancient Greek ruling class whose leisure was secured through slave labor. He therefore seeks to dismantle the assumptions through which such oppressive beliefs continue their hold on us, but does not address the means by which the ruling power was secured in the first place. At other times he locates the source of oppression in capitalist economics. He holds that the deliberate rejection of moral standards as the basis of economic decision making in industrialized countries is responsible for the unjust state of affairs in which we find ourselves. He also blames moral philosophers for placing economic considerations "on a lower level than either morals or politics." They make a great mistake because "the life which men, women and children actually lead, the opportunities open to them, the values they are capable of enjoying, their education, their share in all the things of art and science, are mainly determined by economic conditions" [LW4:225].

He does not, however, pursue the sources of oppression far enough to reflect on why the need to develop and consolidate one's own power is so often understood as requiring denying it to others. And in his conscientious concern with the plight of those who are unjustly treated and strenuous efforts to overcome case after case of specific instances of injustice, he seldom exhibits the anger and angst characteristic of those who practically suffer from bigotry and therefore he does not convey the urgency of their situation. The initial optimism I felt when first coming across references to women's subordination in hitherto unsuspected places in Dewey's writings was often followed by a feeling of disappointment that the examples were used to illustrate some other point and were not introduced in order to deepen a feminist analysis. In *Democracy and Education*, for example, he criticizes Aristotle's theoretical separation of the practical and the intellectual because such a metaphysical position legitimates and extends an unequal and unjust social order [MW9:260–70]. He attributes Aristotle's hierarchical dualism to the fact that he wrote when most men and all women were stuck in menial labor and were used as mere means for the intellectual ends of others. Dewey's explicit goal is to promote social democracy and the educational practices and theory necessary to achieve it. He therefore encourages the development of a curriculum that uses intelligence and theory as "a guide of free practice *for all*." Both his genealogical account of the origin of the separation of theory and practice in the inequalities of class and gender and his liberatory intent to transform education to be inclusive are feminist positions worth developing. They are insufficient, however, insofar as they fail to name the patriarchal appropriation of slave and women's labor as one of exploitation or oppression or to follow up by exploring how the working classes and women are affected by such oppression. Such explicit analyses are necessary in order for his recommendations for overcoming the illicit separation of theory and practice to be effective.

These strengths and weaknesses are illustrated in two talks Dewey gave in which he directly addressed issues of discrimination, one concerning the plight of blacks and the other supporting women's suffrage. In an "Address to the National Association for the Advancement of Colored People" in 1932, Dewey recognizes the greater discrimination and suffering that blacks endure in the midst of the Great Depression, but he thinks this is a quantitative rather than a qualitative difference [LW6:224–30]. He says to them that blacks as a group have doubtless

> suffered more than any other, more keenly, more intensely. Doubtless you are the first, on the whole, to lose employment and the last to be taken on. You are quite likely the last to get an equal opportunity to share in whatever measures of relief or constructive public work, to tide over the depression, undertaken. But none the less, the causes from which all are suffering are the same. [LW6:225]

Like Marx, he thinks that economics is the basic cause of both racism and classism, that those in control politically and economically consolidate their power through encouraging suspicion and divisiveness among the working-class poor. The solution is coalition building among all minority groups who should break with both national parties and start a third party "which will help bring about a social and economic reconstruction in the interest of a society which is cooperative and human" [LW6:230]. With the end of economic slavery, all other forms of slavery will also be overcome.

This blindness to the virulence of racial prejudice—exacerbated no doubt by the severe economic crisis—makes Dewey's analysis of the problem and suggestions for resolving it less effective than they could be. Dewey says to the NAACP audience: "I submit to you the thing I would submit to any white group that is also at a disadvantage, since your fundamental difficulties do not come through color or any other one thing" [LW6:229-30]. But he then says that they *are* due to one thing: "Why were you kept in slavery except for economic reasons? What was slavery except a manifestation of the motive for private gain? Why is it that the denial of civil liberty, of cultural equality still continues, except as an aftermath of that economic oppression from which you once suffered?" This economic aftermath is so devastating because of its emphasis on competition: "What is the economic order in which we live today excepting one of competition? Fundamentally, the disadvantages, or the inequalities—civil, political, and cultural,—of the colored group, of every under-privileged group in this country, exist because we are living in a competitive order which, because it is competitive, has to set man against man, brother against brother, group against group" [LW6:229].

He denies that racism is the fundamental problem for blacks, attributing the cause of slavery, persecution, and the denial of civil liberties to capitalistic economic oppression. He contends that "those who want the greatest profits and those who want the monopoly, power, influence, that money gives, can get it only by creating suspicion, dislike and division among the mass of the people." They secure their own power by setting disadvantaged groups against each other. He recognizes that blacks have been discriminated against more than others, but thinks that they only suffer to a more intense degree what all laboring groups suffer. The depression has thus disclosed a community of interest among all the minority and oppressed groups of the country, but they have not yet realized that they suffer from a common victimization. Only a coalition of minority and disadvantaged groups can effectively challenge the entrenched political and economic powers. "A cooperative economic and social order is the only kind of order in which there will be a genuine possibility for equality among human beings irrespective of race, color and creed, and of the other things which are now played upon to divide people in order that a few may have a monopoly of privilege, power and influence" [LW6:230].

I concur that a cooperative economic social order that breaks the monopoly of privilege and power would be a powerful means for blacks to advance on many levels. I also agree with Dewey's condemnation of capitalistic exploitation and with his stress on the importance of subjugated groups joining together to fight oppression. But the economic position of blacks by itself does not begin to address the question of why they are feared and despised as well as discriminated against in jobs and housing, why they are the last hired and the first fired, why they are most often at the bottom of the heap in any competitive situation, or why they are scapegoated for crimes and general social unrest. Coalition building among disadvantaged groups is a valuable means for successfully opposing entrenched political and economic power, but it is unlikely to go forward in an atmosphere of hate and discrimination.

In another political forum Dewey shares Addams's belief that the strongest argument for women's suffrage is that it is necessary to complete the democratic movement. He says in "A Symposium on Woman's Suffrage" in 1911 that unless it is completed, the evils due to the imperfect state of democracy will be attributed to democracy itself [MW6:153–54]. In answer to four questions addressed to each of the symposiasts, he says that it is reactionary to put limits, such as moral or property restrictions, on women's access to the vote. He clearly rejects any double standard in morality by arguing that since men's moral standard does not affect their right to vote, then neither should women's. And property restrictions only strengthen the strong influence on government already wielded by those with economic power. "It is the masses—the poor—that most need the protection of the ballot" [MW6:153]. As Du Bois also forcefully argues in regard to blacks in *The Dusk of Dawn*, literacy tests are likewise irrelevant in determining social and political intelligence.

Dewey does not think that militant methods are necessary to secure women's suffrage in America, and therefore it would not be wise to use them. English political life, by contrast, does not make changes except under great pressure and under those conditions "women certainly needed some way of demonstrating that they were in earnest" [MW6:154]. This analysis does not take into account why granting votes to women, an extension of the franchise that is so obviously in keeping with the democratic principles Americans profess, was so fiercely resisted for so long in America, or why women should patiently continue to use tactics year after year that were obviously not succeeding. A glimpse of what women were up against can be gathered from a few incidents out of many in the years following Dewey's remarks, such as the brewers' complicity in the brazen vote counting fraud in the 1912 suffrage referendum in Michigan, a vote against suffrage that was not overturned "despite tremendous public uproar and attempts by the Governor to insure a fair count"; the near riot caused by a suffrage parade organized by Alice Paul, Crystal Eastman, Mary Beard, and others the day before Woodrow Wilson's inauguration in which troops of cavalry and a protecting wall formed by male student volunteers from Maryland Agricultural College were needed to enable the marchers to make their way through a hostile, jeering crowd; and Carrie Chapman Catt's 1916 report to the board of the National American Woman Suffrage Association that "the first anti-suffrage organization of importance to be effected in the South has been formed in Alabama with the slogan: 'Home Rule, States Rights, and White Supremacy.' "[10]

In these and in other writings Dewey does consistently argue against the subjugation of women, racial or ethnic and other minorities, and the working class, and for their emancipation and full participation in society. He thinks that these goals can be accomplished through rational persuasion, coalition building, a willingness to use the experimental method, and when all these fail, to overt resistance, such as strikes and public pressure. What is needed to complete his analyses and proposals is a more penetrating account of the sources of inherited prejudice and motivations for beliefs ranging from indifference, to distrust, derision, and violent antipathy toward select groups of people. Since he also believes that agitation and confrontations, especially violent ones, expose a breakdown of communicative inquiry, he also ignores the issue of how to resolve conflicts when those in more powerful positions stubbornly persist in suppressing others. He does recognize that violence can take more subtle forms and that the use of even overt violence can be effectively hidden by those in power to make it look as if confrontation is always the fault of those protesting a misuse of authority. But this recognition does not lead him to revise his theory concerning problematic situations or his methods of resolution.

Perhaps there is no way to persuade those who willingly use force to impose their will on others to stop doing so, except by a more powerful counterforce. Dewey seemed to concede as much when he gave up his pacifism in the face of the enormity of the attack on peoples and nations and the failure of the institutional safeguards of freedom in the two World Wars. He was keenly aware of the horrible price to be paid in settling disputes by force, however, and returns again and again to the question of what needs to be done in the present in order to stave off such confrontations in the future. In doing so, he joins Addams in developing a pacifist feminist model of resistance to the brute use of force to settle disputes as well as a positive program of what should be done to avoid the need or expectation of violence as a legitimate recourse. Women who are victims of domestic violence, blacks, homosexuals, lesbians, and others in society who undergo unprovoked assaults, have, if anything, a greater stake in peaceful resolutions of conflicts as long as their just demands are met. But they also need to be heard and their causes recognized, and this often involves violent opposition by the forces of the status quo which are oppressing them. Dewey thinks that conflicts of all sorts arise through the alienation of others and that the democratic spirit requires breaking down the barriers that divide us into opposing groups. "To take as far as possible every conflict which arises—and they are bound to arise—out of the atmosphere and medium of force, of violence as a means of settlement into that of discussion and of intelligence is to treat those who disagree—even profoundly— with us as those from whom we may learn, and in so far, as friends" [LW14:228]. This is indeed a worthy ideal, but what recourse do subjugated groups have when those who disagree with them are implacable foes?

Dewey's philosophy took a more radical turn because of the threat to the survival of democratic forms of government by the totalitarian regimes of fascist Germany and Japan in the Second World War. Unlike many other intellectuals of his time, he did not embrace jingoistic nationalism and instead took the unpopular position that such "America First" movements expressed the very same attitudes that produced the totalitarianism they were supposedly repudiating. Rather than use the popular revulsion stirred up against enemies in Europe and the Far East to engage in chauvinistic self-congratulation and the stifling of dissent, Dewey warned that the same factors that led to the loss of freedoms abroad were already at work in America. He repudiated the identification of democracy with economic individualism, which actually undermines the will to work together, the essence of cooperation. Uncoerced cooperation as the intent to link one's own well-being with the well-being of all others is central to Dewey's theory of social democracy, which is based on two premises: (1) belief in the potentialities of every human being "irrespective of race, color, sex, birth and family, of material or cultural wealth" and (2) the need for providing conditions that will enable these potentialities to be realized [LW14:226].

In the face of totalitarian threats to democracy Dewey therefore calls for strengthening and deepening these two fundamental positions. In doing so, he begins developing a more acute account of prejudice as an obstacle to his ideal of participatory democracy. He points out that

> to denounce Naziism for intolerance, cruelty and stimulation of hatred amounts to fostering insincerity if, in our personal relations to other persons, if, in our daily walk and conversation, we are moved by racial, color or other class prejudice; indeed, by anything save a generous belief in their possibilities as human beings, a belief which brings with it the need for providing conditions which will enable these capacities to reach fulfillment. [LW14:226-27]

Merely verbal expressions of one's allegiance to democracy remain sentimental unless put into practice every day and are no protection against intolerance and using others for one's own gain. Dewey specifically singles out the evils of racism and anti-Semitism, in addition to classism: "Our anti-democratic heritage of Negro slavery has left us with habits of intolerance toward the colored race—habits which belie profession of democratic loyalty." And he points out that religion has too often been used to foster anti-Semitism before concluding that "there are still many, too many, persons who feel free to cultivate and express racial prejudices as if they were within their personal rights, not recognizing how the attitude of intolerance infects, perhaps fatally as the example of Germany so surely proves, the basic humanities without which democracy is but a name" [LW14:277]. In a 1940 essay, "Contrary to Human Nature" [LW14:258-61], Dewey demonstrates that his appeal to habit as the vehicle of prejudice does not necessarily preclude unmasking and condemning the role of power in societal relations. In this more radical side of Dewey's examination of the place of habit in human development, he shows how those whose power is entrenched not only subjugate others but entice them to collude in their own subjection.

Feminist analyses of misogyny, homophobia, and racism would complement these accounts by calling attention to specific issues that need to be addressed if the effort to develop persons who are sufficiently tolerant and concerned for the welfare of others that they will not resort to violence to settle disputes is to succeed. Charlotte Perkins Gilman, W. E. B. Du Bois,

Jane Addams, and Alain Locke certainly recognized the importance of dealing with these issues and began the process of deepening and expanding Dewey's pragmatist account.

Dewey's Pragmatist Feminist Theory

Neither females nor males, nor isolated individuals make up the basic unit of existence or theory for pragmatists, but concretely interrelated persons within a natural and social environment. Because pragmatism takes the active transaction of organisms and environment as the basis of human action, which is specifically characterized as striving for goals, its feminism is perspectival and pluralistic. Rationality has evolved over time as the power to reflect on the results of our actions on the environment and its effects on us. It is the ability to imagine a future different from the present, to anticipate and feel strongly about future as well as present states of affairs, and to retain from present experiences something that will be of value to future experiences. It is, therefore, exhibited in the everyday lives of women as well as men, of the underprivileged as well as the elite, educated classes, and is not reducible to consistency within formal systems. Women's and men's different experiences lead to different perspectives on the world and different values, not because of their biological differences as such, but only as such biological and psychological differences lead to different experiences and only as they are mediated through specific beliefs, customs, value systems, and institutions.

In one of his more radical addresses, "Philosophy and Democracy" (1919), Dewey explicitly uses his pragmatist principle of perspectivism to argue that women's experiences differ significantly enough from men's to affect the philosophies they develop. He says that "women have as yet made little contribution to philosophy. But when women who are not mere students of other persons' philosophy set out to write it, we cannot conceive that it will be the same in viewpoint or tenor as that composed from the standpoint of the different masculine experience of things" [MW11:45]. He also argues in "Context and Thought" [LW6:20–21] that such differing standpoints will exhibit the limitations as well as the strengths of their points of view and need to be corrected by listening to and interacting with others differently situated. In two letters written to Scudder Klyce in 1915 and 1920, Dewey developed further his views of male domination and women's perspectives.

He criticizes Klyce for claiming that women, as a class, have been restricted by men and that these restrictions have negatively affected their development without his also recognizing that men must also be analyzed as a class shaped by their privileged position. Klyce's failure to do so shows that he takes men as a standard without realizing how his emotional attachment to a masculine viewpoint distorts his judgment. Women who have theorized from their own experiences have recognized that "men are essentially hogs" because they assume that their own work is the most important thing in the world. Moreover, men do not even recognize their own androcentric viewpoint. Dewey also criticizes Klyce for generalizing from too narrow a base of women. In his own experience of "essentially sane women . . . superior in concrete intelligence" Dewey has been struck by how often they surprise him intellectually in ways that men's reasoning never does. He also says that it is his experience that women's observations are more honest than men's and they are more willing to face the unpleasant facts of life than men are.[11]

Dewey also criticizes Klyce's stereotypical view that men are more courageous than women. Klyce mistakenly compares "men" to "ladies," a manifestly artificial product of societal distinction. The conventional definition of courage is too one-sidedly taken from men's experiences and their self-aggrandizement, and it should be obvious from women's childbearing alone that they exhibit superior courage. Men tend to judge women in aggregate because they do not recognize the same individuality in them that they see in other men. This is partly due to the division of labor between women and men and the restriction of women to subordinate and poorly paid positions. The "enormous handicaps" from which women suffer in the labor market can only be overcome by experiments through which new facts about their abilities and the nature of work will become perceptible. Dewey expects that women's entrance into the professions will humanize them, bringing in an element of service to counteract the present overemphasis on profit. Much more experimentation is needed to show what women's potentialities are. As to the criticism that feminists are too shrill and argumentative, Dewey says the wonder is that there is not more protest. The present unequal division of labor fails to give women an "outlet for their individualized capacities *as* they [are] influenced by sex." Women have never had a chance to decide for themselves what, if any, division of labor they want because men have settled the question for them purely on the basis of anatomy. Dewey says that this statement "is the woman question in a nutshell."[12]

Dewey also points out that society has not considered what women should do with their lives beyond their childbearing years. He admonishes Klyce that he could "learn more from 'even' the extreme feminists than [he has] been willing to do." Just as Jessie Taft had argued in her 1913 dissertation on the Woman's Movement, written for the pragmatist philosophy department at the University of Chicago, Dewey attributes the widespread controversies over women's issues to the displacement of their home-based occupations by the industrial revolution.[13] Women who seek fulfillment outside the home are labeled selfish, but he points out that this judgment is made from the perspective of the "unperceived 'very' *longtime* Selfishness of men."[14]

Dewey's feminism is rooted in a central value of his pragmatism, which is that democracy as a way of life ought to guide all other aspects of philosophical analysis and activities. His interpretation of this value was deeply influenced by Jane Addams.[15] Central to his understanding of social democracy is the rejection of the atomistic individualism of liberal democracy as well as of fixed essences and hierarchies. He affirms instead that every existence is unique and irreplaceable and

> does not exist to illustrate a principle, to realize a universal or to embody a kind or class. . . . In social and moral matters, equality does not mean mathematical equivalence. It means rather the inapplicability of considerations of greater and less, superior and inferior. It means that no matter how great the quantitative differences of ability, strength, position, wealth, such differences are negligible in comparison with something else—the fact of individuality . . . [understood as] the incommensurable in which each speaks for itself and demands consideration on its own behalf. [MW11:52–53]

This uniqueness thrives in interaction with other individuals, so that the tendency to isolation and independence inherent in individuality is dynamically balanced in democracy with fellowship or collegiality, that is, continuity, or "association and interaction without limit." Philosophizing from democratic principles can be judged as all other philosophical perspectives are, by whether it leads to better institutions of life. Pragmatist feminists theorize and act against the prejudices and oppressions that hinder the full participation of all in the life of multiple communities of which they are members. Such participation requires the unhindered development of the capacities of each to freely choose and skillfully carry out their choices in interaction with others who are equally valued.

Specific Feminist Issues

In turning from the general contours of Dewey's pragmatist feminist philosophy to his actual explanations of the problems women face in a society organized around men's perspectives and values and in which men wield disproportionate power, the strengths and weaknesses of his own use of pragmatist feminist theory to interpret experience become more apparent. He positively values women's accomplishments and acknowledges their influence on his theories. As we have seen in his support of enfranchising women, he is not afraid to speak out and work for women's radical causes and against misogyny, just as he consistently attacks racial, ethnic, and class prejudice. But sexism is clearly of lesser concern than is classism and racism and he misses many opportunities to follow through in developing specifically feminist analyses. The assumptions underlying his feminist analyses are sometimes quite radical and at other times moderately liberal or even conventional. The way that his pragmatism informs his feminism can be deduced from two specific issues: how privilege and power are hidden behind appeals to human nature and how women are affected by marriage and motherhood.

Dewey continues a long line of feminist analysis at least as old as Mary Wollstonecraft's 1790 work, *A Vindication of the Rights of Women,* and as new as postmodernist deconstructions of mistakenly essentialized identities when he argues that a frequent ploy for opposing social change is to assert that the proposal goes contrary to human nature. At best, such a defense of the status quo diverts attention from a "critical examination of the actual merits of the proposal in question. . . . At the worst," it is merely "an expression of a strong prejudice clothed in the garb of an idea in order to appear respectable. The use of the idea of the unchangeability of human nature as a means of opposition to special projects for political and economic change belongs in the latter class" [LW14:258]. Appeal is made to traits that happen at the time to be associated with human nature, the very beliefs and habits which are being challenged. Since history shows that reforms have always had to overcome the "opposition of habits entrenched in positions of advantage," it is surprising that appeals to human nature have not lost their force.[16] The inertia of established customs is no argument for the constancy of human nature. People's minds as well as actions are in the grip of habit "and while the tendency is most marked in the case of those who obtain onesided advantage from customs as they exist, it is strong enough to hold in subjection many of those who are put at a dis-advantage by those customs." Both those who opposed the abolition of slavery and those who opposed the enfranchisement of women "used the argument that it was contrary to the very laws of Nature and of Nature's God. Such facts prove how strong is the tendency to use well-established habits as the proper standard and measure of what is natural and unnatu-ral" [LW14:259].

Dewey does not expect that merely exposing the will to power hidden in appeals to a fixed human nature will eliminate its negative consequences because the conception of human nature also reifies and essentializes the conserving force of habit in human behavior. He says that "although the argument from fixity of human nature is but a 'rationalization' of existing habits, including prejudices and onesided interests which have become in-stitutionalized, proponents of social changes have something to learn from it." The first lesson is that the stubborn conservatism of habits means that " 'revolutions' never go as far or as deep as they are supposed to go; it takes time, usually a long time and a succession of partial changes, to carry one through, since carrying it through signifies the establishment of habits which will be as deep-seated and as 'natural' as those which have been dis-placed" [LW14:260]. The second lesson is that features of human nature that are more constant than habits can be appealed to in order to challenge rather than perpetuate the inequities of the present social order. A healthy, vigorous life is such a feature, which the capitalist economic system can be faulted for not meeting. Means must be found for satisfying other basic human needs besides the need for food and health, such as "the need for companionship, for freedom of choice, for rivalry or emulation, for secu-rity, etc." [LW14:261].

Both liberal and radical reformers would be less disillusioned if they recognized that no single prescription for transformation of the social or-der can succeed as its followers expect. This should lead not to discourage-ment, but to more effective efforts that recognize the complexity of the conditions of oppression. Doubtless this makes policy change more diffi-cult to implement, but both history and experience provide evidence that simple solutions, though valuable for energizing reformers and revolution-aries, are bound to fail because they inevitably leave out some of the con-ditions contributing to the oppressive situation.

Another set of feminist issues has to do with sex, marriage, and the fam-ily. In the first decades of the twentieth century in America, prohibitions on the open discussion of women's sexuality contributed to psychological problems and unwanted pregnancies. Dewey supported Margaret Sanger, Charlotte Perkins Gilman, and other feminists who challenged the suppression of sexual information and the prohibition of birth control. In 1928, for example, he protested Mary Ware Dennett's conviction on the charge of sending obscene material through the mails.[17] The supposedly offensive material was an educational pamphlet called *The Sex Side of Life*. In defense of her right to publish on issues of sexuality Dennett responded with *Who's Obscene?* and included Dewey's letter of support in it. Dewey wrote that as both an educator and father of seven children, he welcomed the distribution of *The Sex Side of Life* to parents and youth and condemned its suppression, since there was nothing obscene or indecent in accurate information on sex, but there was in the suppression of such information.

Although Dewey often recognized how patriarchal forms of marriage and family life oppressed women and therefore sought to eliminate their negative effects, he did not always adopt such a feminist perspective. It is mostly absent, for example, in "War's Social Results," written in 1917, in which Dewey made some uncharacteristically utopian predictions about the new social democracy that would emerge after the allied victory of the First World War.[18] He predicts that supply and demand capitalism will be replaced by industrial democracy. The domination of the upper classes will cease and the great amounts of money taken from them for the war effort will continue to be exacted by the state after the war but will instead be spent on the needs of the common people. Although he says that "it is not at all clear what the reign of the hitherto submerged classes will be like," he thinks that the family will undergo a most radical change and may even cease to exist [LW17:23]. Love, marriage, and romance may come to mean very different things than they do in the present. He is not so optimistic about whether these changes will be for the better. He is careful to say, for example, that he is not advocating changing the ideals of marriage or a revolution in sexual morality, but only observing that tremendous changes are on the way. Most of the changes have to do with the diminished role of the father, who was at one time supreme. The change is due primarily to the transition from feudalism to capitalism. Under capitalism the individual, not the family, became the economic unit and it was natural "that children threw off the yoke of patriarchal rule" [LW17:24]. Dewey does not explicitly name women's oppression by patriarchal rule, but he does say that its overthrow is most clearly illustrated in the free selection of marriage partners and the increasing importance of romance.

Marriage, however, was not thereby strengthened but divorce became more common.

According to Dewey, the war has accelerated a new economic epoch and with it has come "three most startling changes in the social status of women." With millions of eligible young men killed or rendered unfit for marriage, women will vastly outnumber men and many cannot expect to find husbands. Even more importantly, "women never had so little use for husbands as they have in France and Germany to-day" [LW17:24]. During the war women took men's jobs and many proved that they were more efficient than men. Having acquired economic power, women were starting to gain political power. They could decide to abdicate in favor of men after the war in order to get husbands, but with little prospect of that for most women, he wonders what they would receive that would cause them to relinquish these gains. Finally, with the great loss of lives, all the nations have advocated childbearing and the states have granted children a right to be born and to be educated. Because the state assumes responsibility for children, fathers and husbands are left with less responsibility than ever. Dewey predicts that changes will occur in morality to fit the new conditions. Exactly what they will be he cannot say except to note that there will be some shifting from the ideals of "marital monopoly."

In this essay Dewey clearly both predicts and supports radical changes in the postwar period. He hopes that a socially responsible industrial democracy will replace the predatory practices of unbridled capitalism and that the lower classes will be emancipated from the control of the upper classes. But his assessment of the results of the emancipation of the submerged class of women is ambiguous. He seems more worried that the status quo will be overturned than confident that a new era in gender relations will emerge that will be beneficial to women and to society in general. His masculinist biases are revealed by the fact that he recognized the great social and economic changes in women's lives brought about by the war but only seems concerned with how such changes will impact on men's lives. He does not emphasize women's newfound economic independence and freedom from patriarchal control in marriage as a necessary step in their emancipation or even call them positive gains. In fact, he distances himself from radical challenges to the institution of marriage and to sexual morality. He is more concerned with the rising divorce rate as a result of the diminishment of the supreme role of the father than he is with its impact on women's subordination.

Since Dewey recognizes that economic changes accelerated by the war have led to three startling changes in the social status of women, he raises our expectation that the significance of these changes for women and for society will be examined. Instead, he treats them as causes for alarm. What he is really worried about is how women's changed status will affect men's. He notes that women have made real economic and political gains and as a result have little use for husbands to support them. What this might mean for women is not considered. He wonders what will happen if women do not voluntarily abdicate their newly acquired economic power when men return home from the war. He does not raise the issue of why women should want to abdicate power or why men should expect them to do so. Oddly enough, the third change only indirectly concerns women, but it does directly impact on men's traditional role of supporting a family. It has to do with the state's newfound zeal for children's rights because of the importance of replacing people lost in the war. Dewey's only comment on this changed state of affairs is that giving more responsibility for children to the state will diminish men's responsibilities.

Dewey concludes the essay by predicting that whatever changes men have undergone as a result of their war experiences will largely determine postwar society. Despite his recognition of women's very different war experiences and newfound emancipation from economic dependency and patriarchal control, no such claim is made about their experiences or influence. Therefore, despite his call for a reconstruction of morality due to changed conditions, he failed to follow through with developing or even advocating a feminist ethics adequate to postwar realities.

By 1930 Dewey seems to have made a complete about-face. He clearly asserts that "present ideas of love, marriage, and the family are almost exclusively masculine constructions." Rather than lamenting men's reduced role in the family, he recognizes that upholders of conventional marriages and traditional beliefs about love and sexuality are "idealizations of human interests that express a dominantly one-sided experience," namely, that of men. "They are romantic in theory and prosaic in operation." Dewey's findings have long been recognized by an earlier wave of feminist theory that has emphasized the suffocating restrictions such prosaic practices imposed on women and by later waves of feminists, who have explored the even more deadly consequences of domestic abuse. Dewey also connects men's sentimental idealization of relationships developed to further their interests with a legal system that supports their dominance. He counters such sentimentalization and legalization by appealing to the realities of the relationships of men, women, and children, which have been covered over in both the idealizing accounts and the legal system. He now asserts, furthermore, that "the growing freedom of women can hardly have any other outcome than the production of more realistic and more human morals. It will be marked by a new freedom, but also by a new severity. For it will be enforced by the realities of associated life as they are disclosed to careful and systematic inquiry, and not by a combination of convention and an exhausted legal system with sentimentality" [LW5:276]. Since Dewey's own pragmatist ethics begins with the realities of associated life, he is deliberately including feminist concerns with the domestic sphere within pragmatist ethics.[19]

But in the fuller explication of "Marriage and the Family," which is the last chapter of his 1932 *Ethics*, Dewey, along with his coauthor, James Hayden Tufts, takes the realities of associated life as a strong argument for supporting the permanence of commitment to heterosexual marriage, which should combine sex with friendship. He responds to the assaults on the institution of marriage by the new Freudian emphasis on sexual satisfaction and the modern emphasis on individual fulfillment.[20] Several aspects of the exposition are troubling from a feminist perspective. The first section, which briefly sketches the history of the family, clearly states that—except for a brief matriarchal period—the present form of marriage derives from a patriarchal model of "father right" that was not even displaced by the Protestant reformation, which retained the "subjection of women" in marriage. The problem is that this insight does not inform the rest of the analysis. In fact, this first section is the only part of the chapter not rewritten from the 1908 version of the *Ethics*, where it introduced a more radical critique of women's oppression by the patriarchal family. Where the first edition emphasizes and is plainly concerned about women's alienation, the second edition is mainly concerned that women's economic, educational, and political emancipation threatens the institution of marriage. The earlier sources of conflict between women and men are now merely "irritations" not needing further reflection.

As was intimated in "War's Social Results," divorce is seen as a mostly selfish act by those not willing to make the sacrifices necessary to continue the institution of marriage. The forces encouraging "casual attachments instead of permanent unions" are examined first "from the point of view of the man and woman" and then as they affect children [LW7:447]. Despite the acknowledgment that women's social roles have been more profoundly changed than men's as a result of industrialization, and that the working class's experiences differ from the middle class's, their interests are not considered separately from men's or from the perspective of the middle-class family. By contrast, in the first edition, the conflicts generated by the fact that women's and men's perspectives diverge due to their different situations and social pressures, combined with the fact of men's blindness to women's plight, were such important issues that Dewey spoke of a "masculine fallacy" and a "feminine fallacy" by analogy with William James's term, "psychologist's fallacy" [MW5:525]. The psychologist's fallacy, according to James, was confusing one's own point of view with that of other persons in the situations under examination. By assuming that women's and men's interests in preserving marriage are the same and in discounting the effect on newly emancipated women of his admonition to subordinate their selfish interests to the good of the family, Dewey commits the very masculine fallacy that he had earlier warned against. Jane Addams had already argued in 1902 that the priority of higher social values over individual good could not be used to condemn women for being selfish when they refused to subordinate themselves to family claims when it was their very recognition of wider social demands that led them to choose a career outside the home in the first place.[21]

Dewey emphasizes that marriage must evolve from an authoritarian form to one in which there is equality and mutual consideration, respect, and cooperation, and he is careful to talk about the responsibilities of *parents* in child rearing. But the fact remains that it is women's newfound individualism, as evidenced in the extension of the suffrage, the unconventional communities of women in the settlement movement, the more extensive opportunities for education opened to women, and the choice of career over marriage by 20 percent of female college graduates, that is seen as a threat to the stability of marriage and a contributing factor to the decline of births among middle- and upper-class women.[22] Marriage should be seen as a high social obligation and women and men should work together to create something not yet experienced that will exemplify new values. Although women are said to have an equal right to education, political participation, and gainful employment outside the home, and despite the recognition that some women rightfully choose career over marriage, the interests of men and women are still seen in stereotypically sexist terms. "Ambitious young men" are appealed to, for example, to "find an opportunity for self-development and for usefulness in the community" in a stable marriage as well as in professional advancement [LW7:452]. On the other hand, it is said that "if we have healthy bodies . . . one of the ways in which we may make our contribution is through bringing new life into being, and giving to our children the best in our power" [LW7:454]. Women are blithely told that although it is still difficult to combine professional careers and marriage, there is no need to choose between them, since the fact that some women already combine both shows that it is not impossible. It is pointed out that women in industry, that is, blue-collar workers, have been doing it for an even longer time. How they do so and maintain a good environment for children is not clear, however, since "impersonal care by experts" in child-care settings is thought to be less desirable than "long and intimate physical union between mother and offspring" [LW7:456–57 and 461].

The chapter ends by referring to Ellen Key, who declares that the family does not have to be destroyed in order to secure women's personality and the proper development of children. Dewey says that the family will survive because it an indispensable part of moral life "and life means power to adjust to changing conditions" [LW7:461–62]. But a more radical analysis of just what changes are required is thwarted by a belief stated more clearly in the earlier version of *Ethics*. There it says that no matter how much the family is reinvented, it cannot alter "one fundamental division of labor between men and women," one which married women wisely accept. In Helen Bosanquet's words, it is "the obvious fact that the man is incapable of the more domestic duties incident upon the rearing of children" [MW5:531]. Destroying this myth has been one of the persistent themes of feminist theory. One might hope that Dewey recognized this more clearly than his coauthor Tufts, since in the same work he is unambiguously "the lover of children," confident that childhood best expresses the essence of humanity. Dewey clearly believed that "it is not only meet, but a joy, that fathers labor for the children" [MW5:520]. He did not experience such work as drudgery and in his early educational work even defended teaching domestic chores to young boys as a valuable learning experience.

Another indication that the more reactionary aspects of the chapter on marriage in the 1932 *Ethics* may be attributable to Tufts rather than to Dewey is the fact that in it birth control clinics—which were as controversial then as abortion clinics are today—are defended as legitimate, but specifically to reeducate "the poor and ignorant" and substitute medically approved procedures for their violent and criminal methods [LW7:460]. Dewey's defense of birth control in the same time period was not class based, and he supported it unequivocally as part of his effort to wrest science and technology away from military and capitalistic control and use it instead for social good and individual empowerment. In "Education and Birth Control," for example, he says that opposition to the birth control movement is part of the larger resistance to newly discovered knowledge that affects the conduct of life [LW6:146–48]. "Ignorance, prejudice, dogma, routine, tradition" come into play in the ongoing conflict between the old and entrenched and new ideas and discoveries. Such conflict is inevitable in human beings affected by a past and anticipating a future. Knowledge always means increased control and the birth control movement provides a means for intelligently controlling the processes of procreation and conception. It puts a blind natural process under human direction. Laws and public sentiment formed in ignorance of such means of control newly developed by science block public access to knowledge that will give persons more complete control of their conduct. Since "suppression and secrecy breed unfairness, mental and moral disorder," arbitrary restrictions to the intelligent control of nature must be removed. Dewey points out that mass education was being criticized for failing to develop the individual capacities of children, but policies whose effect is to increase the numbers of people born without any regard to their quality of life work against this very respect for the individual. If parents had the power to make the quality of life supreme in their homes, then the problem of mass education would disappear.

The issues at stake in a bill seeking to legalize birth control, which was introduced in the United States Senate in the early 1930s, have chilling parallels with issues regarding abortion rights in the 1990s. In "The Senate Birth Control Bill," Dewey asks, for example: "Can anything more absurd be imagined, than that clinics should be established for the care of women, and that a reputable physician should be guilty of a crime if he gives information as to the location of these clinics, to a woman needing care?" [LW6:388]. In lobbying for the bill he seeks to broaden its appeal by diffusing accusations that it is too radical. He points out that it is conservative in restricting those authorized to give out information to those deemed competent, such as the government, medical societies, schools, and journals. He predicts that later generations would compare criminalizing those distributing scientific information about birth control to the dark ages when witches were hunted down. The bill is also conservative in that it seeks to "conserve human life and well-being, that of mothers, of children, of families." Unimpeded access to safe forms of birth control would lessen the need for abortions and it would lessen the injury caused by unscrupulous quacks. The bill neither compels those opposed to it to distribute information about birth control nor does it prohibit groups from dissuading their members from employing contraceptive measures. But it would be "un-American, undemocratic, and despotic" for such groups "to attempt to use legislation to create crimes, in order to impose their special moral views upon others" [LW6:389].

Conclusion

Dewey's pragmatist feminism has many facets, only a few of which have been explored in this chapter. Most importantly, he argues for the continuity of theory and practice and that philosophy has an explicitly emancipatory goal. Because of his recognition that experience is had before it is interpreted, he astutely criticized the intellectualist fallacy represented today in the exaggerated claims of formalist epistemology, and he developed a powerful model of concrete experience. These positions have many resources for contemporary feminist analyses, just as contemporary feminist theory reveals absences and failings in the earlier pragmatist theory. The background conditions of the context of understanding and the operation of selective interest opens a space for recognition of the multiple prejudices that feminists examine. Reflection on these background conditions also reveals the embeddedness of human understanding in the histories, values, and multiple relationships through which persons are constituted in interaction with others. The limitations of perspectivism that follows from its particularity also suggest a remedy to pragmatist feminists in that it requires inclusiveness of points of view as a means to achieve objectivity and therefore a justification for including those traditionally excluded.

Intelligence is explicitly linked to "free communication: the method of conference, consultation, discussion, in which there takes place purification and pooling of the net results of the experiences of multitudes of people." That this is no trivial requirement is emphasized by Dewey's pointing out that during the Second World War when this assertion was made "hundreds of thousands of persons who have been tortured, who have died, who are rotting in concentration camps, prove that talk may also be tragically costly, and that democracy to endure must hold it immensely precious."[23] The multiplicity of points of view as well as the multiple relations constitutive of persons support feminist claims to having insights to contribute to philosophizing that have so far been missing and whose absence has distorted what is there. It also gives good reasons for de-emphasizing essentialist analyses of gender and provides a model for theorizing about the multiple relationships through which we are constituted and which have been distorted through homophobia, racism, classism, and colonialism, as well as sexism. As in quotations where Dewey links the conditions for objectivity in knowledge with democratic values, his emphasis on the continuum of means and ends deliberately collapses the distinction of pure and applied theory. It thus supports the specificity of feminist analyses of housework, sexual relations, abortion, job discrimination, and the myriad problematic situations that women in all our variety encounter as necessary steps to theorizing about reality as well as to attaining justice.

Notes

1. Phyllis Rooney, "Gendered Reason: Sex Metaphor and Conceptions of Reason," *Hypatia* 6, 2 (Summer 1991): 97–98.

2. See Lorraine Code, *Rhetorical Spaces: Essays on Gendered Locations* (New York: Routledge, 1995), esp. chap. 1.

3. Simone de Beauvoir, *The Second Sex* (New York: Vintage, 1952), p. xxii. Jane Addams, *The Long Road of Women's Memory* (New York: Macmillan, 1916).

4. John Dewey, *Art as Experience* [LW10:23]. See also pp. 42–44 and 142–45.

5. Joyce Antler, *Lucy Sprague Mitchell* (New Haven, Conn.: Yale University Press, 1987), p. 62.

6. W. E. B. Du Bois, *The Autobiography of W. E. B. Du Bois* (New York: International, 1980), pp. 146–47.

7. See Herbert Aptheker, "Introduction," in W. E. B. Du Bois, *Darkwater: Voices from within the Veil* (Millwood, N.Y.: Kraus-Thomson, 1975), p. 14.

8. Lucy Sprague Mitchell, *Two Lives* (New York: Simon and Schuster, 1953), p. 74; and Du Bois, "Of the Ruling of Men," *Darkwater*, pp. 134–59.

9. For Dewey's explanation of experience as the interaction of persons and some aspect of the world in terms of undergoing and doing, see *Art as Experience* [LW10:50–52, 137]; in terms of action-undergoing, see *Experience and Nature* [LW1:28–30].

10. Eleanor Flexner, *Century of Struggle* (Cambridge, Mass.: Harvard University Press, 1975), pp. 268, 272–73, 284.

11. Dewey to Klyce, 5 July 1915, Huntington, New York [number 03542], Library of Congress, Klyce Papers.

12. Dewey to Klyce, 8 May 1920, Nanking, China [number 04621], Library of Congress, Klyce Papers.

13.   Jessie Taft, *The Woman Movement from the Point of View of Social Consciousness* (Menasha, Wisc.: Collegiate Press, George Banta, 1915).

14.   Dewey to Klyce, 8 May 1920.

15.   See Jane M. Dewey, "Biography of John Dewey," in *The Philosophy of John Dewey*, ed. Paul Arthur Schilpp (Evanston, Ill.: Northwestern University Press, 1939), 30; and Paul Kellogg, "Twice Twenty Years at Hull-House," in *Eighty Years at Hull-House*, ed. Allen F. Davis and Mary Lynn McCree (Chicago: Quadrangle Books, 1969), p. 171.

16.   Dewey uses a strange circumlocution; isn't it the case that it is persons, and not habits, who are entrenched in positions of advantage?

17.   John Dewey, "In Defense of Mary Ware Dennett's *The Sex Side of Life*" [LW17:127]. Dennett's conviction was later reversed [LW17:560 n. 127.5]. See also Constance M. Chen, "*The Sex Side of Life*": *Mary Ware Dennett's Pioneering Battle for Birth Control and Sex Education* (New York: New Press, 1996).

18.   Dewey, "War's Social Results" [LW17:21–25].

19.   See Seigfried, chap. 10, "Social Ethics," in *Pragmatism and Feminism* (Chicago: University of Chicago Press, 1996), pp. 224–58.

20.   Although Dewey co-wrote the book with Tufts, who wrote the chapter on marriage, they reprinted the preface to the first edition, along with the new preface, and it states that because of suggestions and criticisms by each of the other's work, they consider the book to be jointly authored throughout.

21.   Addams, chap. 3, "Filial Relations," in *Democracy and Social Ethics* (Cambridge, Mass.: Belknap Press of Harvard University Press, 1964), pp. 71–101.

22.   Eugenicist fears are also expressed that the "children of diseased or feeble-minded parents" and "other elements of the population" are reproducing at a greater rate than those of prosperous, healthy, educated parents, such as the families of "scientific men" [LW7:454].

23.   Dewey, "The Basic Values and Loyalties of Democracy" [LW14:276].

11 The Contemporary Significance of the American Philosophic Tradition: Lockean and Redemptive

Thelma Z. Lavine

What is distinctive about the American philosophic tradition is that among the various competing philosophies that survive in the contemporary western world, the classical American tradition alone attempts to identify and to reconcile the conflicting philosophical traditions of the modern West. Among the influential classical American philosophers—Royce, Peirce, James, Dewey, and Mead—only Dewey perceived the axial significance of the conflicting philosophical frameworks which had emerged in the modern era; it was Dewey who devoted his lifelong career to exploring the multifactoral causes, the consequences for social practice, and the prospects for mediation and reconciliation of the philosophic contestations of modernity.

It is only in the ending decades of the twentieth century that western intellectual culture, European and American, has attained sufficient reflective distance from its philosophic conflicts to begin to frame a conception of modernity and its contentions, traditions, and interpretive modes. References to the Enlightenment and Romanticism are now sprouting in unexpected places, in modes of philosophic discourse that had been characteristically estranged from history and culture. It is becoming increasingly recognized that the contestation within the era of modernity is between the Enlightenment tradition deriving from Locke and Newton in the seventeenth century and the counter-Enlightenment tradition deriving from Rousseau and the Romantic and idealist German, English, and American philosophers and poets, first emerging at the end of the eighteenth century.

Each tradition has its own thought-style. Enlightenment Modernity as the first cognitive framework of modernity begins with the scientific breakthrough of Newton and the political breakthrough of Locke. Both breakthroughs are founded on reason and share the claim to offer truths that are universal, absolute, realistic, and objective. Scientific reason yields laws of nature (physics, astronomy, chemistry, physiology, with the instrumentality of mathematics) and technologies. Substantive reason yields the truths of inalienable individual natural rights; government by consent of the governed; the rule of law and equality under the law; liberation by reason from dogma, myth, tradition, and prejudice; and the maintenance of a civil society of free and open social and economic relationships.

Romantic Modernity spawns ideas that oppose, scorn, and fear the power of Enlightenment thought and practices to discredit traditional political, religious, ethnic, and economic modes of group and personal life. Counter-Enlightenment thought-style opposes abstract universal reason with the human significance of spirit, will, imagination, creativity; it opposes objective science with subjectivity, and with the arts and culture as the paths to truth; it opposes the politics of the autonomous individual and natural rights democracy and a free-market economy with a collectivist politics, a statism of left or right and a command economy; it opposes the self-interest of the individual with the primacy of the needs and aspirations of the community; it opposes the functions of civil society with a concern for the victims of civil society—the marginalized, the poor, the oppressed, minorities, and rebels.

America was born into Modernity in 1631 under the shield of the Protestant Reformation in search of religious freedom. By the third quarter of the eighteenth century, the errand into the wilderness, having endured the hardships of nature, Puritan theocracy, colonialism, and separation from European centers of commerce, and having experimented with local self-government, mounted and won the war of independence from Britain. America became the "first new nation";[1] its national and legal identity lay in Enlightenment truths of natural rights and constitutional government. These were Americanized as the inalienable natural rights, freedom, and equality of Jefferson's Declaration of Independence and Madison's Constitution with its separation of powers and its machinery of representative democracy.

The founders provided in the Declaration, the Constitution, the Federalist papers, and the Bill of Rights, a political theory of principles based closely upon Locke's Second Treatise of Civil Government. The principles entailed in Lockean liberalism were freedom and equality of the individual, universal inalienable rights, representative democracy, constitutionalism and the rule of law, due process, and redress of grievances.

For the framers of the Constitution, political theory had come to an end. The ancient dream of the Stoics for a republic of individual freedom from the oppression of the Roman Empire had been realized in the new nation, the millennial nation. Built into the Constitution were mechanisms that allowed for mediation in governmental and economic conflict, enabling in principle the new nation to be stabilized and to run by itself. The American republic, unlike all previous historical republics, which had been short-lived and disastrous, was also unlike the traditional nations of the West with which America shared the Enlightenment truths of individual rights and constitutional government.

In the western traditional societies that embraced Enlightenment political truths, these new ideas were filtered through, modified, and colored by the long years of feudal and church domination, by memories of oppressive hierarchy, by longstanding traditions of social stratification, and by the religious and moral philosophies that legitimated them.

In America, by contrast, the political principles of the Enlightenment were unfiltered through older visions of religious and political hierarchy. The Declaration, the Constitution, the Federalist papers, and the Bill of Rights boldly defined and promoted the principles of the Enlightenment as the political and moral foundation of America. These Enlightenment principles set the course of the nation, evolving into the widespread consensus of belief that Gunnar Myrdal's celebrated study, *An American Dilemma*, identified in 1940 as "the American Creed" (later incorporated by contemporary sociologist Seymour Martin Lipset and political scientist Samuel Huntington, among others).

> These ideals of the essential dignity of the individual human being, the fundamental equality of all men, and of certain inalienable rights to freedom, justice, and a fair opportunity, represent the essential meaning of the nation's early struggle for independence . . . in the clarity and boldness of the Enlightenment period.
>
> The ideals of the American Creed have thus become the highest law of the land. . . . These principles have been hammered into easily remembered formulas. . . . The schools teach them, the churches preach them. The Courts pronounce their judicial decisions in these terms.

And Myrdal continues, "Sometimes one gets the impression that it is the prevalence of 'wrongs' in America, wrongs judged by the high standards of the national Creed— which helps make the ideals stand out so clearly. America is continuously struggling for its soul."[2]

Ironically, and ineluctably, the very "clarity and intellectual boldness" that Myrdal perceived as the American formulation of its Enlightenment principles set the stage for the long and continuous history of American counter-Enlightenment dissent from consensus and for the specifically American version of the contestations of Modernity.

In 1955, the publication by Louis Hartz of *The Liberal Tradition in America* raised the question that no political sociologist and no political theorist of America has since been able to ignore: Why has socialism not developed into a politics for America? Hartz follows de Tocqueville's perception of America as heavily weighted toward a consensual politics of democracy, a democratic will toward equality even at the expense of liberty, and the tyranny of the majority over inequalities of intellect and wealth. More than a hundred years after de Tocqueville, Hartz's famous explanation of the failure of socialism in America is based upon an absence (of feudalism) and a presence (of Lockeanism). The absence of feudalism leaves America without any historical memory of oppression (a beast of Babylon) to be overcome; no repertoire of horrors exists in the American imagination that can be revived (as in Europe) to inspire revolutionary action in times of social upheaval.[3] Hartz's explanation in terms of presence invokes the presence of Lockeanism, the central liberal consensus that individuals have a "natural right" to acquire property through their labor and dispose of it as they choose. American Lockeanism reflects a general acceptance of the value of material prosperity and the opportunity to achieve it that the American economy and polity provide to the citizen. Even the disputations of political parties in America, Hartz notes, reflect without significant disagreement the Lockean consensus with regard to property. Moreover, in America, Hartz argues, there is no aristocracy to look down upon middle-class materialistic values and no Marxist proletariat to attack them.

From the historic influence of de Tocqueville upon Hartz comes the major source of the concept of American exceptionalism. The American nation is exceptional among the nations of the western world in being founded upon political principles; it is exceptional also in its consensus politics of the pursuit of material goods, through individual labor and equal opportunity and expectation. The presence of these shared Lockean principles and the absence of a feudal past effectively immunize America from socialism.

Deeply disappointed by the failure of American society to break out of its ignoble Lockeanism and to heed the call of European socialism, Hartz fails to see that American politics supplies its own homegrown replacement for the oppression of European feudalism. Although feudalism is indeed absent from America's historical memory, American culture provides a substitute for feudalism's perceived domination and oppression. America's substitute oppression is the omnipresence of the political system that the Constitution dictates, the democratic capitalism that it underwrites, and the impoverished life-world of the American people that is their consequence.

Hartz could be satisfied only by the advent of Marxist socialism, for which he and many others longed in their current political climate. He did not see that the Lockean domination of economics and politics had assumed for some the image of an oppressor to be overcome and the opening of a path to a possible socialist turn in American politics. No one argued more succinctly than John Dewey that America had generated its own oppressor in the rapidly expanding industrial economy of the early years of the twentieth century. In *Human Nature and Conduct* Dewey writes: "The new industrialism was largely the old feudalism, living in a bank instead of a castle and brandishing the check of credit instead of the sword" [MW14:148].

The Marxian rhetoric of capitalist oppression and its overturn that resonates in Dewey's identification of American industrialism with the old feudalism reflects the increasingly influential currents of Marxist counter-Enlightenment in America from the turn of the century. But the Romantic counter-Enlightenment had already entered America with Emerson and the Transcendentalists and flourished from the 1830s to the 1850s. Emerson and the Transcendentalists signal the first philosophical breakout from the structures of American Lockeanism.

Long before Dewey, the Transcendentalists had rejected Jefferson's self-evident truths and Madison's machinery of government and Unitarianism's dry religious rationalism. They questioned the capitalist system and the struggle for security and material goods that it engenders; they rejected the externalities of science; they rejected both the conformity of contemporary mass society (de Tocqueville's tyranny of the majority); and also the accretions of the past, including the Enlightenment founding of America. What was their vision? They sought out Goethe and Coleridge and Wordsworth and Carlyle and returned with the subjective counter-Enlightenment Romanticism of the "inward path," the spiritualization of self and nature, the idea of the infinite potentiality of the human spirit, and a rediscovery of the Puritan idea of renewal, the power to renew oneself, to change one's life. But this poetic Romanticism offered no replacements for the American social and economic structures that it repudiated. The Transcendentalist breakout left no viable social philosophy for America. Its heritage appears in an underground stream of antinomian personal mysticism and in the long Romantic tradition of American literature and its discontents with the prevailing American life-world.

The Progressive Movement, from the 1890s to World War I, reflects a second major intellectual breakout from Enlightenment America. It occurred in the face of a national crisis that followed upon monopolistic post–Civil War industrialization and the dislocations of modernization throughout the society. *In this troubled context arose classical American philosophy* as an attempt to rethink the American Enlightenment tradition in the light of alternative counter-Enlightenment, European philosophies. It was also an attempt to pursue an integration of Enlightenment and counter-Enlightenment modes of modernity for an America whose national and legal identity lay in Enlightenment truth. Dewey more than Peirce, Royce, James, or Mead grasped the immensity of this undertaking. Such an American philosophy would venture to interpret the conflicting frameworks of modernity within their own problematic situations; to identify their consequences in practice; and to explore the philosophic issues of their integration. *Of all American philosophers of pragmatism, Dewey was the most sensitive, personally and theoretically, to the countercurrents of modernity and the challenge of their unification.* Dewey himself provides the key to understanding the theme of unification that dominates the development of his thought. Reflecting upon his early response to reading Hegel, he sees that "[It] supplied a demand for unification that was doubtless an intense emotional craving . . . that only an intellectualized subject-matter could satisfy." By contrast to that satisfaction, Dewey speaks of

> the sense of divisions and separations . . . divisions by way of isolation of the self from the world, of soul from body, of nature from God, brought a painful oppression—or, rather, they were an inward laceration. [LW5:153]

The pursuit of satisfying the demand of unification that Hegel had opened up for Dewey is discernible as a recurrence of the Transcendental breakout from Enlightenment America—in Emerson's pursuit of the mystical unification of the spiritual self with nature and the Over-Soul. In the rhetoric of Emerson and Dewey there flows the same poetic symbolism of a sanctified unification of the self with a larger self, with nature, with community, with some source of divinity. The goal is *redemption through the process and experience of unification, through a sense of wholeness that over-comes self-interest and "gaps, gulfs and divisions" between self and other.*

But Dewey's mode of redemption is transmitted through his reflective philosophical argumentation. Dewey's mode of redemption is neither the immediate luminous experience of oneness with God in moments of religious mysticism, nor is it exhausted by the Emersonian personal experience of crossing Boston Common at twilight and becoming a transparent eyeball in which oneness with reality is achieved without mediation.

No one knew better than Dewey that a sense of redemptive wholeness is something that Enlightenment rational principles can never deliver. Yet Enlightenment democratic and scientific principles are constitutive of the modern world. Thus, Dewey's mode of redemption could be won only through a philosophic struggle to achieve the *reconciliation* of the conflicting Enlightenment and counter-Enlightenment traditions of modernity. This had been the challenge that had called classical American philosophy into being. Dewey was not alone in this struggle. This pursuit of a via media, of a mediating wholeness, which is the *secular salvation sought by Dewey*, had already been sought by Hegel, Marx, Comte, and Burke in the nineteenth century, and in the twentieth century by Weber, Freud, Durkheim, Mannheim, and, most recently, by Habermas—in all cases with problematic success.[4] How does Dewey negotiate philosophically the dynamics of oppression and redemptive liberation in America? How does Dewey negotiate philosophically the conflicts of modernity in America?

By contrast with Louis Hartz's brokenhearted conviction that America was exceptional in being immunized from socialism by its Lockean consensualism and by the absence of an oppressive beast to be overcome, Dewey perceptively finds the oppressor at home in America. Following Marx's symbolic world history, in which each stage until the socialist "world to come" has its oppressor to be overcome and its slaves to be liberated, Dewey sees modern industrial America as a re-run, a repetition of "the old feudalism," as he says, "living in a bank instead of a castle and brandishing the check of credit instead of the sword" [MW14:148]. Dewey's social philosophy can be seen from this perspective as a philosophy of American liberation from the oppression of corporate capitalism to a new communal world of socialism.

Dewey's development of his political philosophy (*Reconstruction in Philosophy* [1920], *Human Nature and Conduct* [1922], *The Public and Its Problems* [1927], *Individualism Old and New* [1930], *Liberalism and Social Action* [1935]) emerged in response to the pre-war Progressive movement, the boom years following World War I, and the collapse into the Great Depression—periods of social turmoil within a political culture that was under the pervasive and persuasive influence of socialist theory and the presence of Soviet socialist practice.

By the time of the Progressive Era (1890–1920), the American economy was being transformed from family-owned small businesses and farms to interlocking systems of corporations owned by stockholders. The rise of corporate capitalism was widely seen as a threat to basic political ideas of liberty, equality, the private ownership of small property, and the supremacy of the individual over the state. Progressivism was engaged in reconciling corporate capitalism with the traditions of American liberalism. As a movement of reform, progressivism produced more legislative alterations in American political and economic life than occurred at any other period in American history, beginning with the Interstate Commerce Act of 1888 and followed notably by the Sherman Anti-Trust Act of 1890, women's suffrage, direct election of senators, initiative, referendum, and recall.

Dewey's response to the corporate threat was socialist, not that of progressive reform, nor populist restoration of the old individualism. For him, the problem of corporate power could be solved only by turning over ownership and control of production to a central authority. Dewey's proposal was plausible in the bitter years of the Depression, in which millions of Americans lost their jobs, their homes, their savings, and one-fourth of the labor force was unemployed. No federal relief existed to cope with any of these disasters.

But the concept of centralized authority, with its associations with absolute power and what is currently viewed as statism (the coexistence in a society of a command economy and an authoritarian polity), is incompatible with Dewey's "liberal socialism" (or "social democracy"). The absolutism, fixity, and class conflict of Marxist and Soviet social and political thought were abhorrent to Dewey's conception of social democracy. Without resting upon Marxist concepts and argumentation, Dewey's liberal socialism had no place for the capitalist system, individual rights, or private property. Dewey rejected those concepts and institutions as obstructive to democratic formation of social policies that would lead to a fulfilling and redemptive life for all members of the community.

What, then, does Dewey mean by centralized authority? Reflecting the considerable interest during the years 1918 to 1920 in British social philosopher G. D. H. Cole's guild socialism and industrial councils, Dewey seems to regard centralized authority as the function of a planning group, using Dewey's method of intelligence, supplemented by newly developed modes of organization to further community fulfillment. Beyond this, Dewey does not spell out the meaning of centralized authority, organized intelligence, or a directive council.

With Franklin Delano Roosevelt and the New Deal, a new wave of governmental politics intervened by federal control of the banks and the stock market and the introduction of social security and governmental agencies to provide employment. This was a statist turn in opposition to the liberties of the individual and the beginning of America as a welfare state. Dewey, however, did not support the measures introduced by the New Deal, on the ground that they were makeshift by contrast with socialism. Dewey argued that the power of corporate capitalism is underwritten by a political regime that he described as "the agent of a dominant economic class" [LW11:40]. "Liberalism," he urges in Marxist language, "[must now be] prepared . . . [to] socialize the forces of production" [LW11:62].

Dewey's writings on social philosophy purposefully utilize counter-Enlightenment strategies to undermine and delegitimate the structures of traditional Enlightenment America. Process, change, whether Hegelian, Darwinian, Marxist, or historicist, is for him the primary trait of reality and functions as a universal solvent for all claims to foundations, immutable truths, inalienable rights, or other "fixities." In place of all absolutes he offers his theory of inquiry, the key to which is his powerful concept of the problematic situation. A problematic situation is theorized as one in which disunities have been identified and explained, and an interpretive hypothesis resolving the difficulty is proposed and subjected to verification. All beliefs and cognitive claims are seen as interpretive resolutions of past problematic situations and are subject to change, re-evaluation, or obsolescence as new situations emerge.

Dewey's theory of the problematic situation is his most effective attack upon the Enlightenment principles that founded the American republic. From the perspective of the problematic situation, the Declaration, the Constitution, the Bill of Rights, and their underlying Lockean political and economic individualism are seen as interpretive resolutions of past problematic situations; with vast changes in America these old solutions to past problems become dysfunctional, archaic, obsolete, and obstructive to change. With this argument, Dewey seeks to delegitimate and desacralize the arguments of the founding documents and the resulting American creed.

But although he attacks the Enlightenment politics of America, Dewey retains from the Enlightenment ensemble of contributions to modernity the crucial twin concepts of science and democracy. How can he accept these fixities of the Enlightenment tradition? He strips science and democracy of their cognitive complex of principles and reconstructs ("redescribes") both as counter-Enlightenment group processes, functions of social communities.

Community is the unifying concept that Dewey offers to oppose Enlightenment individualism. Community is characterized by communication and the sharing of meanings, interests, values, and goods. Community is the effective authority in support of beliefs and values. But since a community, like all structures, cognitive, moral, social, institutional, is subject to change, its authority is presumably temporary and time bound. Within Deweyan community the rational autonomous individual of the Enlightenment, endowed by his creator with inalienable rights, becomes a social self whose rights are endowed by his or her community, and for whom the attainment of self-realization and redemption is achieved by surrendering self-interest to the shared interests of the community.

Dewey's strategic opposition to Enlightenment individualism by utilizing the concept of community appears also in his strategic use of history. In the case of history, Dewey's repudiation of individualism leads him to the strategy of *erasure*: his social philosophy omits any account of the Revolution, the Declaration, the deliberations of the Constitutional Convention, and the Federalist papers, in which the founding was theorized and the philosophy of individual rights and democratic constitutionalism was explored. The erasure by Dewey of the historic founding of America and its philosophy of individual rights results in the further scandal that America's foremost social philosopher has no philosophy of human rights and no contribution to the global discourse on human rights that has exploded in the current political scene. *What the whole world knows, emulates, or fears—American political and economic liberty, individual rights, due process, and the rule of law under a constitution—is unknown in Deweyan social philosophy.*

In Dewey's political writings of the 1920s, unification has become explicitly unification within a socialist society. "We are in for some kind of socialism, call it by whatever name we please," he insists in *Individualism Old and New*, "and no matter what it will be called when it is realized" [LW5:99]. And he argues in *Liberalism and Social Action* that a liberalism that is sincere "must will the means . . . [of] achieving . . . its ends. Regimentation of material and mechanical forces is the only way by which the mass of individuals can be released from regimentation and consequent suppression of their cultural possibilities" [LW11:63]. What is necessary for the liberation of Americans from the regimentation of traditional America, he is saying, is the new regimentation by "organized intelligence" through a "coordinating and directive council." But in what sense is unification under the regimentation of organized intelligence and its council compatible with the method of inquiry by a testable problematic situation? And how can the regimentation of life under the new socialism of organized intelligence be reconciled with the spiritual redemptiveness that Dewey had offered to America as "a common faith," as the sacramental aspect of shared human experience? (Dewey's cautious response is that a mentality which would be "congruent with the new social corporativeness" cannot be predicted.)

In the sharing of democratic human relationships, in the experience of the scientific mode of searching for clarity and evidence in deliberating over common problems, in the natural piety of communion with nature, Dewey had tried to sublimate traditional religious faith into a secular religion embracing the modes of the modern world—the Romantic quest for unification and the Enlightenment principles of democracy and science. We hear in Dewey the Emersonian Romantic longing for transcendence, for escape from regimentation, for a spiritual union of self and nature, self and humanity, reaching to a mystical sanctified unification. Dewey in 1920 ends *Reconstruction in Philosophy*:

> And when the emotional force, the mystic force one might say, of communication, of the miracle of shared life and shared experience is spontaneously felt, the hardness and crudeness of contemporary life will be bathed in the light that never was on land or sea. [MW12:201]

And at the end of *Human Nature and Conduct* (1922), Dewey expresses his view of religion: "Religion as a sense of the whole is the most individualized of all things, the most spontaneous, undefinable and varied. For individuality signifies unique connections in the whole" [MW14:227]. And for Dewey everyday life in industrial America is sacramental and is lifted up into Romantic mystical unification and intimations of immortality:

> Within the flickering inconsequential acts of separate selves dwells a sense of the whole which claims and dignifies them. In its presence we put off mortality and live in the universal. The life of the community in

which we live and have our being is the fit symbol of this relationship. The acts in which we express our perception of the ties which bind us to others are its only rites and ceremonies. [MW14:227]

Unfortunately, the gap between unification under Dewey's imposed socialist "regimentation of material and mechanical forces" [LW11:63] and the spiritual unification of Dewey's redemptive common faith cannot be closed. Nor can Dewey's lifelong pursuit of a redemptive via media, reconciling the modes of modernity, bridge the gap between the conflicting substantive structures of modernity and Dewey's own process of inquiry, which dissolves all such structures, thus nullifying their reconciliation and the possibility of redemption.

After the fateful year of 1989 and the collapse of Soviet socialism as a command economy and an authoritarian political system, we have learned that such statist installations of counter-Enlightenment ideas are human disasters. The socialism for which Dewey and Hartz longed, we now see, however painfully, through newly released archives as potentially the road to serfdom, perceptively foreseen by Friedrich Hayek. But although state socialism as a political and economic system is dead, socialism lives as the counter-Enlightenment thought-style of modernity, expressive of truths, perceptions, and values at odds with the Enlightenment. *As long as liberal democracy and the Constitution of the American republic prevail, so long will counter-Enlightenment socialist dissent prevail and find expression in American cultural and political life.*

Since 1989 we have also gained sufficient distance to perceive the structure and substance of the contesting modes of modernity. Each side, Enlightenment and counter-Enlightenment, closes off, excludes, ignores, undermines, and denies the truths, perceptions, and values of the other side. Left-wing liberalism as the Americanized version of socialism assumes the role of the counter-Enlightenment in American politics: its role is to identify the dark side, the negativities of Enlightenment liberal capitalism: its self-interested atomistic individualism; its moral and spiritual vacuity; its marginalization of race, ethnicity, and gender; its insensitivity to the human insecurities endemic to a capitalist society. But the counter-Enlightenment has its own dark side: its lack of universal principles; its consequent particularism, which engenders divisiveness, hostility, and conflict between nations, and between ethnic, racial, and gender groups and the host society and among each other; its proclivity toward statist politics and command economics; its moral and spiritual Babel of voices;

and its repudiation of the American Constitutional tradition of political and economic individualism, and its self-serving attempt to represent this repudiation as redemptive.

By this last decade of the twentieth century, Enlightenment America has developed a mixed "welfare capitalist" economy and a "civil rights" democracy. These changes were in response to a growing counter-Enlightenment quest for community, contempt for monetary greed, guilt in the presence of poverty, suffering, and discriminatory practices against racial, minority, and gender groups. Although these new policies are for the most part adaptations of European socialist measures, they are not identified as such in America but only within the contestations of American liberal democracy. The political right and center accept these policies reluctantly as rational, utilitarian reforms; the political left in America sees these policies as redemptive payment for the sufferings caused by the American social system.

In American party politics at the end of the twentieth century, the left wing of the Democratic party remains the voice of counter-Enlightenment socialist-style protest against the right wing and center of the Republican party and its Lockean principles and policies. The contestations of Enlightenment and counter-Enlightenment modernity are now being played out by the contesting political parties of America.

The contemporary significance of the American philosophic tradition is that among all remaining philosophies of the West, only American pragmatism addresses and seeks to theorize the contestations of modernity. The American philosophic tradition is consequently entrusted with a mission: to respond after 1989 to the challenge of historically understanding and reconciling the great conflicting traditions of the modern world, the challenge that first called American philosophy into being and has called forth as well celebrated European responses. The challenge to the contemporary American philosophic tradition is approaching with the millennium: Can the American Creed and the American philosophic tradition, Lockean and redemptive, speak to a millennial challenge?

Notes

1. See Seymour Martin Lipset, *The First New Nation: The United States in Historical and Comparative Perspective* (New York: Norton, 1979).

2. Gunnar Myrdal, *An American Dilemma: The Negro Problem and Modern Democracy* (New York: Harper, 1944).

3. Hartz fails to note that for blacks in America there is indeed a historical memory of oppression, one which has important national consequences.

4. On the concept of a via media, see James T. Kloppenberg, *Uncertain Victory: Social Democracy and Progressivism in European and American Thought, 1870–1920* (New York: Oxford University Press, 1986).

Joseph Margolis

I

The academy is not particularly hospitable to efforts to compare in a close way the distinctly homogeneous work of Anglo-American analytic philosophy and the sprawling diversity of what, in a plainly derogatory spirit, is collected as continental philosophy. And yet, the comparison is implicated in the mere juxtaposition of labels. On "both sides," the implied comparison is dismissive—and unhelpful. The analysts regard the continentals as inept and distracted; the continentals regard the analysts as barbarian and blinkered. There is some truth in both charges; but nearly all that is said there smacks more of tribal loyalties and self-congratulation than of the generosity of first philosophical wonder (about which we have heard so much). I hope to put such bickering behind me.

Within the run of American philosophy, largely from the turn of the century to the end of John Dewey's life and, since then, in a surprisingly vigorous revival that will probably enter the twenty-first century as a continuing force, pragmatism, which in a curious way is thought to share the salient features of the work of both the "analysts" and the "continentals," is increasingly invoked as a conceptual bridge between the nearly incommensurable labors of the others. This may have been hit upon more as a convenience than anything else. But since there are, now, undeniably serious doubts (even in the analytic camp) about the ultimate validity of the best current analytic practice,[1] what is now being recovered as the admirable balance, breadth, resilience, strategic power, and humanity of pragmatism begins to encourage (in its own right) a comparison between the work of the pragmatists and of both the analysts and the continentals.

There is a surprising body of work that collects one or another pragmatist and one or another continental thinker: for example, George Herbert Mead and Maurice Merleau-Ponty,[2] and Charles Sanders Peirce and Karl-

Otto Apel (and Jürgen Habermas).[3] The development is a relatively new one (very much on the increase), in the sense that the original wave of pragmatism reviewed in Europe was largely centered on the somewhat uncomprehending reception of William James—and, later, Dewey—as representing a distinct American philosophical movement (effectively the first of its kind) judged to be more or less correctly summarized in James's rather unfortunate rendering of the pragmatist's conception of truth, later haltingly revised. The fate of this first reception—in British, and eventually, by a curious rebound, in American analytic philosophy—was conspiratorially managed through Bertrand Russell's dismissive reviews of James's treatment of truth and Dewey's conception of logic.[4] All that is past now. We see the dubious motives and argumentative gaffes on all sides, and we are now, at the end of the century, drawn into an altogether different phase of the philosophical contest. Russell and G. E. Moore are hardly reliable totems any longer; positivism and the unity of science are nearly museum pieces; logicism is dead; and the superseded pragmatists and marginalized continentals are livelier than their opponents had ever supposed.

It would not be unfair to single out Richard Rorty's 1974 essay, "Overcoming the Tradition: Heidegger and Dewey,"[5] as one of the earliest influential accounts of this last turn in English-language philosophy—a turn that was originally meant to be instructive to Americans but was received with a remarkable mixture of curiosity, enthusiasm, bafflement, and ridicule in Western Europe—and now globally. No one could have anticipated its reception, deliberately linking (as it does) Dewey and Wittgenstein and Heidegger as Rorty's avowed philosophical mentors and as the essential clue to what has come to be understood as the "end of philosophy."[6]

Rorty's essay is a very good one, very likely one of his best. But it fails, nevertheless, primarily because it does not really capture the essential difference, within the terms of Rorty's own contrived convergence, between Heidegger and Dewey, and because, failing to isolate the first, Rorty hurries to draw his own rather arbitrary, cranky, hardly supported legitimation for bringing philosophy (canonical philosophy, it's true) to an "end." What Rorty says is very nearly a caricature of the well-known caricature attributed to Dewey on the occasion of someone's having presented him with a copy of Heidegger's *Sein und Zeit* and asking him what his impression of it was. According to the hearsay I've collected (from several sources), Dewey is supposed to have said that it read like a Swabian peasant trying to write like Dewey![7]

Fine. But that only signifies—returning to the point of Rorty's essay—that Dewey probably misunderstood Heidegger and Heidegger would have misunderstood Dewey (according to Rorty's gloss) in the same way Rorty himself effectively misunderstands the difference between the two. The reason for Rorty's having missed the point is simply that his own "postmodern," "ethnocentrically" local reading of both is, ultimately, little more than a sly endorsement of the very features of current analytic philosophy—chiefly, Davidson's[8]—which Rorty pretends to supersede via Dewey, Wittgenstein, and Heidegger.[9] Also, of course, there have been a number of substantive efforts earlier than Rorty's to reconnect with care the main thrust of Dewey's philosophy and hospitable tendencies in earlier European philosophy—for instance, those linked to Marxist sources.[10] In any case, Rorty's reading is, I think, dead wrong.

The irony is that Rorty does touch on the essential theme—well, touches on it eccentrically—but he very nearly misses altogether (certainly, he does not feature) the distinction needed. Here is what he says—I mention it because it is the sole passage in which he himself mentions the decisive term (or, rather, a clue regarding it): "It is when Dewey proceeds to view *philosophies*—the thought of Plato, of Thomas, of Hegel—in the same way as an engineer views ore-bearing regions of the earth that Heidegger would recoil. To treat the thought of Hegel as a *Weltanschauung* is to view him as an object of exploitation rather than a possible occasion of revelation. It is to treat philosophies as if they were means to the enhancement of human life."[11] This goes wrong in two ways: first, because it suggests that Heidegger would not have thought technology (the "technological" use of philosophy) to be worth debating or to be even philosophically coherent: Heidegger's thought is rather that the "technological" yields a profoundly false kind of philosophy, one utterly unresponsive to Being (*Sein*); second, because it fails to explain the sense in which philosophy *is* an "occasion of revelation" either in the essays following the *Kehre* or in *Being and Time*, and because it does not address the question of whether Dewey and Heidegger could possibly have meant similar things by the revelatory power of philosophy. The answer, of course, is that *they could not*. In short, neither Heidegger nor Dewey ever meant to bring philosophy to an "end"—in Rorty's sense. Rorty grants this in Heidegger's case and misses it completely in Dewey's—as he does as well in reading Wittgenstein. In all these cases, as it happens, he fails—pursuing his own private ends.

This is perhaps no more than gossip. But the fact remains that, with allowance for a difference in idiom, *both* Heidegger and Dewey would "agree" that Dewey's philosophy *is* a *Weltanschauungsphilosophie* and Heidegger's is meant to oppose and reject the adequacy of the other; each thinks that philosophy, reformed along the lines he recommends, would be correctly oriented at least.

I do not find any such recognition in Rorty, though it surely marks the most important difference between Dewey's and Heidegger's philosophies, whatever further comparisons we might favor between Dewey and continental thinkers, *and* the possible bearing of Dewey's thought on any rapprochement between analytic and continental philosophy.

Look a little more closely, therefore, at Heidegger's notion of *Weltanschauungsphilosophie.* Heidegger condemns the notion, signaling—not particularly politely—his contempt for Karl Jaspers's frank admission that the label applies to his own vision.[12] Heidegger explicitly disjoins *Weltanschauungsphilosophie* and "scientific philosophy": "*being,*" he says, "*is the proper and sole theme of philosophy.* . . . philosophy is not a science of beings but of *being* or, as the Greek expression goes, *ontology.*"[13] Of *Weltanschauungsphilosophie* he adds the following, pointedly in reaction to Jaspers's account:

> the world-view . . . always arises out of the particular factical existence of the human being in accordance with his factical possibilities of thoughtful reflection and attitude-formation, and it arises then *for* this factical Dasein. The world-view is something that in each case exists historically from, with, and for the factical Dasein. A philosophical world-view is one that expressly and explicitly or at any rate preponderantly has to be worked out and brought about by philosophy, that is to say, by theoretical speculation, to the exclusion of artistic and religious interpretations of the world and Dasein. This world-view is not a by-product of philosophy; its cultivation, rather, is the proper goal and nature of philosophy itself. In its very concept philosophy is world-view philosophy, philosophy as world-view. If philosophy in the form of theoretical knowledge of the world aims at what is universal in the world and ultimate for the Dasein—the whence, the whither, and the wherefore of the world and life—then this differentiates it from the particular sciences, which always consider only a particular region of the world and the Dasein, as well as from the artistic and religious attitudes, which are not based primarily on the theoretical attitude.[14]

If you keep this in mind, you cannot fail to conclude: (1) that, for all his bluster, Heidegger's own philosophy cannot but be a *Weltanschauungsphi-*

losophie; (2) that Dewey celebrates philosophy as *Weltanschauungsphiloso-phie*; (3) that Dewey and Heidegger are utterly and irreconcilably opposed to one another's conception of what philosophy is all about and what it is capable of achieving; and (4) that Rorty deforms the vision of both in his zeal to promote his own deflationary view of philosophy and, in the bargain, fails to grasp the significance of the opposition between Dewey and Heidegger—as well as the sense in which Wittgenstein as well is (in the *Investigations*) committed to a project implicitly opposed to Heidegger's vision and closer to *Weltanschauungsphilosophie*.

In a word, Rorty is the worst possible guide here, though with the best possible familiarity with the writings of all three of his mentors. You may confirm the finding unmistakably—it is worth confirming—by reference to any number of Rorty's summary comments on the nature of philosophy, for instance the following, from another well-known essay, "The World Well Lost":

> "the world" is either the purely vacuous notion of the ineffable cause of sense and goal of the intellect, or else a name for the objects that inquiry at the moment is leaving alone, those planks in the boat [in Neurath's metaphor] which are at the moment not being moved about (treated philosophically). It seems to me that epistemology since Kant has shuttled back and forth between these two meanings of the term 'world', just as moral philosophy since Plato has shuttled back and forth between 'the Good' as a name for an ineffable touchstone of inquiry which might lead to the rejection of *all* our present moral views, and as a name for the ideally coherent synthesis of as many of those views as possible. This equivocation seems to me essential to the position of those philosophers who see "realism" or "the correspondence theory of truth" as controversial or exciting themes.[15]

What is at stake is not a purely textual matter, however: it bears on the very prospects of philosophy. For Rorty's fashionable view does not merely misrepresent Dewey and Heidegger, it fails to come to terms with the obvious fact that *both* "agree" (with Rorty) in dismissing realism in the correspondentist sense, a fortiori in dismissing the correspondence theory of truth; *and*, in doing that, acting to reclaim the positive work of philosophy—hence, the positive prospects of a theory of reality and truth!

Were it not for the fact that Rorty's extraordinary influence in shaping our reading of the relationship between pragmatism (as well as analytic philosophy) and Heidegger (and other continental philosophers) has bordered on the cultish, I would simply drop the matter. But, for good or bad, the clarification of what to make of a comparison of Dewey's and Heidegger's philosophies—and between Dewey and other continental figures—must, in current American terms, possibly in the Anglo-American tradition at large, pass through Rorty's prism. That lens, I say, blinds us to the true facts. The point of referring to "the world"—in Dewey and Heidegger—is to orient philosophy rightly: in Heidegger, to escape the confinement of what (*we* learn) *he* cannot possibly escape; in Dewey, to confirm that there's no benefit in attempting to escape at all and that the best work of philosophy lies in acknowledging same.

I'll venture one last remark of Rorty's and then move on. "One may say of Heidegger," he observes, closing the essay linking Dewey and Heidegger, "what he himself says of Nietzsche: misled by a superficial understanding of the Platonic ideas, he tried to replace them, but instead only translated Platonism into a newer jargon. By offering us, 'openness to Being' to replace 'philosophical argument,' Heidegger helps preserve all that was worst in the tradition he hoped to overcome."[16] Here, Rorty obviously believes that Dewey, more sensibly than Heidegger, "turn[ed] away from philosophy as a distinctive activity altogether, and toward the ordinary world" and that Heidegger "hoped that a new path [the one mentioned] would open."[17] But the truth is, neither turned *away* from *philosophy*; both tried to direct philosophy away from the played-out models Rorty correctly identifies. The difference between them is that *they* believed philosophy was on the point of taking a turn for the better and *he* believes there is no such possibility if that means reclaiming the problems of reality, knowledge, truth, goodness, and the like. "The ordinary world," for Rorty, means the abdication of philosophy; for Dewey, it means the only possible site for philosophy; for Heidegger, it means what we must escape if we are ever to do philosophy or to secure what is best in philosophy!

One cannot understand Dewey, therefore, or the point of comparing Dewey and continental philosophers if one follows Rorty's recommendation.

II

It is true that the comparison between Dewey and Heidegger is the most rewarding if we really mean to interpret Dewey's philosophy perspicuously in the company of the continental philosophers. I shall give that first comparison some further scope, but one must bear in mind that it is not the only comparison worth making. In fact, the analysis will ultimately take an unexpected turn—linking pragmatism and phenomenology more than merely Dewey and Heidegger. The best beginning, I suggest, is one that features Dewey's curious characterization of "the problematic situation" which, in a way, organizes the distinctive labor—a failed labor, I must say—of his *Logic: The Theory of Inquiry*.[18]

I don't believe Dewey's *conception* of logic is a failure, as I shall try to make clear; rather, it's the attempt, hopelessly literal-minded, "schizzy," perhaps even ultimately incoherent, to accept in the first place the standing categories of the usual canonical logic and then to reinterpret *them* in the intended dynamic terms of his own revision. That can't be done. I cannot see why Dewey ever invited such troubles, when, obviously, what was called for was a general conception of how the same effective intelligence that attends to questions of logical consistency (while exploring and manipulating the world) tries to regularize as well its sense of the categories of formal argument and reasoning. There was never any point in construing, piecemeal, the structure of standard propositional forms in terms of the very process of thinking or *praxis*, though there might have been a point to reinterpreting (en bloc, in Dewey's case) the actual import of formal logical structures and principles, somewhat as Peirce does, in reinterpreting the standard (dyadic) categories of syllogistic logic in terms of his own notion of a triadic or interpretive account of "inquiry"—as the reinterpretation of the principles of noncontradiction and excluded middle confirm.[19]

In fact, Dewey is explicit about his "great indebtedness" to Peirce: "As far as I am aware," he says, "[Peirce] was the first writer on logic to make inquiry and its methods the primary and ultimate source of logical subject-matter." You would be right to see in this the essential clue to Dewey's dutiful—but entirely impossible—reinterpretation of logic in Peircean terms (as he understands matters) as well as the point of his actually citing, almost in justification of his analysis of the various kinds of propositions, Peirce's rather offhand remark: "We ought to construct our theories so as to provide for such [later] discoveries [scientific propositions being subject to doubt as a result of further inquiries] by leaving room for the modifications that cannot be foreseen but which are pretty sure to prove needful."[20] One has here a sign of Dewey's characteristic simplification of Peirce's enormously subtle and dense way of pondering the deeper significance of well-known standard logics. There's very little in Dewey to compare with Peirce's cast of mind. All the more reason Dewey should not have tampered with the usual canonical distinctions he does in the piecemeal way he does.

Here, the point of observing the provenance of Dewey's *Logic* and the better policy of reading what he says in terms of his conception of inquiry and not (primarily) in terms of his interpretation of particular kinds of propositions and operators prepares the ground for a more interesting comparison with Heidegger. Dewey's logic is still Peircean in an obviously derived sense that pretty well erases Peirce's strenuous metaphysical and methodological distinctions while remaining thoroughly pragmatist in orientation. Ironically, it is Dewey's version of pragmatism that has become the exemplar of the entire field—so much so that, now, Peirce's metaphysics and logic might even be judged to be much less thoroughly pragmatist in spirit than Dewey's way of addressing matters! One can resolve the terminological issue readily enough, if one merely compares Dewey's and Peirce's conceptions of fallibilism. They confirm very different forms of pragmatism; but I shall leave that to one side.[21]

We need a few specimen remarks of Dewey's here, if, in the middle of some particular *praxis*, we are to fix his sense of inquiry and the bearing of generating the categories and conceptual distinctions by which we ordinarily achieve the proper ends of any inquiry. With that in hand, we should be able to make an effective comparison between Dewey and Heidegger. (It will, I promise, throw new light on the anecdote reported earlier about Dewey's having scanned Heidegger's *Sein und Zeit*.)

Very early in his account Dewey remarks: "That inquiry is related to doubt will, I suppose, be admitted. The admission carries with it an implication regarding the end of inquiry: *end* in both senses of the word, as end-in-view and as close or termination. If inquiry begins in doubt, it terminates in the institution of conditions which remove need for doubt. The latter state of affairs may be designated by the words *belief* and *knowledge*. For reasons that I shall state later I prefer the words 'warranted assertibility.'"[22] This may be as good a clue as any to the usual simplification and reshaping of Peirce's theory of inquiry that Dewey effects. Dewey goes on in the same passage to say: "*Belief* may be so understood as to be a fitting designation for the outcome of inquiry. Doubt is uneasy; it is tension that finds expression and outlet in the processes of inquiry. Inquiry terminates in reaching that which is settled. This settled condition is a demarcating characteristic of genuine belief."[23] The addition will seem unexceptional until one fixes the sense in which the very process of *inquiry* is to be understood. It is there that the full benefit of comparing Dewey and Heidegger makes itself felt. (That is what Rorty misses.)

The obvious focus of Dewey's theory of logic concerns the nature of what he calls "inquiry," but its true focus lies with the analysis of "an indeterminate situation." Inquiry is formally defined in a way that rather ingeniously recalls Peirce's notion of the "vague" and the "indeterminate." Both thinkers construe inquiry in existential terms—if that is taken to signify that the formal distinctions (the "vague" and the "indeterminate") do accurately characterize features of the real world encountered, as such, in human *praxis*. Inquiry is actually defined as "the controlled or directed transformation of an indeterminate situation into one that is so determinate in its constituent distinctions and relations as to convert the elements of the original situation into a unified whole."[24]

One would be seriously mistaken, however, if one construed this formulation as some sort of informal or instructional metaphor. Dewey intends it in a metaphysically serious way: "it is of the very nature of the indeterminate situation which evokes inquiry to be questionable; in terms of actuality instead of potentiality, to be uncertain, unsettled, disturbed." Here are some of his most pointed warnings about how to read his remarks:

> It is the *situation* that has these traits. *We* are doubtful because the situation is inherently doubtful.[25]
> The habit of disposing of the doubtful as if it belonged only to *us* rather than to the existential situation in which we are caught and implicated is an inheritance from subjectivistic psychology. . . . It is, accordingly, a mistake to suppose that a situation is doubtful only in a "subjective" sense.[26]
> The unsettled or indeterminate situation might have been called a *problematic* situation. This name would have been, however, proleptic and anticipatory. The indeterminate situation becomes problematic in the very process of being subjected to inquiry. The indeterminate situation comes into existence from existential causes, just as does, say, the organic imbalance of hunger. There is nothing intellectual or cognitive in the existence of such situations, although they are the necessary condition of cognitive operations or inquiry. In themselves they are precognitive. The first result of evocation of inquiry is that the situation is taken, adjudged, to be problematic. To see that a situation requires inquiry is the initial step in inquiry.[27]

Now, one cannot fathom correctly what Dewey says here if one does not take note of the fact that a footnote is appended to the last of the passages cited, in which, without further attribution, Dewey explicitly notes the *formal* inadequacy of a "two-valued logic" (a bivalent logic); he says that "such a logic is necessarily so truncated that clearness and consistency in logical doctrine are impossible. Being the matter of a problem [he explains] is a primary logical property."[28] Of course, this is the most abstract possible rendering of Peirce's treatment of the logic of vagueness and indeterminacy—or of Peirce's rationale for denying the ubiquitous applicability of the principles of noncontradiction and excluded middle.[29]

There's no doubt that there is, here, a touch of the old argument in favor of "panpsychism" drawn from the German idealists, which affects Peirce as well as Dewey and which is, perhaps, remotely linked to Emerson's influence. It's not unrelated to what is often said to be the "Hegelian" cast of Dewey's philosophy.[30] But it is also true that there is almost nothing that is actually Hegelian in Dewey's philosophy. Dewey expressly opposed the Hegelian turn;[31] he was more of an evolutionist than a historicist, and whatever we say is Hegelian is pretty well exhausted by his well-known rejection of all the principal forms of disjunctive dualities: the subjective and the objective, the real and the apparent, the private and the public, the biological and the cognitive, the psychological and the social, experience and nature, and the like.[32] Roughly speaking, Dewey biologized what he drew from Peirce and Hegel. I think that is the only way to read what I've cited from the *Logic*. The associations with Peirce's logic and Hegel's critique of Kant are "there" all right, but Dewey erases the need to refer to them as more than penumbral metaphysical themes implicated in the biological priorities he favors. When they are actually made explicit and read in determinately "realist" terms, Dewey avoids them—or reinterprets them generally as no more than instrumentally justified.

I take most of the usual Peircean and Hegelian elaborations of what Dewey offers in this spirit to be subtly off the mark. Its real purpose is to allow the informal "metaphysics" of the indeterminate situation to be read as: (1) post-Kantian, in the sense of ensuring an escape from all the dualisms overcome in the tradition that moves from Kant to Hegel (including those that may be rightly attributed to Kant and Hegel themselves); (2) biologized and *praxis*-centered, in the sense that all regularized determinacies regarding the putatively real structures of the world emerge, instrumentally, locally, in a more or less progressively explicit and stable manner, never more than contingently or heuristically or impermanently (if projected beyond the immediate "situation" that is the begin-all of inquiry); and, most important, (3) natural or "naturalistic," in the sense that the cognitive and active resources of the human organism are the only resources we have, are deemed adequate (qua natural) for the needs of life, are never privileged in any way, are never more than the reflexive effectiveness of powers and processes already present in nature at large, and take form (reflexively) from existence itself. If you grant all that, you see the benefit of comparing and contrasting Dewey and Heidegger.

III

What Dewey means here is difficult to capture in words. Try an awkward rendering first: I shall try to unpack it.

The alien quality of Dewey's formula, which his readers imagine "must" be akin to certain themes in Heidegger's *Being and Time*, centers on the concept—more than the image—of the gathering doubt, and the gathering process of resolving that doubt's *subjective* (hence, dawningly cognitive) manifestation. (Doubt is the reflexive cognitive dawning of an "indeterminate situation.") Dewey treats it as nothing less than the natural site (telically described) *of* a larger, *prior, existential* process that reflexively evolves in an orderly way *we then* anthropomorphize—or, describe in an exaggeratedly psychological, insular, detached way—*by* insisting on the dualism of subject and object. Dewey's strange idiom is the consequence of applying a scruple that adheres at all costs to the requirement that such a dualism must be overcome. I don't deny that the theme is genuinely *phenomenological* in Dewey. But it is not Heideggerian any more than it is Husserlian. If I must choose, it would be fairer to say it was akin to the conviction one finds in Merleau-Ponty, in *The Visible and the Invisible*, where Merleau-Ponty finally grasps the verdict that to ensure the validity of phenomenological inquiry he must make a clean break with Husserl and *must deny that there is any discontinuity between the natural and the phenomenological.*

I'm certain the key to what one finds mysteriously promising in Dewey regarding a rapprochement between Anglo-American and continental European philosophies lies here. The clue is this: both pragmatism and phenomenology address the conceptual knot we know as Cartesianism—which links, indissolubly, the advocacy (*a*) of supposedly apodictic powers and the concession (*b*) of an insuperable dualism at the heart of (*a*). Husserl may be thought to risk a skepticism inseparable from (*b*), in the name of ensuring (*a*), by producing a super-Cartesianism. Heidegger, Sartre, and Merleau-Ponty are unable, finally, to endorse Husserl's extraordinary—quite impossible—solution. One will find the supporting evidence already in Husserl: for instance in the curious episode of Husserl's deep annoyance at Heidegger's "anthropologizing" the new draft of his *Encyclopaedia Britannica* article and in his inviting Eugen Fink to prepare materials for a sixth meditation to be added to *Cartesian Meditations*.[33]

One will also find a profoundly equivocal solution of the Husserlian puzzle in Heidegger's *Being and Time*. I shall come to it in a moment. But the point of its novelty lies in overcoming Husserl's Cartesian dualism, avoiding (therefore) Husserl's apodicticity, and yet (somehow) reserving a privilege meant to govern the unprivileged pronouncements of naturalized or worldly cognition—"ontologically," *not* (it seems) epistemically. Heidegger's solution is an ingenious one, but it fails, because it falls back (but denies that it does) to something akin to Husserl's apodicticity. One sees this in the notorious "Letter on Humanism," which is obliged to reinterpret truth oracularly in order to protect its flank against the charge of repeating Descartes's and Kant's appeal to the apodictic.

In Merleau-Ponty, by contrast, the "pre-given" world, the world that precedes conceptual analysis but informs it, is itself conjecturally supplied, wherever determinately specified, *from* the "second-order" vantage of naturalized inquiry. In the limit, in *The Visible and the Invisible*, Merleau-Ponty tries to reclaim the inseparable bond between the pre-thematized world of the "lived body" and the normalized world of a threatening dualism by the fantastic device of inventing, in exquisite detail, matching uses for all the familiar "subjective" categories in the "objective" world and for all the familiar "objective" categories in the "subjective" world. In that way, Merleau-Ponty construes the search for the apodictic as internal to the form of life we manifest—which generates the quest but cannot ensure the capture of its prize. Merleau-Ponty's idiom is, finally, illegible.

What I am sketching here is the ground for a plausible rapprochement between a pragmatist and a phenomenological resolution of the Cartesian knot. Peirce supplies the clue; Dewey deploys it in his analysis of the "indeterminate situation." (Peirce, of course, was explicit about the commitment of pragmatism to dismantling the Cartesian project.[34]) On the phenomenological side, Husserl *was* a super-Cartesian. The best of the phenomenologists certainly know (that is, they eventually realize) that they cannot save the Cartesian (Husserl's) confidence if they would also save the phenomenological contribution *to* the full analysis of our (natural) cognitive powers.

Heidegger tries to hold on to *a privileged source that never issues in privileged truth-claims* (in, say, the correspondentist sense of truth): that's why he falls back to *aletheia* in *Being and Time*. Here is one of the most explicit of Heidegger's pronouncements on the matter:

> because the *logos* is a letting-something-be-seen, it can *therefore* be true or false. But here everything depends on our steering clear of any conception of truth which is construed in the sense of 'agreement'. The idea is by no means the primary one in the concept of *aletheia*. The 'Being-true' of the *logos* as [alethically informed] means that in [their being drawn from phenomenal experience] the entities *of which* one is talking must be taken out of their hiddenness; one must let them be seen as something unhidden (*alethes*); that is, they must be *discovered.*[35]

You see how, in admitting "true or false" in the sense of *aletheia*, Heidegger (1) preserves the *priority* of the phenomenological precondition of discursive truth-claims; (2) denies a merely discursive role *to* the phenomenological itself; yet (3) assigns it a pertinent role (ultimately "ontological," in Heidegger's special idiom) in constraining the validity of the *discursive* use of "true" and "false"; hence, (4) implicates a cognitive privilege for the phenomenological vis-à-vis ordinary ("natural") discourse. Conditions (1)–(4) betray the Cartesian and Kantian character of Heidegger's failed attempt to escape Husserl's super-Cartesian resolution of the Kantian problem.

Now, the point to be secured is this. Heidegger is bound to locate the play between the discursive and the alethaic sense of "true" in the "ontology" of a certain unique being (*Seiendes*): because *it* is capable on the one hand of holding discursive truth-claims to their dependence on the ultimate alethaic source (*Sein*) and because, on the other hand, it can do that inasmuch as its own "being" inherently bridges and indissolubly joins the "ontic" powers of discursive thought (as in Descartes and Kant) to the "ontological" resource that Heidegger now claims to have discovered. That entity, of course, is *Dasein*, which Heidegger characterizes in a transparently contrived way:

> Dasein [he says] is an entity which does not occur among other entities. Rather it is ontically distinguished by the fact that, in its very Being,

that Being is an *issue* for it. But in that case, this is a constitutive state of Dasein's Being, and this implies that Dasein, in its Being, has a relationship towards that Being—a relationship which is one of Being. . . . [Hence,] *understanding of Being is itself a definite characteristic of Dasein's Being.* Dasein is ontically distinctive in that it *is* ontological.[36]

This would make no sense unless the *concepts* or categories of the "ontic" were separable from, but dependent on, the "*existentialia*" of the "ontological." But, of course, Heidegger renders the distinction ad hoc, suspicious, ultimately unconvincing, because he himself admits that *Dasein* has a "relationship" with Being, in spite of the fact that Being (*Sein*, as distinct from plural *Seiende—Dasein* included) has no discursive, categorically accessible structure of its own. (If it did, there would be no room for the "ontological" dimension of *Being*. But, of course, the distinction does indeed collapse: after all, it can be discursively reported.)

We need a further linkage. Bear with me. One should now anticipate that Heidegger will have to "duplicate" everything that is discerned "in nature"—in the natural world, discursively, ontically—by supplying their "prior," "ontological" *Doppelgänger* that authentically dawn in the space of *Dasein's* relationship to *Sein* (aletheia). That is, the conceptually undifferentiated source (*Sein*) of beings (*Seiende*) *is* authentically disclosed as a world of plural beings—*to* and only to that uniquely privileged being, *Dasein,* that, because of *its* "ontic-ontological" structure, *has* that exclusive function! Nothing could be prettier! This explains why Heidegger provides, in *Being and Time,* a formulation that many think is similar to Dewey's notion of "the indeterminate situation." But there is no equivalence there. Furthermore, where one imagines a convergence, the impression is due to reading Heidegger's extravagance in the more concessive, eventually conciliatory terms favored by Merleau-Ponty. The lesson is worth drawing out, because it explains what is so promising in Dewey's pragmatism, what justifies a sense of rapprochement between pragmatism and continental European philosophy (particularly phenomenology), and what is so characteristically lacking in the more extreme analytic currents of Anglo-American philosophy.

There are a good number of passages in *Being and Time* in which Heidegger introduces the dialectical idiom of *Vorhandenheit* ("presence-at-hand") and *Zuhandenheit* ("readiness-to-hand") that corresponds in a way to the equally dialectical idiom (Dewey's) of "indeterminacy" and "determinateness." It will pay to have Heidegger's wording before us—we already have Dewey's:

> 'Nature' is not to be understood [Heidegger says] as that which is just present-at-hand, nor as the *Power of Nature*. The wood is a forest of timber, the mountain a quarry of rock; the river is water-power, the wind is wind 'in the sails'. As the 'environment' is discovered, the 'Nature' thus discovered is encountered too. If its kind of Being as ready-to-hand is disregarded, this 'Nature' itself can be discovered and defined simply in its pure presence-at-hand. . . . Thus along with [our usual] work, we encounter not only entities ready-to-hand but also entities with Dasein's kind of Being—entities for which, in their concern, the product becomes ready-to-hand; and together with these we encounter the world in which weavers and users live, which is at the same time ours.[37]

Heidegger dutifully warns us how we should and should not read this formula: "To lay bare what is just present-at-hand and no more, cognition must first penetrate *beyond* what is ready-to-hand in our concern. *Readiness-to-hand is the way in which entities as they are 'in themselves' are defined ontologico-categorically.* Yet only by reason of something present-at-hand, 'is there' anything ready-to-hand."[38] Heidegger's solution is, verbally, straightforward enough:

> The [natural or ontic, the discursive or categoried] world itself is not an entity within-the-world; and yet it is so determinative for such entities that only in so far as "there is" a world can they be encountered and show themselves in their Being, as entities which have been discovered. But in what way "is there" a world? If Dasein is ontically constituted by Being-in-the-World, and if an understanding of the Being of its Self belongs just as essentially to its Being, no matter how indefinite that understanding may be, then does not Dasein have an understanding of the world—a pre-ontological understanding, which indeed can and does get along without explicit ontological insights?[39]

I shall not pursue the full elaboration of Heidegger's rather complicated invention. One sees the sense in which Heidegger improvises—skillfully, it must be said—in order to ensure the formal coherence and seeming adequacy of his scheme. *Dasein* must look to *Sein*, which has no antecedent structure, in order to make the case *that* the particular entities human beings (as manifestations of that *Dasein*) discern or encounter in the world are *then* precisely what they are because such disclosure counts as authentic or alethaic. The *categoried* treatment of particular entities (say, along Kantian lines) is then seen to be in tow to the prior "ontological" power of *Dasein* to mediate between our categories and the existential dawning of our first encounter with the world (*Sein*) *before* it is actually categorized. The latter (discursive categorization) is what Heidegger means by readiness-at-hand (a "reserve" of manageable things in "normal" form); the former (presence-at-hand) is what makes that possible; and even the former presupposes a deeper inexpressible encounter between *Dasein* and *Sein*.

IV

There are too many idiosyncrasies in Dewey's and Heidegger's separate idioms to make close comparison an entirely straightforward affair. Nevertheless, it is a very good intuition that encourages risking a comparison between the two—one that goes well beyond their own particular visions but catches up their best insights nevertheless. At any rate, I am myself sufficiently convinced of the importance of attempting a comparison that I urge a measure of patience in wading through Heidegger's extraordinary verbiage and Dewey's curiously matter-of-fact treatment of "the indeterminate situation."

There are at least two essential themes that, once broached, help to bring the intended comparison into clear focus and yield an important lesson. One must begin by recognizing that pragmatism and post-Kantian German philosophy agree in opposing the pre-Kantian conceptual strategies of early modern philosophy. Their common motivation is, of course, that the nested forms of skepticism that may be abbreviated as the threat posed by "representationality" (addressed in Kant's first *Critique*) and the further threat posed by "correspondence" (entrenched by Kant's very treatment of representationality and addressed in Hegel's *Phenomenology*) must be exorcised if philosophy is to proceed without self-referential paradox. I endorse the good sense of that conviction: I take it to be shared by Peirce, James, and Dewey, though I also concede there is no common body of doctrine that may be usefully labeled pragmatism.

In any case, the picture is entirely different, seen from the side of phenomenology. Husserl begins with an appreciation of how the Kantian question challenges Descartes's own naive confidence, but what Husserl then dreams of is, precisely, what *correcting Kant's Cartesian naïveté* would permit and encourage us to reclaim as an even stronger Cartesianism. One may glimpse something of this, in Husserl, from the following passage, which touches on the relationship between transcendental phenomenology and the movement of early modern philosophy from Descartes to Kant:

> Part of transcendental philosophy's own meaning was that it arose out of reflections on conscious subjectivity through which the world, the scientific as well as the everyday intuitive world, comes to be known or achieves its ontic validity for us; thus transcendental philosophy recognized the necessity of developing a purely mental [*geistige*] approach to the world. But if it had to deal with the mental, why did it not turn to the psychology which had been practiced so diligently for centuries? Or, if this no longer sufficed, why did it not work out a better psychology? One will naturally answer that the empirical man, the psychological being, himself belongs, in soul as well as body, to the constituted world. Thus human subjectivity is not transcendental subjectivity, and the psychological theories of knowledge of Locke and his successors serve as continued admonition against "psychologism," against any use of psychology for transcendental purposes. But in exchange, transcendental philosophy always had to bear its cross of incomprehensibility. The difference between empirical and transcendental subjectivity remained unavoidable; yet just as unavoidable, but also incomprehensible, was their identity. I myself, as transcendental ego, "constitute" the world, and at the same time, as soul, I am a human ego in that world.[40]

There is a dilemma in Husserl that Husserl never successfully overcame—could never overcame—that is, the unwelcome choice between a radical disjunction between transcendental and "natural" cognitive powers and a thorough embedding of would-be transcendental (second-order or legitimative) powers *in* the cognitive resources of our natural (mental) life. To choose the first option is to insist on a form of apodictic privilege that is both utterly arbitrary *and* oddly alien vis-à-vis the "natural" categories it pretends to examine in testing the phenomenological "constitution" of the world. By contrast, to choose the other option is, effectively, to abandon altogether the very idea that phenomenological and natural(istic) inquiry have different cognitive resources (though they obviously pursue different philosophical questions) *and*, to abandon, as a consequence, any principled disjunction between the two inquiries. (I trust it is clear that what we should mean by the mental or psychological is a troubling question as well.)

In fact, on the second option, there can be no sense in denying that phenomenology, transcendental or not, *is* "psychologistic" in precisely the sense in which the exploration of natural reason is said to be psychologistic.[41] But if that is so, then phenomenology raises deeper questions than Kant's about how to construe the "sources" of our natural cognitive competence—for instance, whether the supposed invariance of the Kantian forms of intuition and categories of understanding *are* rightly understood, *are* genuinely complete, *are* demonstrably invariant. Here, theorists like Merleau-Ponty and Heidegger came to realize that Husserlian phenomenology was unable to surmount its original dilemma.

Merleau-Ponty was originally unwilling to abandon the Husserlian project: he sought a safer haven for its seeming privilege and found it, as in the early *Phenomenology of Perception*, in "the world as directly experienced": "it is [he says] a question of recognizing consciousness itself as a project of the world, meant for a world which it neither embraces nor possesses, but towards which it is perpetually directed—and the world as this pre-objective individual whose imperious unity decrees what knowledge shall take as its goal."[42]

"Looking for the world's essence," Merleau-Ponty goes on, "is not looking for what it is as an idea once it has been reduced as a theme of discourse; it is looking for what it is as a fact before any thematization. . . . The self-evidence of perception is not adequate thought or apodictic self-evidence. The world is not what I think, but what I live through."[43] Here, Merleau-Ponty overcomes any division between the "worlds" of natural and transcendental experience; he does not accord phenomenology a determinate cognitive privilege but ensures its regulative role nonetheless; and he specifically subordinates the *validity* of science and natural discourse to what role he can recover as the regulative constraint of our pre-discursive, "pre-thematized" existence and experience. It is for this reason that he warns, "The whole universe of science is built upon the world as directly experienced, and if we want to subject science itself to rigorous scrutiny and arrive at a precise assessment of its meaning and scope, we must begin by reawakening the basic experience of the world of which science is the *second-order* expression."[44] We cannot recover the pristine world of direct experience apodictically or directly; but we can, it seems, qualify and correct our "second-best" discursive conjectures by what remains vestigially of that experience.

Merleau-Ponty arrives at an absolutely stunning challenge to Husserl's—and his own former version of—phenomenology when, reflecting on Husserl's worry about the empirical researches of Lucien Lévy-Bruhl, he queries Husserl's late formula, "transcendental subjectivity is intersubjectivity." Here, he asks, "if the transcendental is intersubjectivity, how can the borders of the transcendental and the empirical help becoming indistinct?" He goes on to affirm, "the transcendental [then] descends into history."[45]

What I am leading to is this: Dewey, from the side of pragmatism—itself directed (as with Peirce) against "Cartesianism" and (in Dewey in particular) against all forms of dualism—*converges with Merleau-Ponty, not Heidegger*, from the side of phenomenology. Phenomenology, of course, originally opposed, though in a peculiarly equivocal way, the ("naturalized" or "psychologized") dualisms and apodictic pretensions of the tradition from Descartes to Kant. My own way of putting this is to insist that Merleau-Ponty grasps—though neither Husserl nor Heidegger does—the indissolubility of experience, knowledge, reason, and whatever of reality each resource claims to address. In short, on Merleau-Ponty's view, naturalism without phenomenology is blind and phenomenology without naturalism is empty; and their "relationship" is neither additive nor hierarchical in any way.

Heidegger was obliged to reject anything close to this formula in the manner favored, say, by Merleau-Ponty and (if one allows the liberty) Dewey. Because, for one thing, Heidegger was an uncompromising opponent of *Weltanschauungsphilosophie*—which, in the final analysis, cannot be said of Merleau-Ponty (given his view of Marxist humanism) or, of course, Dewey; for another thing, Heidegger was driven (finally) by the logic of his own position to decouple the already attenuated Kantian-like connection between the "ontic" and the "ontological" in order to ensure (after the *Kehre*, in "Letter on Humanism") the oracular privilege of the supposed pronouncements of Being (*Gelassenheit*) that then can no longer be challenged by any naturalistic *or* phenomenological or existential correction. The result is that the seemingly promising comparison between Dewey's treatment of "the indeterminate situation" and Heidegger's dialectic of *Zuhandenheit* and *Vorhandenheit* is simply a misunderstanding. It is only when phenomenology rids itself of its own dualistic, privileged pretensions that one finds (judging from Husserl's and Heidegger's strategies) that the convergence between pragmatism and phenomenology yields a most important lesson.

One may be startled, then, to see, in the so-called "Working Notes" published together with *The Visible and the Invisible*, the extraordinary convergence between Dewey's formula and Merleau-Ponty's. Consider the following excerpt, for example:

> Reversibility: the finger of the glove that is turned inside out—There is no need of a spectator who would be *on each side*. It suffices that from one side I see the wrong side of the glove that is applied to the right side, that I touch the one *through* the other (double "representation" of a point or plane of the field) the chiasm is that: the reversibility——
>
> It is through it alone that there is a passage from the "For Itself" to the For the Other——In reality there is neither me nor the other as positive, positive subjectivities. There are two caverns, two opennesses, two stages where something will take place—and which both belong to the same world, to the stage of Being.
>
> There is not the For Itself and the For the Other. They are each the other side of the other. This is why they incorporate one another: projection-introjection——There is that line, that frontier surface at some distance before me, where occurs veering I-Other Other-I——[46]

This theme may be excerpted at will throughout *The Visible and the Invisible* and the "Working Notes"—both with regard to different selves and with regard to the subject/object duality. It affords an unintended clue to the proper reading of Dewey's puzzling remarks in *Logic*. It confirms, that is, that *if one seriously means to overcome the dualisms and cognitive pretensions of the early modern tradition—which, on reflection, prove to be entrenched in the late tradition as well, down to the end of the century—one must: (a) grasp the indissoluble unity of pragmatism and phenomenology; and (b) grasp as well that the contingency of the cultural formation of our cognitive powers, which are biologically given but not biologically fixed, as the competencies they are, lead us inevitably to admit the historical diversity of those culturally formed competencies.*

I must leave the matter here. I take it to indicate the most promising line of inquiry for recovering and resolving the master questions of philosophy, capturing (1) the tradition's solutions of the various threats of skepticism; (2) rejecting all forms of cognitive privilege; and (3) admitting that, under constraints (1) and (2), our cognitional competences are themselves historically constituted. Pragmatism insisted on (1) and (2); phenomenology originally saw that our "natural" powers of cognition *and* (accordingly) "its" cognized world must be constituted "phenomenologically." Phenomenology then found itself obliged to admit (with Merleau-Ponty against Husserl and Heidegger) that (3) our phenomenological (as well as "natural") competence was itself historically or culturally constituted. In that convergence, one will also find explained the characteristic pre-Kantian weakness of analytic philosophy (which, at long last, it is beginning to admit).

One final caveat may be helpful, therefore. The convergence between Dewey and Merleau-Ponty hardly requires the extravagance of either's idiom. If I have put the matter rightly, then the convergence between pragmatism and phenomenology holds only in a holist sense, *not* distributively. There's room enough for any number of alternative idioms—within the space defined by (1)–(3)—of how to understand the ingredient function of the "subjective" and the "objective." That remains to be decided in the new century. Dewey's and Merleau-Ponty's formulas ("the indeterminate situation" and the "chiasm") do not positively require confounding our usual distinctions between the subjective and the objective. What they favor is better viewed as an instructive metaphor opposing any and all forms of Cartesianism and pre-Kantian philosophy than as an exemplar of what is required of any specific argument that claims to have caught either of their lessons.

Their shared lesson is easily missed or misread. Neither Dewey nor Merleau-Ponty answers any carpentered questions within his ken. Each shows, rather, what to expect of any set of such questions and answers. Very broadly put, they demonstrate how pragmatism and phenomenology converge—and, in doing that, promise what is (to my mind) the best general strategy we now possess for meeting the entire range of philosophical puzzles. The unity of pragmatism/phenomenology saves the advantages of what has been tallied as items (1) and (2), brings them into full accord with the deeper conditions of history (3); and, now, (4) problematizes all the usual questions of logic, epistemology, and metaphysics that analytic philosophy has never really been willing to consider. I cannot see any better prospect in the offing. It signals a "naturalism" ampler than the fashionable "naturalizing" of late analytic philosophy—because it refuses to deny the relevance and distinctive logic of second-order questions;[47] and it lays the ground for recovering, within its terms, whatever a naturalized phenomenology may contribute to our legitimative inquiries.

What that means, ultimately, is that Dewey and Merleau-Ponty have, respectively, isolated the minimal themes pragmatism and phenomenology contribute to the soundest philosophies of the new century, without quite matching, for their own part, the precision and power of the detailed work of Peirce and Husserl, which, respectively, they have themselves reinterpreted in less vulnerable ways—and (of course) holistically. The adequacy of each requires the implicated contribution of the other.

Having come this far, I close with a more pointed finding. The sense I have of what Merleau-Ponty marks as "second-order"—our discursive grasp of the world—is also, on his best (late) reading, the source from which we recover (as well as we can) what is "pre-thematized," that is, prediscursive in our way of living in the world. Merleau-Ponty is sanguine about what remains of such prediscursive clues in our "languaged" world. But the critical point is that the prediscursive must be "anthropomorphized" in discursive terms: otherwise, phenomenology cannot fail to be privileged—as indeed it is in Husserl, who, of course, disjoins language and thought (partly at least) to secure that benefit.

Now, what Heidegger says about *Zuhandenheit* as well as about the "ontological" side of *Dasein* strikes me as very cleverly designed to recover the ambiguous role of a prediscursive grasp of *Seiende*: a role that *is* privileged but not discursively. Since Heidegger also abandons Husserl's strategy of eidetic variation, it is simply not clear how *Dasein's* resources bear on the rigor of discursive knowledge itself. If I understand Dewey rightly, then Dewey's account of "the indeterminate situation" is *never* meant to ensure any such epistemic privilege. It affords instead a sense of what we should mean by "inquiry" under the condition of avoiding all forms of dualism and of confirming the contingent continuity of cognition and life and the inseparability of that continuum and the embedding of human life itself in its environing world. But if that is so, then there is very little that is genuinely similar in Dewey and Heidegger.[48] What is similar in Dewey and Merleau-Ponty may be what will be surest in the philosophy of the next century.

Notes

1. I share those doubts, I must confess. See Joseph Margolis, "Donald Davidson's Philosophical Strategies," in Carol C. Gould and Robert S. Cohen, eds., *Artifacts, Representations, and Social Practice* (Dordrecht: Kluwer, 1994); and

idem, "A Biopsy of Recent American Philosophy," *Philosophical Forum* 26 (1995).

2.   See Sandra B. Rosenthal and Patrick L. Bourgeois, *Mead and Merleau-Ponty: Toward a Common Vision* (Albany: State University of New York Press, 1991).

3.   See Karl-Otto Apel, *Charles S. Peirce: From Pragmatism to Pragmaticism*, trans. John Michael Krois (Amherst: University of Massachusetts Press, 1981); and Jürgen Habermas, *Knowledge and Human Interests*, trans. Jeremy J. Shapiro (Boston: Beacon Press, 1971).

4.   See Bertrand Russell, "Dewey's New Logic," in Paul Arthur Schilpp, ed., *The Philosophy of John Dewey*, 3d ed. (New York: Tudor, 1951); and "William James' Conception of Truth," *Philosophical Essays* (London: Longmans, Green, 1910).

5.   Reprinted in Richard Rorty, *Consequences of Pragmatism (Essays: 1972–1980)* (Minneapolis: University of Minnesota Press, 1982).

6.   I have tried to assess the reception of Rorty in my "Situer Rorty en philosophie," *Archives de Philosophie*, forthcoming.

7.   My most reliable source for this story is Abraham Edel, who, I think, attributed it to Sidney Hook. The remark may appear in print, but I haven't bothered to track it down. I may also not be citing it altogether accurately. But the fun of it hardly lies with that sort of accuracy.

8.   See Richard Rorty, "Pragmatism, Davidson, and Truth," in Ernest Lepore, ed., *Truth and Interpretation: Perspectives on the Philosophy of Donald Davidson* (Oxford: Basil Blackwell, 1986).

9.   See Richard Rorty, *Philosophy and the Mirror of Nature* (Princeton, N.J.: Princeton University Press, 1979).

10.   See, particularly, Richard J. Bernstein, *Praxis and Action: Contemporary Philosophies of Human Activity* (Philadelphia: University of Pennsylvania Press, 1971).

11.   Rorty, "Overcoming the Tradition," p. 50. Here, Rorty explicitly draws his remark from a reading of Heidegger's late essay, "The Question Concerning Technology," that is, a paper written after the fateful *Kehre*. For that reason, it is not a reliable clue as to the meaning of Heidegger's position in *Being and Time* and the *Phenomenology*. I shall come to that in a moment.

12.   See Karl Jaspers, *Psychologie der Weltanschauungen*, 3d ed. (Berlin: Springer, 1925).

13.   Martin Heidegger, *The Basic Problems of Phenomenology*, trans. Albert Hofstadter (Bloomington: Indiana University Press, 1982), p. 11.

14.   Heidegger, *The Basic Problems of Phenomenology*, pp. 6–7.

15.   Richard Rorty, "The World Well Lost," *Consequences of Pragmatism*, p. 15.

16.   Rorty, "Overcoming the Tradition," p. 54.

17. Ibid., p. 53.

18. John Dewey, *Logic: The Theory of Inquiry* (New York: Henry Holt, 1938). [*The Later Works of John Dewey, 1925–1953*, vol. 12, ed. Jo Ann Boydston (Carbondale: Southern Illinois University Press, 1986).]

19. See *The Collected Papers of Charles Sanders Peirce*, ed. Charles Hartshorne and Paul Weiss (Cambridge, Mass.: Harvard University Press, 1963), 5.446–50, 505.

20. Dewey, *Logic*, p. 9, n.1 [LW12:17]. See Peirce, *Collected Papers*, 5.448.

21. See Joseph Margolis, "Peirce's Fallibilism," in C. J. Delaney, ed., *New Studies in the Philosophy of C. S. Peirce* (New York: Fordham University Press, forthcoming).

22. Dewey, *Logic*, p. 7 [LW12:14–15].

23. Dewey, *Logic*, p. 7 [LW12:15].

24. Dewey, *Logic*, pp. 104–105; italics in original [LW12:108].

25. Dewey, *Logic*, pp. 105–106 [LW12:109].

26. Dewey, *Logic*, p. 106 [LW12:110].

27. Dewey, *Logic*, p. 107 [LW12:111].

28. Dewey, *Logic*, p. 107 [LW12:111, n.5].

29. See *Collected Papers of Charles Sanders Peirce*, 5.448.

30. On this general matter, see James T. Kloppenberg, *Uncertain Victory: Social Democracy and Progressivism in European and American Thought, 1870–1920* (Bloomington: Indiana University Press, 1986); and Richard Rorty, "Dewey between Hegel and Darwin," in Dorothy Ross, ed., *Modernism and the Human Sciences* (Baltimore, Md.: Johns Hopkins University Press, 1994).

31. See Dewey's remark cited in James Campbell, *Understanding Dewey* (Chicago: Open Court, 1995), p. 12; but also *Praxis and Action*, pt. 2.

32. These are the master themes, of course, of John Dewey, *Reconstruction in Philosophy*, enl. ed. (Boston: Beacon Press, 1957), originally published in 1920 [*The Middle Works of John Dewey, 1899–1924*, vol. 12, ed. Jo Ann Boydston (Carbondale: Southern Illinois University Press, 1982)] and *Experience and Nature* (Chicago: Open Court, 1925) [*The Later Works of John Dewey, 1925–1953*, vol. 1, ed. Jo Ann Boydston (Carbondale: Southern Illinois University Press, 1981)].

33. See Walter Biemel, "Husserl's *Encyclopaedia Britannica* Article and Heidegger's Remarks Thereon," trans. P. McCormick and F. Elliston, in Frederick Elliston and Peter McCormick, eds., *Husserl: Expositions and Appraisals* (Notre Dame, Ind.: University of Notre Dame Press, 1977); and Eugen Fink, *Sixth Cartesian Meditation: The Idea of a Transcendental Theory of Method*, trans. Ronald Bruzina (Bloomington: Indiana University Press, 1988).

34. See, for instance, *Collected Papers of Charles Sanders Peirce*, 5.264–65.

35. Heidegger, *Being and Time*, p. 33 (in the German edition), p. 36f. (in the translation).

36. Ibid., p. 12 (p. 32 in the translation).

37. Ibid., pp. 70–71 (p. 100 in the translation).

38. Ibid., p. 71 (p. 101 in the translation).

39. Ibid., p. 72 (p. 102 in the translation).

40. Edmund Husserl, *The Crisis of the European Sciences and Transcendental Phenomenology*, trans. David Carr (Evanston, Ill.: Northwestern University Press, 1970), pp. 201–202. See also, Edmund Husserl, *Cartesian Meditations: An Introduction to Phenomenology*, trans. Dorian Cairns (The Hague: Martinus Nijhoff, 1960), Fifth Meditation; and *Phenomenology and the Crisis of Philosophy*, ed. and trans. Quentin Lauer (New York: Harper and Row, 1965).

41. For a sense of the issues, see J. N. Mohanty, *Husserl and Frege* (Bloomington: Indiana University Press, 1982), and Joseph Margolis, "Late Forms of Psychologism and Anti-Psychologism," *Philosophy and Rhetoric*, forthcoming.

42. Maurice Merleau-Ponty, *Phenomenology of Perception*, trans. Colin Smith (London: Routledge and Kegan Paul, 1962), pp. viii, xvii–xviii.

43. Ibid., pp. xv–xvii.

44. Ibid., p. viii; italics added.

45. Maurice Merleau-Ponty, "The Philosopher and Sociology," in *Signs*, trans. Richard C. McCleary (Evanston, Ill.: Northwestern University Press, 1964), p. 107. Husserl wrote a letter to anthropologist Lucien Lévy-Bruhl in 1935, fully ten years before the publication in France of *Phenomenology*. But it is also obvious from the very first page of Merleau-Ponty's preface to *Phenomenology* that he was already concerned about the import of Eugen Fink's questions about *Cartesian Meditations* and the apparent "contradictions" identified by the kind of inquiries Lévy-Bruhl's work might expose in Husserl. (Some, I may say, profess not to find the formula, "transcendental subjectivity is intersubjectivity," in Husserl.)

46. Maurice Merleau-Ponty, *The Visible and the Invisible*, ed. Claude Lefort, trans. Alphonso Lingis (Evanston, Ill.: Northwestern University Press, 1968), Working Notes, p. 263.

47. This goes against the master theme urged by W. V. Quine, "Epistemology Naturalized" in *Ontological Relativity and Other Essays* (New York: Columbia University Press, 1969), since Quine disallows noncausal explanation. The same is true in Rorty's version of postmodernism and Davidson's naturalism. See, further, Donald Davidson, "A Coherence Theory of Truth and Knowledge," in Ernest LePore, ed., *Truth and Interpretation: Perspectives on*

the *Philosophy of Donald Davidson* (Oxford: Blackwell, 1986); and Rorty, "Pragmatism, Davidson, and Truth."

48. The theme of *Logic* appears as well in *The Quest for Certainty* (New York: Minton, Balch, 1929) [*The Later Works of John Dewey, 1925–1953*, vol. 4, ed. Jo Ann Boydston (Carbondale: Southern Illinois University Press, 1984)].

Selected Works about Dewey

For a comprehensive bibliography of works about Dewey, see *Works about Dewey, 1886–1995*, edited by Barbara Levine. Carbondale: Southern Illinois University Press, 1996. The CD-ROM edition contains a supplement to the print edition.

Alexander, Thomas M. "The Human Eros." In *Philosophy and the Reconstruction of Culture*, edited by John J. Stuhr, 203–22. Albany: State University of New York Press, 1993.

———. "John Dewey and the Roots of Democratic Imagination." In *Recovering Pragmatism's Voice: The Classical Tradition, Rorty, and the Philosophy of Communication*, edited by Lenore Langsdorf and Andrew R. Smith, 131–54, 297–301. Albany: State University of New York Press, 1995.

———. *John Dewey's Theory of Art, Experience, and Nature: The Horizons of Feeling.* Albany: State University of New York Press, 1987.

Bernstein, Richard Jacob. "Action, Conduct, and Inquiry: Peirce and Dewey." In his *Praxis and Action*, 165–229. Philadelphia: University of Pennsylvania Press, 1971.

———. *John Dewey.* New York: Washington Square Press, 1966.

———. *The New Constellation: The Ethical-Political Horizons of Modernity-Postmodernity.* Cambridge, Mass.: MIT Press, 1992.

Boisvert, Raymond D. *Dewey's Metaphysics.* New York: Fordham University Press, 1988.

———. "Heteronomous Freedom." In *Philosophy and the Reconstruction of Culture*, edited by John J. Stuhr, 131–49. Albany: State University of New York Press, 1993.

Boydston, Jo Ann, ed. *Guide to the Works of John Dewey.* Carbondale: Southern Illinois University Press, 1970.

Browning, Douglas. "Necessity in Dewey's Logic." In *Frontiers in American Philosophy*, vol. 1, edited by Robert W. Burch and Herman J. Saatkamp, Jr., 221–29. College Station: Texas A & M University Press, 1992.

Bullert, Gary. *The Politics of John Dewey.* Buffalo, N.Y.: Prometheus Books, 1983.

Burke, Thomas. *Dewey's New Logic: A Reply to Russell.* Chicago: University of Chicago Press, 1994.

Cahn, Steven M., ed. *New Studies in the Philosophy of John Dewey.* Hanover, N.H.: University Press of New England, 1977.

Campbell, James. *The Community Reconstructs: The Meaning of Pragmatic Social Thought.* Urbana: University of Illinois Press, 1992.

———. *Understanding John Dewey: Nature and Cooperative Intelligence.* Chicago: Open Court, 1995.

Coughlan, Neil. *Young John Dewey*. Chicago: University of Chicago Press, 1975.

Damico, Alfonso J. *Individuality and Community: The Social and Political Thought of John Dewey*. Gainesville: University Presses of Florida, 1978.

Deledalle, Gérard. *L'Idée d'expérience dans la philosophie de John Dewey*. Paris: University Presses of France, 1967.

Dewey, Robert E. *The Philosophy of John Dewey: A Critical Exposition of His Method, Metaphysics, and Theory of Knowledge*. The Hague, Netherlands: Martinus Nijhoff, 1977.

Dykhuizen, George. *The Life and Mind of John Dewey*. Carbondale: Southern Illinois University Press, 1973.

Essays in Honor of John Dewey: On the Occasion of His Seventieth Birthday. New York: Henry Holt, 1929.

Garrison, Jim, ed. *The New Scholarship on Dewey*. Dordrecht: Kluwer, 1995.

Gavin, William J. *Context over Foundation: Dewey and Marx*. Dordrecht: D. Reidel, 1988.

Geiger, George Raymond. *John Dewey in Perspective*. New York: Oxford University Press, 1958.

Gouinlock, James. *Excellence in Public Discourse: John Stuart Mill, John Dewey, and Social Intelligence*. New York: Teachers College Press, 1986.

———. *John Dewey's Philosophy of Value*. New York: Humanities Press, 1972.

Hickman, Larry A., ed. *The Collected Works of John Dewey, 1882–1953: The Electronic Edition*. Charlottesville, Va.: InteLex Corporation, 1996.

———. *John Dewey's Pragmatic Technology*. Bloomington: Indiana University Press, 1990.

———. "Nature as Culture: John Dewey's Pragmatic Naturalism." In *Environmental Pragmatism*, edited by Andrew Light and Eric Katz, 50–72. London: Routledge, 1996.

Hook, Sidney. *John Dewey: An Intellectual Portrait*. New York: John Day, 1939.

Hook, Sidney, ed. *John Dewey: Philosopher of Science and Freedom*. New York: Dial Press, 1950; New York: Barnes and Noble, 1967.

John Dewey: The Man and His Philosophy. Addresses Delivered in New York in Celebration of His Seventieth Birthday. Cambridge, Mass.: Harvard University Press, 1930.

Keenan, Barry. *The Dewey Experiment in China: Educational Reform and Political Power in the Early Republic*. Cambridge, Mass.: Harvard University Press, 1977.

Lamont, Corliss, ed. *Dialogue on John Dewey*. New York: Horizon Press, 1959.

Lavine, Thelma Z. "Individuation and Unification in Dewey and Sartre." In *Doctrine and Experience*, edited by Vincent G. Potter, 149–73. New York: Fordham University Press, 1988.

Manicas, Peter T. "Dewey and the Class Struggle." In *Values and Value Theory in Twentieth-Century America*, edited by Murray G. Murphey and Ivar Berg, 67–81. Philadelphia, Pa.: Temple University Press, 1988.

McDermott, John J., ed. *The Philosophy of John Dewey*. 2 vols. New York: G. P. Putnam's Sons, 1973.

Morgenbesser, Sidney, ed. *Dewey and His Critics: Essays from the Journal of Philosophy*. New York: Journal of Philosophy, 1977.

Ratner, Sidney, and Jules Altman, eds. *John Dewey and Arthur F. Bentley: A Philosophical Correspondence, 1932–1951*. New Brunswick, N.J.: Rutgers University Press, 1964.

Rockefeller, Steven C. *John Dewey: Religious Faith and Democratic Humanism*. New York: Columbia University Press, 1991.

Rorty, Richard. *Consequences of Pragmatism: (Essays, 1972–1980)*. Minneapolis: University of Minnesota Press, 1982.

———. *Contingency, Irony, and Solidarity*. Cambridge, Eng.: Cambridge University Press, 1989.

Rosenthal, Sandra B. *Speculative Pragmatism*. Amherst: University of Massachusetts Press, 1986.

Rucker, Darnell. *The Chicago Pragmatists*. Minneapolis: University of Minnesota Press, 1969.

Ryan, Alan. *John Dewey and the High Tide of American Liberalism*. New York: W. W. Norton, 1995.

Schilpp, Paul Arthur. *The Philosophy of John Dewey*. The Library of Living Philosophers, vol. 1. Evanston, Ill.: Northwestern University, 1939. [Reprinted, with bibliography extended to 1950, by Muriel Murray. New York: Tudor Publishing, 1951. Reprinted, La Salle, Ill.: Open Court, 1970. 3d ed., 1989.]

Sleeper, Ralph William. *The Necessity of Pragmatism: John Dewey's Conception of Philosophy*. New Haven, Conn.: Yale University Press, 1986.

Somjee, Abdulkarim H. *The Political Theory of John Dewey*. New York: Teachers College Press, 1968.

Stuhr, John J. "Democracy as a Way of Life." In *Philosophy and the Reconstruction of Culture*, edited by John J. Stuhr, 37–57. Albany: State University of New York Press, 1993.

Thayer, Horace Standish. *The Logic of Pragmatism: An Examination of John Dewey's Logic*. New York: Humanities Press, 1952.

———. *Meaning and Action: A Critical History of Pragmatism*. Indianapolis: Bobbs-Merrill, 1968. [Shortened version, *Meaning and Action: A Study of American Pragmatism*, 1973.]

Tiles, J. E. *Dewey*. London: Routledge, 1988.

———. *John Dewey: Critical Assessments*. 4 vols. London: Routledge, 1992.

Welchman, Jennifer. *Dewey's Ethical Thought*. Ithaca, N.Y.: Cornell University Press, 1995.

West, Cornel. *The American Evasion of Philosophy: A Genealogy of Pragmatism*. Madison: University of Wisconsin Press, 1989.

Westbrook, Robert B. *John Dewey and American Democracy*. Ithaca, N.Y.: Cornell University Press, 1991.

Contributors

Thomas M. Alexander is associate professor of philosophy at Southern Illinois University at Carbondale. His contributions to Dewey studies include *John Dewey's Theory of Art, Experience, and Nature: The Horizons of Feeling*, "The Moral Imagination and the Aesthetics of Human Existence in Moral Education and the Liberal Arts," and "The Context of Community."

Raymond D. Boisvert is professor of philosophy at Siena College. He received his Ph.D. from Emory University. His essays on Dewey revolve around themes in the philosophy of culture. He has written two books on Dewey: *Dewey's Metaphysics* and *John Dewey: Rethinking Our Time*. In 1991–92 he was Fulbright Professor of American Studies at the University of Lyon in France. He is currently writing on the French philosopher Michel Serres.

James Campbell was educated at Temple University and State University of New York, Stony Brook, and is currently professor of philosophy at the University of Toledo. During the academic year 1990–91 he was Fulbright Lecturer in American Culture and Literature at the University of Innsbruck. He is the editor of *Selected Writings of James Hayden Tufts*, and the author of *The Community Reconstructs: The Meaning of Pragmatic Social Thought* and *Understanding John Dewey: Nature and Cooperative Intelligence*.

James W. Garrison is professor of philosophy of education in the College of Human Resources and Education at Virginia Tech in Blacksburg, Virginia. His publications include "Dewey and the Empirical Unity of Opposites," "Realism, Deweyan Pragmatism, and Educational Research," "Deweyan Prophetic Pragmatism, Poetry, and the Education of Eros," "Dewey's Philosophy and the Experience of Working: Labor Tools and Language," and "A Deweyan Theory of Democratic Listening." He is also the editor of *The New Scholarship on Dewey*, a collection of essays on Dewey's philosophy of education, and a member of the Board of Directors of the John Dewey Society. He is editor-in-chief of *Studies in Philosophy and Education*.

Larry A. Hickman is director of the Center for Dewey Studies and professor of philosophy at Southern Illinois University at Carbondale. He has published essays on American pragmatism, the philosophy of technology, and the history of logic. He is the author of *Modern Theories of Higher Level Predicates: Second Intentions in the Neuzeit* and *John Dewey's Pragmatic Technology*, and the editor of *Technology as a Human Affair*.

Thelma Z. Lavine is Clarence J. Robinson Professor of Philosophy and American Culture at George Mason University. She received her Ph.D. from Harvard University and holds teaching awards from Brooklyn College, the University of Maryland, and George

Washington University. She is the author of a nationally televised PBS course in philosophy, the author of *From Socrates to Sartre: The Philosophic Quest*, and coauthor and coeditor of *History and Anti-History in Philosophy*. In addition, she has written many essays on continental philosophy, sociology of knowledge, psychoanalysis, interpretation theory, and American philosophy and culture—including the introduction to volume 16 of *The Later Works of John Dewey*. She delivered the Fifth Romanell Lecture on Philosophic Naturalism and contributed to *Rorty and Pragmatism: The Philosopher Responds to His Critics*.

Peter T. Manicas is currently director of the Liberal Studies Program and professor of sociology at the University of Hawai'i at Manoa. He has authored many articles and books, including *A History and Philosophy of the Social Sciences* and *War and Democracy*.

Joseph Margolis is currently Laura H. Carnell Professor of Philosophy at Temple University. He is the author of more than thirty books, including a four-volume series under the general title *The Persistence of Reality* (which comprises *Pragmatism without Foundations, The Truth about Relativism, The Flux of History and the Flux of Science, Interpretation Radical But Not Unruly*), and *Historied Thought, Constructed World*.

Gregory F. Pappas is assistant professor of philosophy at Texas A&M University. A recipient of the prestigious William James Prize and a Ford Foundation Grant, his recent articles include "Dewey and Feminism: The Affective and Relationships in Dewey's Ethics" and "William James and the Logic of Faith."

Steven C. Rockefeller teaches religion and philosophy at Middlebury College. He received an M.Div. from Union Theological Seminary and a Ph.D. from Columbia University. He is the author of numerous essays on Dewey and the coeditor of *The Christ and the Bodhisattva* and *Spirit and Nature: Religion, Ethics, and Environmental Crisis*. He is also the author of *John Dewey: Religious Faith and Democratic Humanism*.

Charlene Haddock Seigfried is professor of philosophy and American Studies at Purdue University. She has explored the feminist dimension of pragmatist thought in her latest book, *Pragmatism and Feminism: Reweaving the Social Fabric*, and as the editor of a special issue of *Hypatia* devoted to pragmatism and feminism. Her publications on William James include *William James's Radical Reconstruction of Philosophy* and *Chaos and Context*. Her interdisciplinary interests are reflected in publications in the areas of literature, psychology, communication, rhetoric, drama, education, and American Studies. She is currently president of the Society for the Advancement of American Philosophy and a member of the Executive Board of the Society for the Study of Women Philosophers.

John J. Stuhr is professor and head of the Department of Philosophy at Pennsylvania State University, where he also serves on the faculty of the Graduate Program in Social Thought. Educated at Carleton College and Vanderbilt University, he has taught at the University of New England, Whitman College, and the University of Oregon, where he was director of the Oregon Humanities Center. The author of many articles and essays on American philosophy, social and political theory, and contemporary European thought, he is the editor of *Classical American Philosophy* and *Philosophy and the Reconstruction of Culture: Pragmatic Essays after Dewey*, and the author of *John Dewey* and two forthcoming books—*Genealogical Pragmatism: Philosophy, Experience, and Community* and *Experience and Criticism: John Dewey's Pragmatism*. He currently is working on a book on pragmatism and the future of philosophy.

Index

Experimental method, 52
Experimentation, 54, 62*n*24, 63*n*25; defined, 55
Expression, 16; defined, 10

Facts: and values, 47, 106
Faith: common, 227; democratic, 146;
   Dewey's definition of, 140; Dewey's radical
   liberal interpretation of, 142; moral, 140; so-
   cial, 142
Fallacy: feminine, 211; masculine, 211. *See
   also* Philosopher's fallacy
Feminism: pragmatist, xix, 117*n*6, 190; the-
   ory of, 202–5; and virtue ethics, 117*n*6
Feminist philosophers, 189; first generations
   of, 190–93
Feminist philosophy, 187–216
Feuerbach, Ludwig, 137
Fine art, philosophy of, 16. *See also* Art
Fink, Eugen, 242
Fletcher, Joseph, 119*m*5
Force, 200
Forces, social, 32
Form, 16; defined, 9; as reconstruction, 9
Forms, logical, 169
Foundations, 61*m*8
Frankl, Viktor, 140
Freedom, 91, 94; negative, 74; positive, 74

Galileo, 11
Generic traits, 154, 156, 157
Gilded Age, 44
Gilman, Charlotte Perkins, 201
God, 124–48; meaning of term in Dewey's
   mature writings, 141, 142
God language, 141
Golden rule, 199*m*3
Good, 112, 121*n*26; common, 36, 40
Goods, common, 86
Great Community, xx, 37, 56
Great Society, 37, 56
Green, T. H., 127, 130
Groups, 32, 36; overlapping, 38
Growth, 67, 139; as aim of education, 80; ca-
   pacity for, 77
Guernica, 14

Habermas, Jürgen, 232
Habits, 12, 26, 63, 64, 66, 74, 76, 91, 114, 170,
   205; centrality of, 25; conservatism of, 206;
   and customs, 25; formation of, 74; and hu-
man nature, 206; persistence of, 24; per-
   sonal, 28; social, 75, 77
Haiku, 14
Hall, G. Stanley, 127
Hamlet, 15
Hartley, Marsden, 7
Hartz, Louis, 220, 223
Hayek, Friedrich, 228
Hegel, G. W. F., xx, 127, 136
Heidegger, Martin, ix, xi, xx, xxi, 5, 21*n*9,
   152, 231–56
Hickman, Larry, 19*n*5, 50
Hobbes, Thomas, 19*n*3
Hook, Sidney, 145
Hoover, Herbert, 60*m*2
Hopper, Edward, 7
Hull House, 190
Humanism, naturalistic, 2
Human nature, 65, 201; a new, 94
Husserl, Edmund, xxi, 241, 242, 246, 251
Huxley, Thomas Henry, 124, 126

Ideal, the: and scientific vision, 137
Idealism, 20*n*9, 117*n*3; neo-Hegelian, xvii, 124
Idealists, 151
Ideals, 17, 35, 114; democratic, 78; liberation
   of, 6; moral, 115
Imagination, 4, 78, 80
Immigration, 33
Immortality, 144
Implication, 183
Indeterminacy, 244
Individualism, xi, 88, 91, 94, 224, 226; eco-
   nomic, 200, 225; self-centered, 133
Individuality, 38; and community, 28; foster-
   ing, 39; genuine, 93; sacrifice of, 33; as social
   product, 92
Individuals, self realization of, 94
Inference, laws of, 170
Inquiry, 70, 238; aim of, 168; as an art, 172; as
   behavioral response, 171; as control of habit
   formation, 167; controlled, 72, 177; cooperative, 29; Dewey's definition of, xviii, 72;
   and education, 71; as end in itself, 186; as essential within experience, xx; historical
   context of, xxi; matter and form in, 175; as
   means of adaptation, 167; methodology of,
   194; moral, 108; as organic activity, 167; as
   situated, xi; social, xix, 48, 184; stages of,
   108; theoretical, 101

Virtues, cardinal, 114
Vision, imaginative, 79
Von Helmholtz, Hermann, 127

War, 208–10
Warranted assertibility, xix, 71, 166, 168
Warrants, 167
Weber, Max, 59n2
Welfare, 48
Weltanschauungsphilosophie, 234, 235, 249
West, Cornel, 145
Westbrook, Robert B., 59n3, 145

Whitehead, Alfred North, 137, 152
Whitman, Walt, 132, 143
Wieman, Henry Nelson, 144
Wilde, Oscar, 20n6
Williams, Bernard, 118n2
Williams, William Carlos, 7, 20n10
Wilson, Woodrow, 199
Wisdom, 40, 80
Wittgenstein, Ludwig, ix, 233
Woodbridge, F. J. E., 155
Wordsworth, William, 22n24, 143
Wundt, Wilhelm, 127